✗ T

INTERNATIONAL BUSINESS IN THE PACIFIC BASIN, ed. by
R. Hal Mason. Lexington, D. C. Heath, 1978. 213p 78-2373. 18.00
ISBN 0-669-02189-X. C.I.P.
Mason's book is the published result of a research symposium held at
U.C.L.A. in late 1975. This collection of thoughtful, informative, and
well-written essays deals with various aspects of doing business in the
nations of the Pacific basin, with particular emphasis on the U.S., Japan,
and the developing countries of the Far East. Contributors include
educators and business executives with wide-ranging experience in the
Pacific area. There are chapters on the political environment, industrial
development strategies, recent economic and trade developments, host-
nation policies on foreign investment, and technology transfer. Other
sections discuss the role of Japan in this region, doing business with the
People's Republic of China, market analysis, distribution channels, and
financing of sales, and the operation of foreign-owned banks in California.
The chief deficiency of this work is the three-year time lag between the
symposium and publication; even so, not much is out-of-date. This is
recommended reading for anyone wanting to become better informed about
this important and rapidly changing part of the world. Some chapters are
footnoted.

D1206511

International Business in the Pacific Basin

International Business in the Pacific Basin

229778

Edited by

R. Hal Mason
University of California,
Los Angeles

Lexington Books
D.C. Heath and Company
Lexington, Massachusetts
Toronto

Library of Congress Cataloging in Publication Data

Main entry under title:
    International business in the Pacific Basin.

    Based on a research symposium held at UCLA.
    1. Pacific area—Commerce—Congresses. 2. International business enter-
prises—Congresses. I. Mason, Robert Hal.
HF4030.7.A25   382'.099   78-346
ISBN 0-669-02189-x

Published simultaneously in Canada.

Printed in the United States of America.

International Standard Book Number: 0-669-02189-x

Library of Congress Catalog Card Number: 78-346

Contents

List of Tables and Figure

Preface

This book is the result of a research symposium held at the University of California at Los Angeles. It deals with certain aspects of doing business in the Pacific Basin with special emphasis on the United States, Japan, and the developing countries of the Far East. This volume is the initial effort of a recently established Center for Pacific Basin Studies within UCLA's Graduate School of Management. Financial support for this effort was provided by the General Knit Corporation of California, a subsidiary of C. Itoh, one of Japan's largest trading groups. We are grateful to General Knit for their generosity and to Mr. Mickey Steckler, who was then president of the corporation.

List of Contributors
and Panelists

Contributors to the Volume

Thomas W. Allen, Formerly, Executive Director
National Investment and Development Authority
Papua-New Guinea. Now Director, The Implementation and Management
Group Pty. Ltd., Sydney

Claude A. Buss
Professor of Far East Area Studies, Navy Postgraduate School, Monterey,
California
Emeritus Professor of Far East International Relations, Stanford University

Noel Capon, Assistant Professor of Marketing
Graduate School of Management
University of California, Los Angeles

David Eiteman, Professor of Finance
Graduate School of Management
University of California, Los Angeles

Charles W. Hostler, Formerly, Deputy Assistant Secretary for International
Commerce
U.S. Department of Commerce. Now President, Hostler Investment Company, San Diego

Steven W. Kohlhagen, Assistant Professor
School of Business Administration
University of California, Berkeley

Harvey E. McCoy, Vice President (Retired)
Sears Roebuck Overseas—Far East

R. Hal Mason, Professor of International Business
Graduate School of Management
University of California, Los Angeles

Byron Miller, Formerly, Director of International Sales, Australia and Southeast
Asia
The Boeing Airplane Company. Now, Director of Marketing, Frederick B.
Ayer and Associates, Inc., New York City

Robert R. Miller, Professor of International Management Studies
University of Texas at Dallas.

Hans Schollhammer, Associate Professor of International Business
Graduate School of Management
University of California, Los Angeles

Peter Suchman, Formerly, Deputy Assistant Secretary for Enforcement, Operations and Tariff Affairs, U.S. Department of the Treasury. Now, Attorney
with Sharretts, Paley, Carter and Blauvelt, New York City

xiv

Panelists

Richard Baum, Associate Professor
　　Department of Political Science
　　University of California, Los Angeles
Richard Conlon, Senior Vice President
　　Business International
Harold Hecht, Chairman of the Board (Retired)
　　J.W. Robinsons
William Hosken, Vice President (Retired)
　　Cyprus Mines
Richard King, President
　　Los Angeles World Trade Center
Barry M. Richman, Professor of International Business
　　Graduate School of Management
　　University of California, Los Angeles
Shinsaku Sogo, Director Overseas Public Relations
　　Japan External Trade Organization, Tokyo
Mickey Steckler, Formerly President
　　General Knit of California
Gordon Stiegler, Vice President Asia/Pacific
　　The Carnation Company
Michael Yoshino, Professor of International Business
　　Harvard University

**International Business
in the Pacific Basin**

1

Introduction

R. Hal Mason

Trade and foreign investment are growing rapidly within the Pacific Basin. Until recent years, within this context, the United States provided the primary force of leadership. However, with its own withdrawal from South Vietnam, a lowering profile in Southeast Asia, and the emergence of Japan as a major economic power, the leadership roles between the United States and Japan have been altered substantially. Japan is shedding its earlier reluctance to bear the mantle of leadership, partly because of proddings from the United States.

In addition to the changing relationships between the two major industrial powers, most of the developing countries in the region have been maturing.

The interdependence among the Pacific Basin countries is quite evident: Japan and the United States depend on the developing group for raw materials and labor-intensive manufactures, while the developing group depends on the industrial powers for industrial goods, investment capital, technology, and managerial systems. Also, the United States is a major supplier of foodstuffs to most countries in the Basin.

U.S. trans-Pacific trade already equals its trade with Europe. Some 40 percent of U.S. trade is with Pacific Basin states. Japan heavily depends on the entire region for raw materials and markets. Some 60 percent of Japan's exports go to Pacific Basin States. Despite these growing linkages, however, the Basin's developing nations are seeking even more rapid industrialization, greater access to U.S. and Japanese markets, and greater access to investment capital and technology—and all this with fewer strings attached than in earlier years. Simultaneously, both the United States and Japan have become more sympathetic to the developing countries' arguments along these lines. However, it is also true that economic events have weakened both countries' ability to back their resolve with real resources aimed at fostering economic development among the less-developed countries in the Basin. This condition may be temporary, but even if it is not, there is an air of cooperative good will and many old enmities, while perhaps not resolved, are nevertheless being laid aside in the interest of economic development and intercountry exchange and cooperation. there is an air of cooperative good will and many old enmities, while perhaps not resolved, are nevertheless being laid aside in the interest of economic development and intercountry exchange and cooperation.

One cannot ignore the role of China,[a] in the Far Eastern region of the

---

[a]Throughout this book, "China" refers to the People's Republic of China, and the Republic of China is called by its more popular name, Taiwan.

Pacific Basin. Once isolated and cut off from normal economic intercourse—to some degree at U.S. insistence with its Pacific Basin neighbors—China is emerging as a Pacific power. Although that power is being exerted delicately, the Southeast Asian nations, South Korea, Taiwan, and Japan have been affected, which is evident in their policy stances. This in turn has influenced relationships between the United States and Japan and their relative roles in the economic development of the area. While the United States has not withdrawn entirely— nor does China so wish—the U.S. military presence has diminished. Moreover, both the Philippines and Thailand are pushing for a further diminution of the U.S. military presence. This in turn has spurred a more vigorous diplomatic effort among all the countries concerned with the aim of establishing normal diplomatic relations throughout the area. China, however, continues a go-slow attitude toward an opening of its borders to trade and cultural exchange. Despite this, China's vast reserves of raw materials cannot fail to beckon Japan in its efforts to secure long-run supplies of nonrenewable resources. These raw materials can also be expected to influence long-standing economic relationships in the Basin.

While there have been discernable improvements in international relations among Basin states over the past few years, the area is not without its problems. With exception of Canada, the United States, Japan, Australia and New Zealand, most Basin countries are woefully underdeveloped. There are some success stories, including those of Singapore, Hong Kong, Taiwan, and, more recently, South Korea. The Philippine Republic continues to show promise but has yet to demonstrate sustained economic and civil progress. The remaining nations in the Basin, while well endowed with natural resources for the most part, are among the least developed in the world: Thailand, Cambodia, Vietnam, Malaysia, Indonesia, and Papua-New Guinea on the western rim of the Pacific; and Chile, Peru, Columbia, Ecuador, the Central Americas, and Mexico on the eastern rim.

Much of the international trade and investment in the region is being affected by a continuing, and perhaps intensifying, nationalism within the Basin, particularly among the less-developed countries. The Andean group, most members of the ASEAN group, and Mexico have some form of foreign investment law that tends to discriminate against foreign investors. Joint ventures are increasingly preferred. Some sectors are reserved for local capital. Technology transfers are being more closely scrutinized, and the payments for technology are being questioned. Unfortunately, these conditions may frustrate the process of economic development.

As mentioned in the preface, this volume is the product of a research symposium held at UCLA in late 1975. The purpose of the symposium was to bring together academic, government, and business scholars with an interest in international developments in the Pacific Basin and their impact on business relationships there. The sequence of chapters in this book does not necessarily follow the actual order of presentation at the symposium.

The chapters attempt to provide a pragmatic guide to businesspeople and others having an interest in trade, investment, technology transfer, and development in the Pacific Basin. We begin with Claude Buss's overview of some of the political realities in the Far East. His chapter is followed with a review of some recent economic developments by Charles Hostler. In chapter 3, Peter Suchman examines some of the problems of trade negotiation in the Pacific Basin and elsewhere, which are an outgrowth of the Trade Act of 1974. Next, Robert Miller analyzes U.S. policies toward importing and exporting, with emphasis on "export platforms." In the two following papers, Thomas Allen and Steven Kohlhagen provide a detailed analysis of the investment regulations in the Southeast Asian developing countries. This is followed by my own analysis of technology acquisition strategies that countries use to attempt to disengage the technology from direct foreign investment.

Chapters 9 and 10 deal with special aspects of Japan and China: in chapter 9, Hans Schollhammer examines Japanese foreign investments, and in chapter 10, Byron Miller presents a description of his first-hand experience of negotiating a large contract with the People's Republic of China.

The final three chapters deal with specialized aspects of doing business in the Pacific Basin. Harvey McCoy examines methods, channels, and financing of purchases in the Far East for importation to the United States. In chapter 12, Noel Capon reviews some of the problems of applying marketing principles in cross-cultural situations, and finally, David Eiteman discusses some of the differences between U.S.-based banks and Far Eastern-based banks operating in California.

The following is a more detailed summary of each chapter:

Claude A. Buss focuses his analysis on the political environment in the Pacific Basin, with emphasis on the Far East. He is optimistic about the region's political stability, which mainly results from the countries' desire to maintain present conditions. Even the People's Republic of China is motivated by practical rather than ideological considerations in its foreign policy. Japan is satisfied with the present security treaty, which enables it to devote attention to and resources for economic expansion by exporting technology and capital to its neighbors in exchange for raw materials.

According to Charles W. Hostler, the Pacific Basin is the world's most dynamic and perhaps greatest trading region: (1) the region has abundant resources of energy and minerals and plentiful labor supplies that favor the development of the textiles and electronics industries; (2) Japan has set up manufacturing operations to nearby countries; (3) most countries have a better balanced economic development than in the past; and (4) the Basin countries are politically stable. A general feeling of optimism in these countries was not checked by the temporary economic downturn in 1974. Hostler cautions, however, that the passage of the Trade Act of 1974 and the restrictions placed on the generalized system of preferences (GSP) might hinder free trade in this region.

In chapter 3, Peter Suchman is more pessimistic about the Pacific region because of recent disturbing trends in informal trade relations. The Trade Act of 1974 by the United States seems to be a departure from the most-favored-nation (MFN) principle. The MFN concept is consistent with the General Agreement on Tariffs and Trade, which has been largely responsible for the enormous growth in international trade for the past forty years. Preferential trading areas, such as the European Economic Community, are a departure from the MFN concept. The generalized system of preferences, adopted by a number of major industrial countries—and put into effect in the United States on January 1, 1976—is another disturbing trend. There has been increased intervention in the market-place in recent years, such as in export restraints, subsidies, countervailing duties, and government procurement. The U.S. policy of stabilization—stable prices, stable market shares, stable employment, stable growth rates, stable grain reserves, etc.—might result in more government intervention in the private sector.

Robert R. Miller takes a position similar to Suchman's in stating that the United States is abandoning the most-favored-nation doctrine in favor of preferential tariff concessions. This change is in response to internal political pressure, mainly from labor. Although the traditional labor union viewpoint is toward free trade, labor now favors protectionism and attacks multinational corporations for "exporting" jobs. Miller mentions that the comparative advantage of the United States lies in agricultural exports and land-intensive, high-technology industries. The U.S. imports from the Pacific Basin are mainly manufactured products, in contrast with its imports from other developing areas. In general, the United States is heavily dependent on the agriculture sector to generate surpluses to overcome deficits in manufactured products and fuel. The recent U.S. control of agricultural exports, a new development in its trade policy, was undertaken to stabilize domestic prices. Miller examines U.S. firms' "export platforms" and suggests they were developed to meet competition abroad; therefore, he argues, there is a valid reason for U.S. foreign investment, although less jobs will be provided for domestic workers. Miller concludes that the growing trade between the United States and other Pacific Basin nations has been mutually beneficial, and he favors freer trade in this region, including agricultural exports and "export platforms" such as those in the electronics and textiles industries.

Thomas W. Allen, in chapter 6, discusses some industrial development strategies and foreign investment policies in the developing countries of Southeast Asia and the South Pacific. The development strategies have been aimed at import displacement, export promotion, encouragement of foreign investments, expansion of natural resources, and promotion of tourism to earn foreign exchange. Allen discusses the laws regulating foreign investments in these countries. Most deal with "priority areas" of investment, which differ among countries depending on industrial development strategies. Investment laws differ among countries in the region, but all deal with ownership and control. Most countries encourage joint ventures between foreign and domestic capital but are aimed at reducing foreign dominance.

Steven W. Kohlhagen discusses foreign investment policies in the five ASEAN countries—Indonesia, Malaysia, the Philippines, Singapore, and Thailand. His main contention is that the "negative features" of foreign investments by multinational corporations are in response to the incentive schemes of the foreign investment policies that the host countries follow. In Kohlhagen's view, these policies encourage foreign investments in capital-intensive, import displacement industries, rather than in labor-intensive and export-oriented industries.

Chapter 8 discusses the strategies of technological acquisition: direct foreign investment versus unpackaged technology. Unpackaged technology is technology unaccompanied by foreign ownership or control of the operating assets. But the conditions are different today because of the dominant position of international firms, who prefer to own the operating assets. Licensing agreements, technical aid agreements, management contracts, turnkey plants, supply contracts, joint ventures with control vested locally, and some combinations of the above are the methods of acquiring unpackaged technology. Acquisition costs should be the developing countries' main consideration in choosing direct foreign investment versus unpackaged technology. Since industries differ significantly in their characteristics, and since these characteristics influence the acquisition costs, there is no clear-cut general answer as to which method of acquiring technology has the lowest cost.

Hans Schollhammer analyzes Japanese foreign investments, with an emphasis on the Pacific Basin countries. He begins his analysis with a historical perspective on Japanese economic development and examines how this perspective influenced Japan's development strategies. The main thrust of the chapter, however, is an examination of post-World War II events that led to Japan's emergence as an exporter of capital. Schollhammer examines the area and industrial patterns of Japanese foreign investments, providing data that trace recent developments along these lines. Resource-oriented foreign investments have grown, but they now represent a substantially smaller proportion than they did a decade ago. From the data, it is evident that Japan's foreign investment has expanded exceptionally rapidly—it increased nearly ninefold between 1967 and 1975. Schollhammer suggests that Japan's resource-oriented investments will grow rapidly and begin to make up a larger percentage of its foreign investments. Service-oriented investments are expected to make up a smaller percentage over time.

Byron Miller, in chapter 10, offers a personal and fascinating account of his experiences in negotiating the sale of ten Boeing aircraft to China. Miller found that tremendous patience is necessary in negotiating business with China, for the minutest detail is negotiated and then included in the contract. The Chinese demonstrated themselves to be pragmatic but tough businesspeople who expected a fair and just contract for both parties.

Harvey E. McCoy examines the methods, channels, and financing of purchases in the Pacific Basin. Although the traditional distribution channels through local trading companies are still the most important, the trend to more direct distribution is evident. Comparative cost consideration is the key factor in determining the form of the distribution channel. McCoy gives a detailed and authoritive account of the international purchase contract and financing purchases in the Pacific Basin. In discussing purchasing from the People's Republic of China, he points out that China's export program is based solely on the need to develop foreign exchange. As a result, great variation in product availability and pricing occurs from year to year.

In chapter 12, Noel Capon deals with the factors that a firm should examine before deciding to enter an international market. Factors affecting market size, product, and price include: (1) demographic data, such as population growth, based on mortality and birth rates, and age distribution, which affects consumer needs; (2) economic data such as growth rates of gross domestic product (GDP) and population and GDP per capita across countries; (3) economic structure or sectoral composition of GDP over time; (4) shares of foreign trade and investment in GDP over time; (5) transportation; and (6) financial stability as reflected by the value of foreign exchange. Capon discusses the various statistical studies that group countries into classes for purposes of formulating marketing strategies. Countries have been grouped based on geography, GDP per capita, and on more complex bases using twelve environmental and societal attributes. Capon warns that these studies are deficient and difficult to compare because the data come from different time periods and are sometimes out of date. But these variables or factors are important determinants for expanding operations into the Pacific Basin.

In the final chapter, David K. Eiteman attempts to compare the liquidity, leverage, and profitability of Far Eastern Banks in California with those of domestic banks. Using a very small sample of financial statements, he found that foreign banks are generally more aggressive in administering their portfolios of assets because they devote a greater fraction to loans and a smaller proportion to primary reserves than domestic banks do. Foreign banks are also more conservative in having lower deposits relative to stockholders' equity. Using the composite measure of "deposits at risk" to stockholders' equity, none of the foreign banks appear to be more risky than average. The two largest foreign banks seem to be less profitable for their owners than the U.S.-insured commercial banks.

2

Political Realities in the Pacific Basin

Claude A. Buss

For the first time since the end of World War II, peoples and governments throughout the Pacific—particularly in the United States—show a deep interest in long-range developments, issues, and trends as they affect their personal and national political and economic interests.

The United States has grown accustomed to a position of unrivaled power. When World War II ended, U.S. planes dominated the skies, U.S. ships controlled the Pacific, and U.S. advisers helped to shape the destiny of practically every country on the Pacific rim. Only the United States emerged from the ravages of war with enhanced productive capacity and robust economic health.

The collapse of the Kuomintang and the rise of the Communist party in China ran counter to U.S. wishes. The Chinese-Soviet alliance loomed as an international conspiracy to rule the world. In the U.S. government's view, Moscow was the heart and brains of the conspiracy and Peking was little more than a helpless puppet. The "Communists"—all of them—were judged guilty of cynical, naked, and brutal aggression in Korea, and they were fought to a standstill.

After the Korean armistice, the whole world was considered to be bipolar. United States policy was to confront the communists; Soviet-Chinese policy was to overthrow the imperialists. Neither side wasted much sympathy on the neutralists, whose major goals were survival and development. Prince Sihanouk of Cambodia best expressed their attitude when he said, "If the elephants fight, let the ants beware."

In two decades, 1953-1973, it became increasingly clear that the Pacific Basin's problems could not be isolated, let alone solved, without considering the rest of the globe. The number of forces allotted to Korea had to be determined in the light of security considerations in Europe. Trade or aid destined for Africa or Latin America could be made available only in proportion to the needs of Europe or Asia. Official attention given to the Middle East or the India-Pakistan war entirely depended on how much effort could be spared from meeting security needs in Korea, the off-shore islands, or Vietnam.

The overall compelling factor in making Pacific Basin policy did not lie in the Pacific at all, but in Moscow. With its atomic capability and achievements in military technology, the Soviet Union was the one nation with the capacity to confront the United States in diplomacy and to destroy the United States in the event of war. For twenty years the United States dealt with the Soviet-dominated Communist monolith on a cold-war basis, without too much hope for genuine peaceful coexistence.

7

The U.S. government experienced little difficulty in keeping the public's support. Whether Democrats or Republicans were in the White House, they could depend on the votes of most Americans, with whom opposition to communist ideology was a basic article of faith.

But inadequate attention was paid by the United States to the changes taking place in the world. The Communist monolith fell apart. Communism developed problems that might have modified national attitudes on both sides of the iron curtain, had they been accurately assessed. Neutralism became accepted as entirely respectable. The "free world" also lost much of its vaunted solidarity. Client nations demanded more than a certain type of military security from the United States. The spirit of respectable independence galvanized the Third World and challenged the whole concept of "we or they."

Within the leading nations of the free world, especially the United States, problems and attitudes appeared that ruffled diplomacy in the Pacific Basin. Economic cycles raised questions about the monumental costs of security, and factions of loyal opposition protested against the policies of parties in power. New generations of young people, at least partially inspired by idealism, demanded something more substantial—and visionary—from their leaders than the doctrine of "might makes right."

The U.S. experience in Vietnam exacerbated the debates. Five years of frustration tore the U.S. government apart and sharpened the divisions within its allies' governments. The peace of 1973 offered no peace at all. The debacle of 1975 marked the end of an era. It did not blemish the fundamental character of the United States or its people, nor did it tarnish U.S. ideals, principles, or objectives. Rather, it only signaled the end of a disastrous policy. It exposed the need for an agonizing reappraisal of policies toward the Pacific Basin, not only by the United States but by every nation with interests in the Pacific Basin.

The problems of Pacific nations today are the problems of mankind everywhere: air pollution; environmental control; population growth; availability of resources (especially energy); elimination of poverty, hunger, and disease; and avoidance of war. The purpose of this examination of conditions, issues, and trends in Southeast Asia, the Central Pacific, and the North Pacific is to provide more food for thought about how human actions in these geographic areas can inhibit or, on the contrary, can contribute to the achievement of regional peace and universal prosperity.

New Attitudes in Southeast Asia

The most impressive fact in Southeast Asis is that twenty years of hostility have come to an end. For twenty years the attention of every nation in Southeast Asia was riveted on the fighting in Vietnam, and precious little energy was concentrated on the needs of development. The gap widened between the underdeveloped nations and the more developed nations. Future tasks are all the more onerous because the scars of war must be healed before the suffering patients can be given better health and a new life.

Throughout Southeast Asia one senses a new attitude toward the problems of security. No one underestimates the necessity of survival, but the problem is cast within different perimeters. The idea of a bipolar world is admittedly past, and the future equilibrium of power must have a substantial place for the small as well as for the large, for as the saying goes, "it is the shrimps which cause the pain in the belly of the whales." Security will always be important, but so will issues of trade, investment, and international understanding. Friendships and alliances will have to be based on something more substantial than professed anti-Communism on the one side or Communist loyalty on the other.

Governments in power have been forced to take a new look at insurgency. It was too simple to treat insurgency as a segment of a world revolution, guided, financed, and controlled from the outside. Insurgency, as evidenced in the experience of the Philippines and Malaysia, is the result of perceived political grievance, economic inequities, or social injustice. Communists did not cause insurgency; they provided organization, leadership, assistance, and a sense of purpose. Fighting the Communists was attacking the symptoms, not the disease. The so-called insurgents in Vietnam, although dominated completely by the North Vietnamese, owed a large measure of their success to their sense of grievance, their common cause, and their faith in ultimate victory.

The clearest reality in Southeast Asia today is the force of the spirit of nationalism. Nationalism may be anachronistic and imperfect, but it is still powerful. Southeast Asia is an entity in name only. Nations living closely together are increasingly jealous of their own prerogatives. More tariff barriers and other protective measures can be expected, and outsiders will have to do fancy stepping to overcome increasing obstacles. No such thing as free trade will exist; consumers and producers, together with their political associates, will make the fullest use of all the tools at their command for the sake of competitive advantage. Government and business are full partners in economic activity. The relative role assigned to each is as much a matter of history and geography as it is an ideological system.

The evolution of nationalism in the Third World has been dimly perceived and grossly underestimated. Respectable independence is a veritable battle cry. The newly emerged nations demand the same things from their governments that Americans long ago prescribed in their own constitution. They expect their governments to form a more perfect union, insure domestic tranquility, provide for the common defense, promote the general welfare, establish justice, and preserve the blessings of liberty for themselves and their posterity. They do not worry about the precise form of government they choose, whether authoritarian or democratic, military or civil. Democracy is an imprecise word, and the experience of the West cannot be transferred overnight, as it were, to the East.

Democratic values have been distorted and democratic practices abused. The end of government is to serve the people. The form matters less than a decent respect for individual rights.

Generally, Southeast Asians are bound never again to be dominated by any outside power or combination of powers. They are as adamant against U.S. hegemony as they are against China or the Soviet Union. They need, however, to look everywhere on the outside for any economic help that they can attract. They want aid without political strings and they have no prejudices against gift-bearing Communists. Advisers from poor countries are welcomed because they have a better understanding than advisers from rich countries about dealing with conditions in underdeveloped Southeast Asia.

One hears little talk of neo-imperialism. Not too long ago foreign investors and entrepreneurs were condemned as bloodsuckers and exploiters, but the present trend is to look on them as partners in development who are entitled to a reasonable share of the profits. Investment laws are lenient, but they could tighten up in the future. Contracts must make allowances for discrimination or nationalization, and contractors must be prepared for antiforeign manifestations if existing governments decide to turn on the propaganda.

It is not likely that anyone will ever use Asians to fight Asians. Asians are not instruments of foreign policy for big power use. They have not fallen like dominoes but seem to have gained a new confidence in themselves since the U.S. exodus from Vietnam. They are acquiring arms wherever possible, perhaps too many for their own good. Some nations fear the oversupply from the United States. Others fear that North Vietnam will peddle at a discount the supplies left behind in the U.S. retreat. The Southeast Asia Treaty Organization has disappeared, and a new Association of Southeast Asian Nations (ASEAN) will take its place, it is hoped, to convert Southeast Asia into a zone of peace, freedom, and neutrality.

A word might be in order about the special problems of the United States and the Philippines. After the relinquishment of bases in Thailand, the Americans will have foreign bases only in the Philippines. Philippine President Ferdinand Marcos wants recognition of his absolute sovereignty so he can be free to put the bases at the disposal of all nations, for an appropriate fee. He has said that he has no intention of interfering with the capacity of the United States to meet its security needs in the Southwest Pacific and the Indian Ocean, and he seems willing to negotiate some sort of management contract for the bases that would satisfy the Americans.

Economic relations between the United States and the Philippines have not deteriorated since the end of special relations with the expiration of the Laurel-Langley agreement. Business is as usual in spite of Philippine fears that the U.S. Trade Act of 1974 would put an end to the privileged position of sugar and other commodities in the U.S. market. Neither side seems to feel undue pressure in the process of negotiating a treaty of amity and commerce.

Officially, the U.S. government overlooks the demise of democracy and the imposition of martial law. Voices in Congress have deplored the Philippine action and have brought pressure to reduce arms assistance to the Philippines in the light of the authoritarian administration's actions. The use of the English language, the Filipinos' familiarity with U.S. business methods, the large pool of managerial talent and skilled labor, and the hospitable climate for U.S. economic activity make the Philippines a most attractive place for U.S. business.

China and the Pacific Basin

In passing from Southeast Asia to the Central Pacific, the focus shifts to the People's Republic of China, or China for short. The basic reality in any analysis of China is that Mao Tse-tung's leadership has ended. Any forecast of the direction of changes must rest on a sound interpretation of the nature of the Chinese nation-state and its political and economic record.

The national spirit in China is every bit as strong as it is in the fledgling nations of Southeast Asia. The reality is Communist China, not Chinese communism. Communist China is the successor to imperial China, republican China, and national China. Ideology is the adjective, and nation-state is the noun. In dealing with China, one must study its systems, but one must also study the language, culture, philosophy, and history that have characterized the longest-enduring, largest political body on Earth.

The Chinese are pragmatic. They modify their ideological line to suit the times, and they adjust their policies as radically as necessary to reap a national advantage. "Agrarian reform" is a prime example. Once it meant lower rents and reduced interest rates; then it was interpreted to mean land to the tiller; still later it became the banner for the establishment of communes. Chinese leaders have come and gone because they have not been able to keep in step with ideological shifts, to wit the rise and fall of Liu Shao-ch'i and Lin Piao.

Mao Tse-tung and Chou En-lai endured because they were flexible. They could support the tolerance of the Hundred Flowers and subsequently acquiesce in the purge of the dissidents. They could and did insist on leaning to one side in foreign policy and then lead the parade for peaceful coexistence. Subsequently, they turned the Cultural Revolution on and off by mere flips of their political and intellectual switches. They could alternately praise or condemn or befriend the Soviet Union, or curse or bless the United States within the perimeters of their communist ideology. They could insist on autarchy or self-reliance in economic development and at another moment turn 180 degrees and accept foreign trade and aid. Whether communist or not, they acted as responsible national leaders could be expected to act. Chances are that their successors will be equally flexible, whatever the temporary theoretical compulsions of their ideological commitments.

China's internal problems will continue to plague Mao's successors. Given the presumption of party control on the Leninist model, will the party machinery prove equal to the tasks of preserving national unity maintaining stability, solving the contradictions between the central and local governments, and keeping the army in line? Will it be able to handle the enormous administrative problems in the governance of 800 million people? Will it be able to maintain the required level of thought control and permit the individual freedom and initiative that would seem necessary to keep the masses—particularly the young—reasonably happy, prosperous, and confident in the future? The Communist party under Mao's leadership sported a creditable record. Can the successor apparatus do as well?

The national economic record under the Communists is impressive, but the challenge of the future is appalling. The "Good Earth" is limited, the population is growing, and agriculture is the way of life for eight out of ten of China's hundreds of millions. The raw material resources are extensive, especially in energy sources, but the Chinese intend to use those resources only at a pace that will serve the needs of the Chinese masses. The profit motive is out, except in a very small way, and the interest of the consumer, not the producer, is paramount in economic development. National plans aim to keep the development of agriculture, light industry, and heavy industry in balance. Since the unfortunate experience with the Soviets, the Chinese are determined to limit industrialization to their own capacity to manage. Likewise, they place understandable limits on foreign trade. They will sell what they have to buy what they need. What and how much they will trade depend on the national balance sheet, not on opportunities for individual profit.

China's future economic directions depend much more on practical than on ideological considerations. Like any other nation, China needs guns and butter. The Chinese want to be self-reliant but they do not intend to fall too far behind the rest of the world. They will satisfy their needs in airplanes, pipelines, and computer technology where the deal is best. They are not likely to let ideology interfere with their search for bargains. They are just as competent as capitalists in operating in international commercial and financial markets, and in making their economic transactions serve their political ends. Of course they will buy and sell with the United States if it tends to slow down the pace of the U.S.-Soviet détente; and they will even pay premiums in Western Europe to divert Soviet attention from Asia to its European frontiers.

China's acts and attitudes in foreign policy are not too difficult to anticipate, assuming they follow past patterns. In foreign affairs, China has been rational and understandable. Its policy is neither a riddle nor an enigma. China is a great power determined to wipe out past humiliations and determined to be recognized for the greatness it represents. Without seeking hegemony on its own part, it demands equal status with the strongest and the best. To guarantee its own survival, it must develop the capacity to meet any challenge, nuclear or conventional. National survival is the first responsibility of any government, communist or otherwise, in China or elsewhere.

For a long time, Communist China saw the United States as the leader of the imperialist camp and enemy number one. The United States saw China as ruthless, dynamic, and aggressive. Ideological contradictions seemed to place the two nations irrevocably on opposite sides of a bipolar world. The hostility of Korea, the off-shore islands, and Indochina came to a halt with the announcement of détente in 1971. This announcement was not a harbinger of peace and understanding; it was only a recognition that it was better to argue than to fight.

The détente was a matter of timing and political expedience on both sides. No record exists of the thoughts of Richard Nixon and Chou En-lai as they shook hands before the cameras. They might have been something like, "I hate your guts but the time has come to get down to business."

The Shanghai communiqué settled nothing, but it did give each side an opportunity to state its case and affirm its good intentions. Both disclaimed hegemony and agreed to deal with Taiwan as Chinese territory. The way was opened for expanded U.S.-China commercial and cultural relations. Such problems as frozen assets and most-favored-nation status were discussed and yet have to be solved before diplomatic recognition can be accomplished. Both nations indicate a desire for return to normalcy, but both also seem prepared to acknowledge that the road would be long and tortuous.

The United States has given no sign that it believes a change has taken place in the nature of the Communist Chinese regime; it accepts only the proposition that sufficient change has occurred in Communist China's behavior that détente is possible without jeopardizing U.S. security. It has had to admit that there was much more to the fighting in Korea and Vietnam than the mere containment of Communist China. On their part, the Chinese have had to include the United States in their policies for coexistence.

If for no other reason than to counter Soviet power, China seems to have become reconciled to a U.S. military presence in the western Pacific and even on the Asian mainland. China indulges in no more propaganda about capitalist encirclement; it does not seem to want the United States out of Japan, the Philippines, or Thailand, and it is in no hurry to force the United States completely out of Taiwan. China wants peace and stability throughout the region, and for the sake of peace, it is willing to restrain Kim Il-sung and accept the U.S. forces in South Korea.

China's biggest fear is that the United States and the Soviet Union will grow too close. It would be disastrous for China to face up to a U.S.-Soviet agreement on a security pact for the Pacific or an agreement on spheres of influence encompassing Southeast Asia. China does not want to see anything like a Helsinki conference for the Asian area nor further relaxation in Europe between the Soviet Union and NATO, including the United States. China fears Soviet aggression as it once feared the United States, and it is certain to communicate its fears to the United States secretary of state or president on the occasion of every visit of state.

The enmity between China and the Soviet Union is not a new phenomenon. It existed in the days of imperial China and tsarist Russia, and in its current phase it is exacerbated by ideological differences. The true believers have genuinely split, and they criticize each other with venom that is usually reserved for heretics. But the root of their troubles lies in the conflict of national interests. Limited commercial contacts continue between the two nations and perfunctory diplomatic establishments maintain a facade of correct but strained political relations.

China has distrusted the Soviet Union since the airing of their ideological differences in party conferences in the late fifties, and since the Soviet Union's renewed aggressive tactics in Eastern Europe. The recall of Soviet technicians angered the Chinese, and the Soviet advance into Czechoslovakia put the Chinese on special alert. The stationing of a million Soviet troops on the Siberian border and the fear of a pre-emptive Soviet strike to wipe out China's nuclear capacity led to the elevation of the Soviet Union to the position of China's new enemy number one. More than anything, China prepares itself for a Soviet attack, or an attack by the Soviet Union in collusion with the United States. The rhetoric is against hegemony on the part of either or both of the superpowers, but actually the Chinese nation is at work with a hoe in one hand and a rifle in the other so that any invader would be drowned in a sea of blood.

China's relations with Japan are likely to develop in accordance with China's interpretation of the Soviet menace. High on China's scale of priorities is the prevention of either a growing détente between the Japanese and the Soviets or an increasing three-way harmony between Japan, the Soviet Union, and the United States.

China was bitter toward Japan as a result of a half-century of aggression, and at the end of World War II, it was determined to make Japan pay dearly in reparations. As the benign occupation contributed to Japan's resurrection, China became jealous and uneasy. Japanese cooperation with the United Nations in Korea filled China's cup of woe. Japan's ballooning contributions to Taiwan's prosperity prompted China to soften its attitudes, however. It seemed better to woo the new Japan than to indulge in calumny against the old.

China opened commercial relations with Japan—without insisting on a total break between Japan and Taiwan—and invited Japanese Socialist and anti-mainstream Liberal Democratic party politicians to China. (Communist China had little sympathy for most Japanese Communists.) After the China-U.S. détente, China adopted a similar policy toward Japan and pursued more vigorously. China invited increasing numbers of Japanese business executives to Peking, toned down its propaganda, and reached working accords with Japan on fishing, shipping, air traffic, and trade. China made it possible for Japan to play ball both with the People's Republic and with the national government in Taiwan. China and Japan enjoy the advantages of geographic proximity and cultural affinity. They can benefit each other tremendously with their respective resources and capabilities, so the immediate outlook indicates a broad-based, greatly expanded, mutually advantageous political and economic relationship.

China can point to a record of solid achievement in the Third World. (In China's terms of reference, the First World is that of the superpowers; the Second World is the intermediate zone of Japan, Australasia, and Western Europe; and the Third World refers to the emerging nations of Southeast Asia, Africa, and Latin America.) Naturally, China's chief Third World concern lies with its Southeast Asian neighbors. Malaysia, Thailand, and the Philippines have sought normal relations with China, both in trade and diplomacy. And China's quietness has reassured them that Peking does not intend to use the overseas Chinese as antigovernment fifth-columnists and does not intend to export revolution or give any more than sympathetic support to local insurgents.

For a long time China was considered as the heart and soul of revolutionary movements around the world. "Maoism" became synonymous with a hard line until China demonstrated in Bangladesh that it was dedicated only to revolutions that served China's national purposes. China has told all revolutionaries, as Chou En-lai told UAR President Nasser, that it was up to revolutionaries everywhere to make their own revolutions as China had done. China has achieved a reputation for championing the cause of the Third World, and not merely the cause of the revolutionary elements within the newly emerged countries. China has assured the weak that they have nothing to fear from China, neither from outright aggression, from veiled imperialism, nor from manipulated insurgency.

Peking seems to be in no hurry to finalize Taiwan's status. A stronger Taiwan is emerging in the face of diplomatic extinction. Chiang Ching-kuo has proved himself to be a worthy successor to his father, Chiang Kai-shek. Taiwan retains diplomatic ties only with South Korea among its neighbors and has no diplomatic ties with nine out of ten of its best trading partners. Still, its industrial growth has culminated in an impressive list of homemade civilian products as well as F5E jet fighters, Huey helicopters, artillery tanks, and M-14 rifles. Taiwan has strengthened its infrastructure substantially and continues to do as much international trade as the entire Chinese mainland. It has achieved the third highest level of living in Aisa, after Japan and Singapore, and it is inconceivable that Peking will take precipitate action to damage the goose that promises to continue to lay the golden eggs. Taiwan is not entirely convinced that ultimate U.S.-China rapprochement will lead to its own extinction.

China is only a lukewarm supporter of the United Nations. It is gratified with its permanent membership on the Security Council, but it retains the uneasy feeling that the component agencies and the General Assembly itself offer too many opportunities for politicking among the great powers. China wants the U.N. command out of Korea and the annulment of the resolution condemning China for participating in aggression in the Korean War. China believes that a complete overhaul of the charter is long overdue, and it is not at all sure that the U.N. can be an effective instrument for peace and security if confronted by the armed might of the United States and the Soviet Union.

China has publicized its own program for collective security and disarmament. It opposes the nuclear nonproliferation treaty and insists on the right to develop whatever armaments, nuclear and otherwise, it deems necessary for its own protection. It would be satisfied with nothing less than equality in every category: war heads, missiles, bombing planes, and submarines. In the Chinese view, true disarmament can come about only with the complete destruction of existing nuclear stockpiles, a complete ban on the manufacture and use of nuclear weapons, an agreement on "no-first-use," and a nonaggression pact that would cover the entire Pacific Basin.

Changes are bound to occur when the leadership passes from one generation to another. It appears, however, that these changes will be less profound than is generally anticipated. Mao's spirit lives on and may well give China a new sense of unity and renewed vigor for work and achievement. A new constitution appeared (in January 1975), and a new triumvirate has taken over the direction of the affairs of state, dedicated to the objectives of unity and stability. Temporary zigzags may occur in details of party management, government administrative procedures, disposition of the armed forces, thought control, five-year plans, industrialization, foreign trade, and the pursuit of a satisfactory equilibrium of power. The surest bet, though, is that the new generation will be as assiduous as its imperialist, nationalist, or communist predecessors in protecting and promoting the national interests of the Chinese "Middle Kingdom."

Trends in the Northern Pacific

Two fundamental realities emerge from an analysis of issues and trends in the northern Pacific Basin. The first is that Japan and the United States are absolutely vital to each other. The preservation of friendly relations is essential to the security and welfare of both nations and to global peace and stability. The second reality is that Korea is a political time bomb that could explode at any time and involve the larger powers in a wider war. The North Pacific carries more commerce than the North Atlantic and is the arena of some of the liveliest jockeying for power equilibrium in the world today.

In the comparatively comfortable diplomatic atmosphere that existed between the end of World War II and the shattering of the American dream in Southeast Asia, the peace and prosperity of the entire Pacific Basin turned on the Tokyo-Washington axis. American power guaranteed security for both Japan and the United States, and the steady flow of foreign trade contributed to the high standard of living that both nations enjoyed. In 1974 the United States and Japan accounted for 52 percent of the production and 26 percent of the trade of the entire non-Communist industrialized world.

Since the dramatic exodus of U.S. forces from mainland Southeast Asia and the inauguration of détente with the Communist powers, Japan has been obliged to re-examine the utility and viability of the U.S. connection. Japan has asked new questions about U.S. power and intentions and has repeatedly challenged the validity of the premise of containment of communism on which recent U.S. policy has been based. If the United States has found it possible to pursue détente or peaceful coexistence, Japan too can afford to undertake new initiatives toward China and Russia. Some Japanese leaders believe that the time has come for Japan to explore alternative methods to reduce its absolute dependence on the United States. It is not a comfortable feeling to be the junior partner in an unequal alliance.

Japan is not too worried about the future of its own political system, or the immediate danger of an enemy invasion. For the moment it is willing to abide by the restrictions of Article IX in its constitution which denies remilitarization. It does not feel too much pressure to increase its self-defense forces or its expenditures for armaments. The majority of Japanese support the national nuclear policy, which is to accept the protection of the U.S. nuclear umbrella but not to make or possess nuclear weapons of any kind nor to permit their introduction into Japan. Japan has signed and ratified the nuclear nonproliferation treaty. It promotes atomic development for peaceful purposes and has repeatedly demonstrated its sophistication in satellites, rockets, missiles, and delivery systems. It has the capacity and the know-how to become a nuclear power in very short order.

When Japan turns its attention to relations with the United States and the rest of the world, it gives highest priority to economic problems. Although Japan is highly industrialized, it depends on sources overseas for much of its food and most of its raw materials. It lives by its technological and managerial competence, the skill of its labor, and hard work. Trade is its life's blood: Japan could never become self-reliant and still maintain its levels of material prosperity.

Japanese government and business are partners in economic activity. Their cooperation gives the Japanese a competitive advantage that the Americans, with their fierce spirit of independence, cannot hope to match. The United States is at once the most valued partner and most bitter rival of Japan. Traders in both nations want a minimum of political shocks and crises to interfere with the ordinary flow of their competition.

Japan's economic miracle has lost a great deal of its luster. The country is not yet an emerging superstate. It has overcome its fascination with growth and has begun to think more about the quality of life. Of what value are more petrochemical complexes if their fumes pollute the air and obscure the view of Mt. Fuji? The government has been forced to pay more attention to individual welfare than to the gross national product, and to spend money for projects designed more for the public good than for private profit. Japan has lagged woefully in programs designed for social justice.

For Japan, the problem of security is less ominous than the problem of economic welfare. Japan learned a cruel lesson with its defeat in World War II and considered itself fortunate to come under the benevolent wing of the United States for its future protection. Japan now suffers no credibility gap in reassessing its relationship with the United States. It is relieved that the United States has come to its senses and ended its disastrous overcommitment to Southeast Asia. It is convinced that the United States appreciates Japan's importance and will go to war if necessary to come to its aid.

Japan is generally satisfied with the present security treaty. Last renewed in 1970, the treaty seeks to eliminate conflict in international policies and to encourage economic collaboration. It provides that in the event of an armed attack on Japan, the United States will take action in accordance with its constitutional processes. In return, U.S. land, air, and naval forces will be allowed to use facilities and certain areas in Japan. Thus with very little cost to itself, Japan enjoys the protection of the U.S. nuclear umbrella and conventional forces.

The Japanese government shows little inclination to abolish or even amend the security treaty, and the popular demonstrations of "Yankee, Go Home" have practically disappeared since the end of the Vietnam War. But the Japanese were hurt and offended that the United States ignored them when announcing the U.S. policy of détente. Therefore they undertook a more vigorous search for acceptable alternatives to complete dependence on its senior partner. Japan wanted more latitude for independent diplomatic action should the need arise. The search, which is still in progress, aims at hedges around, not at substitutes for, the security treaty.

Japan would like complete freedom of action in dealing with the Soviet Union and China and in deriving the greatest possible advantage from the Sino-Soviet split. Both the Soviets and the Chinese accept the existence of the U.S.-Japan treaty as a fact of life and no longer demand the abrogation of the U.S.-Japan connection. Japan seems to minimize the threat of a nuclear attack by either the Soviet Union or China, and appears to be willing to accept some kind of an agreement that would make northeastern Asia a nuclear-free zone. Ideally, Japan would like to assume a posture of equidistance from both the Soviet Union and China because doing so would constitute the best hope of not becoming involved in any possible Sino-Soviet war.

In dealing with the Soviet Union, Japan has much to offer. It could provide the Soviets with capital assistance and technical know-how in the development of oil, natural gas, railways, and pipelines in Siberia. Japan insists on U.S. participation in ventures of any magnitude, because otherwise it conceivably could be threatened by a monster of its own creation. Japan would like a peace treaty with the Soviet Union that recognizes Japan's claims to disputed northern islands. For its part, the Soviet Union can be expected to adopt reasonably conciliatory attitudes toward Japan, thereby neutralizing as far as possible Japan's disposition to lean farther toward the United States or China.

In discussions with China, Japan seeks the best terms it can get for peaceful coexistence and trade expansion. It is not hindered or embarrassed by ideological considerations or its past relations with Chiang Kai-shek. It has no territorial ambitions of its own, and it is not wedded to the idea of two Chinas. It is content to let Peking and Taipei work out their own formula for Taiwan's future. Japan would like a peace treaty with the People's Republic of China that would lead to the restoration of normal diplomatic relations between Peking and Tokyo. Negotiations are stalled over the issue of a disclaimer of hegemony that Peking insists on, but that Tokyo dismisses as irrelevant and unnecessary.

Japan naturally desires the most extensive economic relations possible with both Taiwan and mainland China. It has built up a huge investment stake in Taiwan, which it is loath to give up. Japan now conducts as much trade with Taiwan as with the mainland; it is sensitive, however, to Peking's feelings about Taiwan and is intrigued by the possibilities of the giant China market. China has a vast store of raw materials that Japan covets, and it offers limitless opportunities for Japanese exports and Japanese investments. The more China industrializes and prospers, the brighter the future for both China and Japan. The Japanese want to make the most of their cultural affinity with the Chinese and to take the fullest advantage of their mutual understanding, without undue deference to the opinions and perhaps the prejudices of their U.S. allies.

Japan has long acted independently of the United States in its guarded relations with the countries of Southeast Asia. It does not see Southeast Asia as a power vacuum, but it acts with a high degree of circumspection largely because of the unpleasant associations of World War II. Japan has won favor through its enlightened reparations payments and makes it clear that it will in no sense succeed the United States as the Santa Claus of foreign aid. It invests heavily in Southeast Asia as a two-way beneficial procedure: the Japanese develop local mines or build ports and railways, which help the Southeast Asians. But Japan's foreign investments also bring profits to Japanese investors and make more raw materials available for the Japanese industrial machine. The Japanese drive hard bargains, and pay much more attention to their own profits than to the ecological effects of their operations on local environments.

The Japanese push for contracts in any country, regardless of political affiliation or ideological inclination. Japan is ready to help Burma or any member of ASEAN; it is also willing to study a new relationship with Indochina, which means that Japan could be of immeasurable help to Hanoi in solving its immense reconstruction problems.

The Japanese have always demonstrated their ability to compete successfully with Americans, Germans, or anybody else in Latin America, Africa, or Western Europe. They have taken on the Indians and the Chinese in the free markets of Hong Kong and Singapore. But they kept economics and politics separate, at least until they encountered the new situation in the Middle East occasioned by the energy crisis. It became expedient for Japan to adopt an independent policy that was less pro-Israel and more pro-Arab than the U.S. policy. This might well be a forerunner of other situations where Japan could turn out to be a political adversary as well as a commercial rival of the United States.

The United States approaches its problems with Japan on a basis of security first and economics second. This approach differs radically from the Japanese scale of priorities. The Japanese want to talk economics; the Americans want to stress security. The Americans are not unhappy over the security treaty, but they would like the Japanese to pay more for their own defense. In the U.S. view, the Japanese could at least build and pay for more submarines and take over more patrol responsibilities along the Japanese coastline. It does not seem quite fair that the Americans should pay so much and the Japanese so little for national defense.

The Americans are caught in a difficult dilemma. If they encourage the further rearmament of Japan, they alarm Japan's neighbors. The alternative to a strong Japan is a strong, costly U.S. military presence in the western Pacific. In either case the objective is mutual security. The U.S. government accepts the proposition that Japan's welfare and security are as important as those of the United States's NATO allies. Japan is the one vital interest of the United States in Asia and the Pacific.

The problem of Korea is scarcely less consequential in shaping the future of the northern Pacific Basin than the problems relating to Japan. After 1969 South Korea was the one nation in Asia that did not want to see the United States pull out of Vietnam and make up with the Communists. The surrender in Vietnam was seen as a ghastly omen that South Korea might be the next sacrificial victim, because it was in the same helpless situation in Northeast Asia that South Vietnam occupied in Southeast Asia.

The armistice in Korea in 1953 left the nation divided, with North Korea in the Communist camp and South Korea a hostage to the United Nations and the United States. The end of the fighting gave each half of Korea the opportunity to construct a political system according to its own ideology, develop its economy, and build up its fighting forces. North Korea talked incessantly of its intention to unify the country by force if necessary, and to assist the "people" of South Korea in their revolution against the government.

South Korea survived under the strong rule of Syngman Rhee until 1960, when a new democratic regime took over. President Park clamped martial law on South Korea in 1972, the better to resist forceful unification by the North. With the help of the United States and Japan, he launched a spectacularly successful economic development program.

As the Americans withdrew from Southeast Asia, Kim Il-sung became more bellicose in words and action. He unleashed commando raids in the South, seemingly prepared to invade while he participated in unification negotiations. He attracted no support from either the Soviet Union or China for a new war, but he threatened constantly to go it alone.

South Koreans now argue over internal politics, but they are unanimous in their hatred of anything identified as communist. Inspired by the cruel memories of the first invasion, they would die to stop another. South Korea does not feel strong enough to stand alone against the North; it needs outside help to counter the assistance that the North might receive from the Soviet Union or China. For a time, perhaps five years, the South wants a U.S. commitment to offset North Korea's air superiority. South Korea has no faith in the United Nations and depends entirely on the United States.

South Korea exhibits many weaknesses in its political and economic structure, but it has achieved extraordinary progress. It has a tremendous reservoir of brainy, courageous, and hard-working citizens. The police state is ruled by an iron hand, but the expertise exists to make democracy work if the opportunity arises. The fear of communism has reached fantastic proportions and has caused the demise of freedom of thought and civil rights. "Resist the North" is the theme for every type of political action.

The national economy has its soft spots. Industrialization was expedited by foreign loans, questionable business practices, and an inordinate amount of corruption, but it came to an abrupt halt with the energy crisis. South Korea, like Japan, struggles mainly for growth without careful consideration for the welfare of individual Koreans. The people in the countryside enjoy plenty to eat, but they have little else. Electric transmission lines go right past villages without bringing simple lights for the peasant homes. Wages are low and jobs are hard to get. Korea competes successfully with its textiles, sweaters, and cheap radios in the world market, but it pays a dreadful price in economic conditions at home. Much of the GNP goes for the support of the army and the government apparatus because of the danger of war, and no relief is in sight before the fear of North Korea disappears.

North and South Korea have been conducting talks looking to unification for the past five years, but neither side is willing to put sufficient faith in the other to accept a compromise. The demarcation line at the 38th parallel still bristles with enmity while troops on both sides of the border walk their patrols in full combat gear. The allies of North Korea and South Korea can put pressure on their clients but they cannot bring about unification without the will and the work of the Koreans themselves. Unification now seems as remote as it did the day that North-South negotiations began.

South Korea pins its hopes for a viable economic future on the United States and Japan. No South Korean leader seems to share Kim Il-sung's burning desire to accomplish unification by force. President Park and his colleagues seem to be content with an independent South Korea for the foreseeable future. They still harbor a skepticism about Japan, which is a heritage of colonial days: they fear they will retain Japan's support only as long as they are useful to Japan.

When Prime Minister Miki visited U.S. President Ford in 1974, their communiqué recognized that the security of the Republic of Korea (South Korea) was essential for the maintenance of peace on the Korean peninsula, and the maintenance of peace on the Korean peninsula was necessary for the peace and security of East Asia, including Japan. They agreed that it was essential, for the moment, to keep U.S. forces in Korea. Subsequently, in Seoul in August 1975, Defense Secretary James Schlesinger told the Koreans that the United States would do everything necessary (implying the use of nuclear weapons) to deter or counter an attack from North Korea.

President Park seemed far happier about the U.S. commitment to Korea than did some members of the U.S. Congress, who saw in South Korea the place where the United States might again become mired in combat on the Asian continent. No congressman advocated the termination of the Treaty of Mutual Defense, which is similar to the security treaty between the United States and Japan, but many congressmen were disgusted with the idea of giving military assistance to a military dictatorship. They wished to give aid on the condition of the relaxation of martial law and the reintroduction of respect for human rights.

Some congressmen disliked the thought of U.S. forces in Korea without provision for systematic reduction or ultimate withdrawal. Most agreed, however, that the U.S. presence was vital for the immediate future. No withdrawal program should be put in operation that would jeopardize South Korea's stability, encourage North Korea, or disturb the delicate relationship between South Korea and Japan. There seemed to be nothing to do about Park's dictatorship until, as one congressman put it, "something beyond our control for better or worse happens to change the situation."

Practically no one outside the United States and Japan has shown a great deal of sympathy for South Korea's plight. Those two countries, however, have made clear their determination that South Korea will not be conquered by force. Whatever changes are brought about for the security of South Korea will have to be accomplished by peaceful means and with the full acquiescence of the government in Seoul.

Conclusions

Can any conclusions be drawn from such a cursory survey of the basic realities in the Pacific Basin? Each reader will undoubtedly interpret the facts as he sees them, and adapt them to his own personal views or business requirements.

Clearly, the Pacific's problems did not begin yesterday, nor will they be solved tomorrow. Their roots go as far back into history as one chooses to trace them. Many conflicts were the results of misconceptions or misunderstandings. Failures, particularly on the part of the United States, were often due to mistaken analyses or faulty situation estimates. The record was marred by missed opportunities.

Now the age of post-war U.S. demicolonialism has come to an end, but the United States will always be a Pacific and an Asian power. The United States has much more than military might to offer to the peoples and nations of Asia, for its strength is much more in its intangible values than in its arms. The United States never has been, and never will be, isolationist as far as Asia is concerned. Whatever happens on one side of the Pacific is bound to make its ripples on the other.

In this period of transition, businesspeople, intellectuals, and government leaders in all countries have the information and the ability to make the new world a better one. May they have the will and the wisdom to make the best use of all the talents and tools that have been placed at their disposal.

3

An Overview of Economic Conditions in the Pacific Basin

Charles W. Hostler

Theodore Roosevelt once predicted that the Pacific, as "greatest of the Seas," would become first in importance. Today his prediction is rapidly being fulfilled. In the past decade, most of the non-Communist countries rimming the Pacific have enjoyed an unprecedented period of economic growth. The Pacific has become the world's most *dynamic* trading region and is *potentially* the greatest. An already enormous market is expanding, while a wealth of natural and human resources still awaits development. As economic activity has intensified, the Pacific Basin has awakened to a new sense of interdependence and a community of interests.

Few people in other parts of the world realize the changes taking place in the Pacific Basin. In some respects the Pacific countries increasingly give the appearance of being an economic entity—for example, almost two-thirds of western Pacific exports go to other countries in the region or to the United States. United States trans-Pacific trade is already substantially greater than U.S. trade with the European community. For example, in 1974 the United States's two-way trans-Pacific trade amounted to $46.8 billion, $5.5 billion more than its trade with the European community. The changes in the Pacific region are steady—not startling, but gradually accelerating along some strong economic base lines so that the effects of effort and progress are clearly visible.

Here are some of the forces at work in the Pacific Basin, which may help businesses to expand export efforts to that area:

1. Exploration and development of new sources of energy and scarce minerals, backed by potential outside investment for related refining, processing, and transportation facilities
2. A widening dispersal of fragmented manufacturing operations among areas of plentiful labor supplies, principally in the textile and electronics industries—for example, televisions assembled in Japan for the U.S. and European markets commonly contain parts made in Hong Kong, Korea, and Taiwan
3. The beginning of a move by the Japanese to shift some manufacturing operations to nearby countries to relieve pollution and congestion at home
4. Better balanced economic development programs in most countries, partly inspired by their success in small parts manufacturing. Food production and infrastructure projects are getting needed attention, and various countries are edging into a higher level of industry. For instance, Korea's new

shipbuilding facility has a three-year backlog of orders, among which are orders for ten ships for Kuwait
5. Economic success and political stability

Economic Viability in the Pacific Basin

The whole Pacific Basin continues to suffer from the economic downturn of 1974, which was brought about by high oil and commodity prices and inflation. Most Pacific nations also were hard hit by a declining export demand resulting from the business slump in the United States and Japan, their main customers. Even so, however, a general feeling of optimism exists. The average Korean is confident that the upturn in the U.S. economy will be maintained, and also is encouraged by developments in Japan. The Japanese managed to pay an additional $13 billion for oil in 1974, and on a balance-of-payments basis still generated a $1.4 billion surplus for the year. Japan also has substantially reduced its rate of inflation.

Technological progress is spreading and is being proudly shared as it is acquired. Taiwan has about 900 technicians at work in agricultural development in Africa, Latin America, and Southeast Asia. All their salaries are paid by the Republic of China. Experts from Taipower, the spectacularly successful government power monopoly, are advising Thailand on nuclear power possibilities and are providing engineering and contracting services to other friendly countries. Japan continues to outpace the rest of the region and, in some respects, the rest of the world. Scarcely twenty years ago this economy was sustained by small-plant, labor-intensive manufacturing just as other countries of the area are today. Both the near-term outlook and the long run for Japan are sound.

Japan

In the larger view, Japan can be seen striding toward world leadership in both trade and industrialization. The Japanese are investing heavily abroad. There is a note of confidence and daring in their investments, some of which are beginning to fall into a new pattern, with control being exerted over the end product and relaxed at the production end of Japanese-financed projects. We see Japanese companies helping to finance energy and mineral projects in remote parts of the world without owning or operating them, and allowing others to handle the processing near the source of supply. After that, however, control over the procurement and shipping of the product passes to the Japanese by virtue of contracts for the projects' output, and by means of deep-water ports, automated warehouses, dock facilities, and special ships that the Japanese provide.

Such arrangements assure Japan's future access to sources of raw materials, avoid much of the risk of nationalization, reduce pollution and labor shortage problems at home, and demonstrate the kind of efficiency most likely to attract OPEC investments for Japan's still more rapid progress.

Australia

Australia is another country where bright future prospects outweigh short-term difficulties. The superboom of the past few years has waned: unemployment is up, the balance of payments has fallen into deficit, and the extensive foreign exchange reserves have dropped, although they still amounted to $3.3 billion in September 1975 when the Australian dollar was devalued 12 percent to try to reverse the trend.

The Australian economy is basically sound, however. In fact, the forces that can generate a resumption of the boom are waiting to be rallied. The Australians are highly skilled, and agricultural, mineral, and other raw material resources are virtually unlimited.

The United States remains Australia's leading supplier. Its share of imports has been more than 22 percent. There will be enormous opportunities for exports of U.S. capital goods as Australian resource development proceeds. The accompanying build-up of Australian industry will further increase the market for high-technology, labor-saving equipment in which the United States specializes. It would be a serious mistake to take the Australian market for granted, however. Between 1969 and 1974, U.S. exports to Australia rose 152 percent, from $1 billion to $2.1 billion. In the same period Japanese exports to Australia increased from $500 million to $2 billion, a gain of 300 percent. United States suppliers have some heavy selling to do in that market, where their competitors are meeting and exceeding U.S. commercial efforts.

Taiwan

Taiwan is pushing ahead pragmatically through economic and diplomatic difficulties, with economic development centered on infrastructure-railroads, ports, highways, airports, and basic industry.

Exports make up half Taiwan's GNP. Together, the United States and Japan account for 55 percent of the exports. The Chinese also look to the economic recovery of the United States and Japan to improve their own condition. American bankers in Taiwan appear to have a good deal of confidence in that country's government: their commitments amount to about $1.2 billion, 80 percent of it in short-term obligations.

Agriculture has been rationalized, fragmented farms consolidated, and productivity increased with the assistance of technical advisers from the central government and credits for fertilizers and seeds. This has released farm workers for industries, just as it did in Japan. The Chinese have become self-sufficient in rice but have found it more economical to import other grains than to produce them at home.

Korea

The Koreans maintain their strong favoritism for the United States. They are somewhat concerned about our reduced military presence but are resigned to the approaching end of the "aid" days. The development loan fund allotted about $25 million in 1975, its last year in Korea.

The Korean goal of military and economic self-sufficiency by the early 1980s is currently obscured by the oil price problem. Inflation is running at a rate of about 30 percent, and GNP growth has dropped from a rate of 15 percent to about 8 percent. Food production, which provided 85 percent of domestic needs in the 1960s, now provides only 67 percent.

The overall Korean development plan is being restudied with a view to slowing down some sectors, particularly petrochemicals, and to speeding up steel and metal industries, with special emphasis on machine tools. Machinery production is being pushed to take advantage of a growing market in Asia for smaller machines that are not readily available from other industrial countries. The Korean shipbuilding industry is beginning to take some business away from the Japanese because of Korea's much lower labor costs.

Indonesia

Indonesia has continued its steady recovery from the mid-1960s, and its mineral and energy resources have assumed major importance. An OPEC member—the only one in the Pacific Basin—Indonesia has much need for its new wealth. Its 130 million people have a per capita income of only about $100. The country still gets aid from the World Bank and the Asian Development Bank, although not on terms as soft as those of the past. Some of the oil revenues will go into power, cement, refinery, and reclamation projects, which are now in the works. Oil export earnings for the 1975 Indonesian fiscal year were expected to triple to a total of $6.4 billion, bringing the total export figure to $8.4 billion. Net foreign exchange reserves are nearing $2.5 billion. New restrictions on foreign investments were imposed in January 1975 and remain to be clarified.

The Philippines

The outlook for the Philippines is good and appears to hinge largely on two steps now being taken: one to improve the infrastructure with new power, port, highway, and other essential projects, and the other to improve fiscal management policies. Tax revenues are enabling the government to move ahead with projects, supplying the "buyer participation" required for credit financing. An extensive supply of skilled labor and an abundance of raw materials are among the national assets.

Thailand

Thailand deserves particular notice for going against the trend: it is backing away from industrialization. Domestically the Thais are enjoying a 5- to 6-percent annual growth rate, and they have a strong holding of foreign exchange reserves, but they show little inclination to build up foreign trade. The Japanese pulled out of a large petrochemical project proposal there last year, so Thailand is taking another look at its plans for a nuclear power plant, with the idea that it may not be needed.

The Far East

The two main requirements for economic development in the Far East are investments and technology. The ideal combination would be OPEC money, because of its free and easy accumulations, and U.S. technology, which is nowhere excelled. However, for reasons already indicated, Japanese investments and technology will be heavily involved in the development of every Far Eastern country. The United States will have Japanese and European competition for all Pacific business, and all Pacific nations will have to compete with the rest of the world for equity and loan capital.

Mexico

Despite Mexico's efforts to diversify its international trade patterns to reduce its great dependence on the United States as a supplier, the current outlook is that the United States will maintain its present market share of around 62 percent of this $6 billion market.

In that regard, there have been some interesting changes: The Mexican import tariff system, modified January 1, 1975, increased duties on one-third of the total tariff classifications, reduced them on one-third, and kept them the same on the rest. Because of these and other changes, the new tariff undoubtedly will have adverse effects on some U.S. exporters while favoring the others, but the effect on U.S. exports in general is not expected to be significant. Another change—one that the U.S. hopes will be only temporary—is the institution of drastic measures during July 1975 to clamp down on imports. All imports were put under a license requirement, and some types of goods have been stopped from entering the country altogether. Others are allowed under the quota system based on the importing company's situation.

The Trade Act of 1974

At the beginning of 1975 the United States prepared to face certain new trading factors, resulting from the passage of the Trade Act of 1974. However, the last-minute restrictions placed on the generalized system of preferences (GSP) were disappointing. The prohibition on extending benefits to OPEC members will exclude an otherwise deserving nation, Indonesia. Although the Latin Americans were among the first to complain, the exclusion of certain textile and apparel articles and of import-sensitive electronic and steel articles is of great concern to many of the U.S.'s Asian trading partners.

For those who recognize that the greatest mutual benefit comes from maximizing both imports and exports, the U.S. government hopes there is support for the position that these rules should be interpreted as liberally as possible. It also hopes U.S. businesses will share its aims of utilizing the new authority of the Trade Act, to negotiate multilateral tariff reductions, eliminate other trade barriers, and reform the general agreement on tariffs and trade (GATT).

The Role of a Free Market

The problem and the opportunities that characterize the economies and the interrelationships of the Pacific Basin point up the validity of the U.S. free-market system, and the need to maintain resiliency. Contrived solutions to problems of supply and demand, no matter how brilliantly conceived by governments, cannot be effective in and of themselves. Free trade with investment policies, supplemented by the interplay of the free-market process that they allow, can achieve success. In this connection the negotiations now going forward within the context of GATT should be of special interest. The U.S. government hopes that those deliberations will result in a flexible policy framework, which is so clearly needed.

4

The Trade Act of 1974: Implications for Trade in the Pacific Basin

Peter Suchman

The talks in Geneva involve subjects of interest to businesses. Of particular interest is the negotiation of an international agreement on subsidies and countervailing duties. I address these subjects with a bit more pessimism than Hostler. There are some disturbing trends loose in the world of international trade, and I do not think those trends are really confined to the developing countries. They also are prevalent among some of our major industrial trading partners and indeed within the United States. Of course my view may be a little distorted by my job, which deals with unfair trade practices. Some of what I have to say has already been mentioned, but I hope I may be able to pull it together and put it in the perspective of U.S. trade policy.

Changes in Trade Policy

The concept of most-favored-nation (MFN) treatment means that a concession granted to any country is granted to all. The United States has pursued an unconditional MFN policy in international trade for the last forty or so years; this policy has been reflected in a series of reciprocal trade acts that have been passed beginning in 1934 and going through the Trade Expansion Act of 1962, which was the basis for the Kennedy round of tariff negotiations. But there have been changes in the MFN concept, which will be discussed later in this chapter. Because of U.S. adherence to the MFN principle, the General Agreement on Tariffs and Trade (GATT), the framework for the multilateral trading system, is grounded on it. It is also grounded on the principle of comparative advantage, which is the other cornerstone of the U.S. approach to trade.

As a result of the MFN system, set up after World War II to include the GATT, and also as a result of the Bretton Woods system, international trade has grown phenomenally over the years. The system has managed to absorb a number of very large shocks recently, especially the huge shifts in payments balances that resulted from the formation of the Organization of Petroleum Exporting Countries (OPEC), the dismantlement of the fixed-exchange-rate system that began in 1971, and the shift to today's flexible-exchange-rate system.

I perceive two major trends that have been developing both within the United States and abroad over the last decade or so that run counter to the two

31

basic premises of this system. The first trend is the erosion of the MFN approach, and the second is a movement away from the marketplace as the determining factor in international trade. Examples of the first trend are the formation of the European Economic Community (EEC), which the United States has supported for various reasons. No one can deny that the EEC is in fact a movement away from the MFN idea. Other preferential trading areas have been created also, for example, the Andean Pact and the Central American Common Market. And now the Generalized System of Preferences (GSP) has been put into effect by a number of major industrial countries, including the United States (on January 1, 1976). This system grants duty-free treatment to the exports of developing countries if they meet certain criteria. The following may come as a shock, but our estimates at the U.S. Treasury, based on a GATT study, indicate that today 65 percent of the world's trade moves through non-MFN channels; i.e., trade takes place on preferential terms. The GSP concept is very simple: it is designed to encourage industrial development in developing countries. Most people will support the policy; the question is whether it will work. Judgment must be reserved for now, but it should be realized that it is contributing to the movement away from unconditional adherence to the MFN policy.

The Trade Act of 1974 marks, or may mark, a turning point in the U.S. approach. First, the act puts forward, for the first time in forty years, the concept of conditional MFN status. This means that concessions will be granted to only those countries who reciprocate, whereas in the past, when a tariff cut was agreed to, it applied to all countries. (As I said, there is a provision in the Trade Act that could lead to a different result in the trade negotiations that are currently under way.) Second, the U.S. Congress is encouraging the executive branch, in the negotiation of agreements or codes on nontariff barriers, to make the advantages of those agreements available only to the countries who sign these agreements. This departure from past practice could prove to be monumental; in effect, it could lead to column-one and column-two treatment for various exporting countries with regard to nontariff remedies. For example, a country might have to find injury before it could impose a countervailing duty on the exports from one country but not on the exports from another.

The second basic premise of U.S. trade policy involves market forces and comparative advantage. The U.S. government has already examined some current developments that question all trading nations' commitments to the concept that those forces are to determine trade flows. We have export restraints, we have subsidies, we have cartels sheltered from competition, and we have the encouragement of government intervention in many ways to distort the market further. Economic institutions are manipulated for short-term political purposes by governments, and the United States has to face the fact that most other countries are more favorably disposed toward government intervention and less inclined to rely on market forces. The United States faces this problem continually in discussing such things as dumping, countervailing duties, standards, government procurement, and so forth.

Effects on Pacific Basin Countries

All these developments are of special interest to the Pacific nations but certainly not confined to them. The developing countries of the area are concerned with the generalized system of preferences. Many will be beneficiaries of GSP and hope to significantly expand their exports of industrial products to the United States as a result of it. Others may well be affected by this conditional MFN approach. In addition, many of those developing countries have special interests in particular commodities, and we all know what is happening in that field with attempts at cartelization. Current discussions—such as the U.N. special session or at the producer-consumer meetings in Paris—are directed at a significant change in the terms of trade for countries exporting raw materials and, in some cases, agricultural commodities.

In line with the above, it should be noted that some Pacific countries are members of OPEC, and all are consumers of petroleum. In addition, the tin agreement will affect countries in the area, and similar agreements have been contemplated for copper, coffee, and cocoa. The old rules of the game no longer apply to a whole range of commodity problems, and it is not yet known what the new rules are. In fact, the current debate can be characterized as a question of whether governments will intervene in the market, in combination, to try to regulate and change drastically the distribution of wealth and income between the developed and developing countries.

Now, these problems are not confined to the developing countries. Among the Pacific's industrial nations—including Canada, Australia, Japan, and the United States—traditional trade policy conflicts, which have been going on for generations, will continue. In addition, however, many new trends symbolize a greater willingness to retreat from the position of allowing market forces to determine the course of trade. Of course, present economic conditions have led to an increase in protectionist pressures, and the United States has certainly been accused of this by its trading partners. But aside from that, more concern should be placed on what seems to be a general agreement that we ought to attempt to stabilize trade. "Stabilize" is a very curious word. Any way you slice it, it turns out to be a major divergence from the free market whether it is in textiles, footwear, steel, or grains. It means that governments or bureaucrats are going to decide what market shares ought to be, who ought to hold what reserves of which commodity, and what prices ought to be in which market. Such problems are different from the kinds of trade policy problems that have generally been discussed in the past.

A wide range of sensitive products lead to these discussions, and they really illustrate the divergence from the liberalization that the United States has long advocated—and that other nations supported—to a concern with stabilization. An example of this new concern that other industries are pointing to is the Multifiber Textile Arrangement, which came to fruition some time ago in Geneva. As a replacement for the long-term agreement on textiles, it provides an umbrella for bilateral restraint arrangements between supplying and consuming countries. Aside from that, there are also great pressures, particularly from Canada, for the trade negotiations in Geneva to concentrate on sectoral arrangements. Again, sectoral arrangements represent cutting off particular commodity areas that will be treated differently: the general rules will not apply. Collectively, trading nations are going to do some things, in effect, that allow governments to regulate trade in particular commodities. In the United States there is no question that there has been a great upsurge in requests by producers for protection from imports of certain commodities and it should be pointed out that these are not limited only to those things already mentioned. They cut across a broad range of things. We have discussed automobiles and there is also a case involving steel. There will be more involving steel but we also have Philippine wall tile and adapters from Japan. There is a long list of products.

Concerns of U.S. Businesses

The requests listed above are legitimate, they are valid under the existing laws, and they will be processed. The case illustrates the fact that certain pressures are building up in the United States, although they are also building up in Japan, Hong Kong, Korea, and Taiwan. The trade involved adds up to well over $10 billion. (Of course, that figure may be somewhat distorted since $7.5 billion is accounted for by automobiles alone.) The main point is that the problem of protectionism is not confined to the United States.

The U.S. system is an open system. Specific criteria are laid down for the exercise of remedies. The courts have been quite willing to intervene when they think the congressional mandate is not being carried out. On the other hand, it is really impossible to know what is going on in some of the other industrialized countries.

I would give you an example of the way we have treated the automobile case in comparison with the way a similar case was treated in the United Kingdom. After the British Prime Minister said that there was a problem with imports of Japanese automobiles nothing further was said about it. Yet there are reports that there has been an agreement between the Japanese exporters and the U.K. government. In the United States, things are much different. When we process a case for protection of domestic producers, somebody has to prove something. That puts us at a very distinct disadvantage in discussions internationally because we published the opinions of our International Trade Commission. Even if the vote is 4 to 2 against providing protection to domestic producers, the two dissenting opinions are still thrown back in our faces by our trading partners. What the U.K. government did in the Japanese auto case we do not know. It was handled behind the scenes. In the United States, the Japanese auto case was a matter of public record and we were criticized even though, unlike the British, we did not provide protection for our domestic automobile producers. This difference in systems is a very difficult one and is not limited to the fact that we are required to be a lot more open in our procedures. In addition, the executive branch is much more limited than in most countries in the authority it has in negotiating agreements. This points to the failure of the American Selling Price Agreement after the Kennedy round. It has given U.S. trading partners a great deal of distress.

Current Negotiations

Current U.S. trade negotiations are quite different from past negotiations, which were purely and simply directed at tariff cuts, with some small, but largely unsuccessful, attempts to negotiate nontariff barrier agreements. Today the major impetus has shifted to nontariff measures, partly because U.S. and EEC tariff levels are very low. Accordingly, other things have sprung up to take their place in trade negotiations.

All past negotiations principally concerned the developed countries, whereas the developing countries are making their demands known in this round. Perhaps the most interesting of their demands is differential treatment of some kind across the entire spectrum of commodities they produce. In general, the United States has supported that demand although it has not yet come forth with any specific proposals. It certainly will be one of the critical factors. I do not think the United States can reach agreements in this round without the developing countries' participation.

Some of the major issues for negotiation involve trade in agricultural products. I do not wish to expand *ad infinitum* on problems with the EEC's and other countries' restrictionist agriculture policies.

In the area of nontariff barrier codes, the subjects most often mentioned are standards. Basically, these standards deal with electronic products but can affect practically anything. Also involved are subsidies and countervailing duties, government procurement, and now renegotiation of the antidumping code that was arrived at in the Kennedy round. Most critically, the United States must address a basic question about whether countries that participate in the multilateral trading system are going to set a new course for international trade over the next few decades. Right now we are in a state of flux. Current negotiations, like those at Bretton Woods, will result in agreements that will be in effect for quite some time. And it increasingly appears that other countries are willing to abandon the benefits that accrue or that we have presumed to accrue through liberalized trade—a system based on the premise that the economic well-being of all is improved by increasing the total wealth available for distribution in the most efficient way possible. The major trading countries, particularly the industrialized countries, are being pressed to abandon this system for the promise of certainty, stable prices, stable market shares, stable employment, stable growth rates, stable grain reserves, and so on. I cannot deny that U.S. policy, in response to these trends, has been somewhat equivocal up to now. The United States must make a choice, which will not be a choice just for the government. It must be reflected in the private sector as well, because if it chooses the path of stability rather than the path it has been following, the United States can count on a great deal more government involvement in the private sector, insofar as it pertains to international trade.

5 U.S. Policies for Importing and Exporting in the Pacific Basin

Robert R. Miller

For nearly forty years, U.S. international trade policy has been predicated on a fairly common set of assumptions. Perhaps most important, it has been based on the notion that the nation's economic welfare is best served by lowering worldwide tariffs and other barriers to international trade. And, too, the United States historically has been firmly committed to the idea that when trade barriers are reduced, they should be lowered uniformly to all nations through the most-favored-nation (MFN) principle. These assumptions have allowed, and indeed encouraged, U.S. participation in a number of bilateral and, more recently, multilateral negotiations with other nations for the purpose of freeing international trade through mutual tariff reductions. U.S. cooperation in discussions under the General Agreement on Tariffs and Trade (GATT) has been made possible through a series of congressional acts beginning with the Reciprocal Trade Agreements Act of 1934 and ending with the Trade Exansion Act of 1962. Recently, the Trade Act of 1974 once again has empowered the president to undertake negotiations to reduce trade barriers. This time, however, there are indications that the assumptions of the past forty years are beginning to change.

The changes that are appearing represent in part a subtle shift in national objectives and in part changes in the international economic environment. Policy alternations reflect an admixture of each. For example, the United States, along with a number of other industrial countries, has begun to discard the idea of uniform most-favored-nation treatment in tariff reductions. Thus far this change has been limited to trade with less-developed countries, which are to be allowed preferential access to U.S. markets for manufactured and processed materials. There are some notable market exceptions, especially from the perspective of Pacific Basin nations: for example, products important to Pacific Basin nations that are not to receive tariff preferences are textiles, shoes, and some import-sensitive electronic and steel products. Even so, abandoning most-favored-nation restrictions represents a rather fundamental change in a long-term policy.

Why did the change occur? The major stimulus came from the concerted efforts of the less-developed countries themselves to gain trade advantages in order to foster industrial development. This pressure coincided with the U.S. government's recognition that earlier programs intended to assist economic development were only moderately successful and that new funds for such programs were becoming much more difficult to obtain. Thus preferential tariff concessions, which inherently mean discarding a part of the older most-favored-nation doctrine, are seen as a device to continue the nation's limited commitment to economic development.

Other policy changes have been motivated by essentially internal considerations, i.e., the desire to maintain domestic employment. As an example, adjustment assistance to firms and workers adversely affected by increased imports from tariff reductions was first incorporated into the Trade Expansion Act of 1962 and has been repeated in modified form in the most recent legislation. This provision recognizes that in any lowering of tariffs, the benefits from greater amounts of imported materials accrue to consumers of these products, whereas the costs fall mainly on domestic industries that fabricate the goods. Two assumptions are implied: (1) overall benefits from imports exceed the costs; and (2) consumers are represented by the taxpaying populace as a whole, while affected firms and workers are more concentrated. Therefore adjustment assistance can be considered a transfer payment from beneficiaries of the tariff policy to the few individuals suffering losses, which, although significant to them, are assumed to be smaller than the community gains from increased trade.

The introduction of such a policy, long advocated by economists, owes its political inspiration to the U.S. labor movement's changing attitude toward free trade. In years immediately following World War II, many unions affiliated with capital- and research-intensive industries actively supported trade liberalization on the grounds that more trade would be beneficial to their memberships. Recently, this position has shifted rather dramatically toward protectionism, and adjustment assistance can be viewed politically as an expedient method to regain residual support for free trade legislation.

The changing labor union viewpoint on trade policy can be seen again in a current issue of particular relevance to Pacific Basin countries. Unions have been vehemently opposed to so-called export platform activities of U.S. multinational firms, much of which has taken place in the Pacific area. Companies establish subsidiaries in such countries as South Korea, Taiwan, or Singapore to fabricate products expressly for export to the United States. Unions attack these firms for "exporting" jobs, and the suggested policy prescription is the Burke-Hartke Bill, thus far rejected by Congress. This bill would severely restrict corporate investments affecting U.S. labor markets. In the years to come, the increasingly protectionist posture being adopted by previously free trade-oriented unions will be an important factor in future trade policy directions.

One other apparent shift in policy concerns the export side of the trade ledger. The quest for domestic price stability has motivated a new policy and, some would say, an insidious form of policy that allows governmental regulation of exports, especially agricultural exports. The purpose of this interference with market processes is clear: by increasing domestically available supplies, prices for goods produced here can be lowered relative to the world price. Although such controls have been commonplace in other countries, they are only a recent development in the United States, at least in the post-World War II period.

The remainder of this chapter is addressed to the topic of trade policies and their origin, with particular emphasis on trading patterns in the Pacific Basin.

Economic Rationale for U.S. Trade Policy

It can be said that, more than for most other countries, U.S. trade policies in the last four decades have been dictated by a belief in the efficacy of the unadulterated theory of comparative advantage. This theory states that world economic welfare is enhanced if each country produces a set of goods for which it is best adapted, and trades to obtain products made more efficiently elsewhere. The particular assortment of goods produced is based on a nation's specific endowment of such productive factors as raw materials, fertile land, skilled and unskilled labor, and capital equipment. Individual countries would be expected to export products that intensively incorporate their most abundant factors. Imports would consist of products cheaper to produce elsewhere because other countries were better endowed with the resources important in their production. Any interference with the free flow of trade would simply short-circuit the process of resources being utilized in the most efficient manner possible.

The appropriate trade policy for the world, if not for each country, under these circumstances is free trade; generally, the United States has maintained this position for many years. To be sure, cynics might argue that such a posture is particularly advantageous for the United States, since it is the largest and most developed industrial nation in the world. Less-developed countries might be forgiven for believing that a policy of unfettered trade is tantamount to accepting a position of permanent second-class citizenship in the world economy. Nonetheless, the U.S. policy position traditionally has been founded on a belief in the correctness of the simple theory of comparative advantage. Successive administrations have worked to reduce not only U.S. barriers to trade but also equivalent impediments in other countries around the globe.

Although the theory has served as a basis for overall U.S. trade policy, its use has been limited in precisely explaining the sources of comparative advantage for the United States. The theory of comparative advantage suggests that the United States should export capital- and land-intensive products because it is particularly well endowed with them. Conversely, since labor is highly paid here, imports should consist of items requiring large amounts of labor. In particular, imports from such Pacific Basin nations as South Korea, Hong Kong, Taiwan, Singapore, the Philippines, and to some degree Japan should consist of manufactured products that call for a large amount of relatively unskilled labor.

Unfortunately for policy-makers, Wassily W. Leontief demonstrated over twenty years ago that the actual situation is considerably more complicated than any simple theory would suggest [7, 8]. In fact, it turns out in Leontief's work that the United States is a net importer of goods incorporating larger amounts of capital and a net exporter of labor-intensive products. In his words, "An average million dollars' worth of our exports embodies considerably less capital and somewhat more labor than would be required to replace from domestic production an equivalent amount of our competitive imports" [7, p. 522]. Needless to say, this finding stimulated a rash of economic research to explain Leontief's seemingly perverse result and to isolate the sources of U.S. competitive strength.

Some researchers have concentrated on the import side, attempting to explain why U.S. imports might be capital-intensive. For example, it has been suggested that the composition of U.S. imports is fairly heavily weighted toward industrial raw materials, such as iron ore, bauxite, and crude petroleum.[a] These commodities, regardless of their country of origin, are typically extracted by capital-intensive production methods. And, too, the rising importance of U.S. multinationals in trade could be a factor in explaining capital-intensive imports. When producing overseas for export to this country, these firms characteristically would use technology similar to technology used in the United States. The evidence indicates little technical adaptation by such firms to take account of differing resource prices in other parts of the world.

Other researchers have investigated exports in an effort to find reasons for expecting that U.S. shipments would be produced by labor-intensive methods. For example, it has been noted that U.S. exports tend to be derived from industries heavily engaged in research and development.[b] Thus the source of the U.S.'s comparative advantage might lie in the innovation of new products and processes. If so, such items frequently are manufactured by non-capital-intensive techniques, particularly during earlier phases of production. Also, research and development in itself is labor-intensive when measured in the usual way.

Unfortunately, measurement problems are a feature of all the empirical research, including Leontief's original work. For example, even in the most detailed studies, a high level of industry aggregation has been utilized. Industry categories used in making generalizations about trade patterns in fact might conceal more than they reveal. An import industry classified as capital-intensive at the three-digit SIC level can include several distinctly labor-intensive subsectors (say, four-digit industries) that account for most of the imports. More detailed studies are needed before much confidence can be placed in research results.

Nonetheless, the available evidence supports the conclusion that U.S. exports flow largely from technologically advanced industries and from factors associated with certain "natural" advantages. Agricultural exports, as an example, are based on an abundance of fertile cropland; even so, farming is a capital-intensive activity in the United States, relative to other producing countries. On the other hand, U.S. imports tend to be industrial commodities

[a]For a complete discussion, see [11].

[b]For empirical verification, see [4], [6], or [1].

and certain tropical food items, together with a wide assortment of manufac- tured products. These manufactured good imports usually are products origi- nating from more mature technologies, although not necessarily technologies favoring low-cost labor supplies.

U.S. Trade Patterns in the Pacific Basin

In analyzing trade patterns between the United States and the Pacific Basin area, one is immediately confronted with a definitional problem: Just what countries does the Pacific Basin comprise? For this chapter's purposes, both Canada and the Latin American nations have been excluded from the Pacific Basin, even though many of these countries do border the Pacific. The omitted areas historically have been closely tied to the United States in trade, and the basis for trade with these regions differs considerably from trans-Pacific trade. For convenience, the Pacific Basin as defined here can be divided into three major groupings:

1. Japan
2. Australia/New Zealand and Oceania
3. Asia (including Burma, Thailand, Malaysia, Singapore, the Philippines, Macao, South Korea, Hong Kong, Taiwan and the Indochinese nations)

Some idea of the pattern of trade with Pacific Basin countries, compared with other regions of the world, can be gained from Tables 5-1 and 5-2, covering the year 1973. On the import side, the figures demonstrate that Pacific Basin nations, with the perhaps surprising exception of Australia and New Zealand, today ship mostly manufactured products to the United States. Even the least-developed areas of the Pacific (mostly in the "Asia" category) concentrate their U.S.-bound export trade in manufactured items. This pattern contrasts sharply with other less-developed regions, exemplified in these tables by Latin America, which ships a preponderance (almost three-fourths of total shipments) of agricultural and industrial raw materials to the United States. An unknown portion of manufactured imports from Asian countries, of course, consists of transfers from U.S.-owned affiliates in these nations.

Some of the more detailed import figures not contained in the tables are of interest. For example, about 40 percent of the category "Manufactured Goods, by Material" comprises iron and steel products, including nails and wire. Most of these shipments originate in Japan; more than half of Japan's exports to the United States in this category are iron and steel products. Textiles, mostly fabrics, are also an important item in this category, accounting for nearly one-fifth of total shipments. Japan is still the largest supplier of textiles (two-thirds), but other Asian countries have made significant inroads and ship

Table 5-1

U.S. Trade, by Region and Product Category, 1973

(In Millions of Dollars, Approximate)

| | Imports | | | | | | Exports | | | | | |
| | | | | Pacific Basin | | | | | | Pacific Basin | | |
	Canada	Latin Am.	W. Europe	Japan	Asia	Aust.	Canada	Latin Am.	W. Europe	Japan	Asia	Aust.
Food; live animals	739	3,104	1,161	272	549	1,041	737	1,199	3,250	1,809	1,143	34
Beverages and tobacco	235	70	852	5	18	1	14	46	568	115	105	33
Inedible crude materials, except fuels	2,873	568	388	60	452	150	683	438	3,063	2,476	883	112
Mineral fuels, lubricants, etc.	2,064	1,732	521	21	288	3	360	233	465	500	33	18
Oils and fats—animal and vegetable	4	42	54	2	133	2	37	171	199	108	41	7
Chemicals	555	105	1,179	229	26	150	833	424	1,902	628	489	210
Mfd. goods, by material	3,096	872	4,450	2,447	992	126	2,003	1,066	1,921	587	534	196
Machinery and transport equipment	7,010	674	7,108	4,746	1,425	29	8,669	3,694	7,448	1,495	1,911	753
Mfd. articles, not elsewhere classified	450	362	2,962	1,759	2,343	11	886	547	1,441	403	189	144
Total	17,026	7,529	18,675	9,541	6,226	1,513	14,252	7,818	20,257	8,121	5,328	1,507

Source: Department of Commerce.

43

Table 5-2
U.S. Trade: Percentage Distribution, by Product Category and Region, 1973

	Imports (%)						Exports (%)					
				Pacific Basin						Pacific Basin		
	Canada	Latin Am.	W. Europe	Japan	Asia	Aust.	Canada	Latin Am.	W. Europe	Japan	Asia	Aust.
Food, live animals	4.3	41.2	6.2	2.9	8.8	69.0	5.2	15.3	16.0	22.2	21.5	2.3
Beverages and tobacco	1.4	0.9	4.6	0.1	0.3	—	0.1	0.6	2.8	1.4	2.0	2.2
Inedible materials, except fuels	16.9	7.5	2.1	0.6	7.3	9.9	4.8	5.6	15.1	30.6	16.6	7.4
Mineral fuels, lubricants, etc.	12.1	23.0	2.8	0.2	4.6	0.2	2.5	3.0	2.3	6.2	0.6	1.2
Oils and fats—animal and vegetable	—	0.6	0.3	—	2.1	0.1	0.3	2.2	1.0	1.3	0.8	0.5
Chemicals	3.3	1.4	6.3	2.4	0.4	9.9	5.8	5.4	9.4	7.7	9.2	13.9
Mfd. goods, by material	18.2	11.6	23.8	25.7	15.9	8.3	14.1	13.6	9.5	7.2	10.0	13.0
Machinery and transport equipment	41.2	9.0	38.1	49.7	22.9	1.9	61.0	47.3	36.8	18.4	35.8	50.0
Mfd. articles, not elsewhere classified	2.6	4.8	15.8	18.4	37.7	0.7	6.2	7.0	7.1	5.0	3.5	9.5
Total	100.0	100.0	100.0	100.0	100.0	100.0	100.0	100.0	100.0	100.0	100.0	100.0

Source: Table 5-1.

the remaining one-third. Even so, textiles, clothing, and accessories represented less than 13 percent of overall U.S. imports from the Pacific Basin area in 1973. Other important products in this category from Asia are wood products and tin alloys, which together constitute over half of the area's exports to the United States.

In "Machinery and Transport Equipment," U.S. imports from the Pacific Basin are also quite concentrated in a few subcategories. For example, more than 60 percent of the import shipments from the whole area comprise telecommunications equipment and motor vehicles, including parts. For Japan alone, the figure is 70 percent. Similarly, over four-fifths of the Asian area imports in this category consist of telecommunications equipment and electrical machinery. In sum, the picture that emerges on imports from the Pacific Basin, in contrast with other less-developed areas, is one of concentration on manufactured products, and further concentration within manufactures on a few specific product lines.

The striking matter to note on the export side of the ledger is the importance of crude and semiprocessed material exports to the Pacific Basin countries, again with the exception of Australia. Over one-half of U.S. exports to the region are products of this type, compared with a figure of about 27 percent for the other regions combined. Especially important are agricultural products, both edible and inedible, which make up fully one-fourth of U.S. exports to Pacific Basin nations. Thus the U.S. pattern of comparative advantage appears to be somewhat weighted toward land-intensive products in the Pacific, relative to other regions of the world, both developed and developing. Considering the population densities in most of these nations, perhaps this finding should not be surprising. Even in its overall trade accounts, however, the United States heavily depends on the agricultural sector to generate surpluses to overcome deficits in manufactured products and fuels. One estimate of this surplus in 1974 is $11.9 billion, offsetting a nonfarm deficit of $10.2 billion. The conclusion is that land-intensive exports are very important to U.S. trade, and especially so in the Pacific Basin.

Details of the export side are less noteworthy than for imports, but a few items are worth pointing out. For example, the importance of land-based products in U.S. exports to the Pacific Basin is enhanced by noting that nearly 20 percent of exports in the "Manufactured Goods, by Material" category consists of paper and wood products, both heavily dependent on West Coast timber resources. And, too, within the various manufactured goods categories, U.S. exports to the Pacific Basin are dispersed widely in subcategories, none of which is markedly predominant. If one were to attempt to isolate a particular determining characteristic, without much more thorough analysis, it would be skill intensity. U.S. exports are spread across such categories as computing equipment, duplicating equipment, jet aircraft, semiconductors, heating and cooling equipment, and aircraft engines. Broadly speaking, each of these industries would employ a disproportionate number of scientists, engineers, and skilled workers, as compared with other industries in this country. However, more confident statements about the determinants of U.S. export strength await more detailed analysis of disaggregated data. As noted previously, almost no published studies exist at this level of analysis.

One recently published study is pertinent here. John Roemer analyzed trends in U.S. and Japanese trade between 1963 and 1971 in an attempt to determine the impact on U.S. trade of Japan's rapid expansion of exports [10]. As usual, the analysis is carried out at the three-digit level. Nevertheless, Roemer's results are interesting. Even without citing details from his book-length work, it can be said that in industry after industry within manufacturing, the Japanese share of worldwide exports is rising while that of the U.S. share is declining. This phenomenon, of course, is in part a natural consequence of Japan's relatively rapid rate of growth in manufactured exports since 1963, but U.S. market share losses occurred mostly after 1968. Between 1968 and 1971, U.S. market shares declined in nearly all manufacturing industries studied.

The precipitate market share losses for the U.S. between 1968 and 1971 suggests more than anything else an inappropriate exchange rate between the dollar and other world currencies, particularly the Japanese yen. The U.S. balance of payments was deteriorating rapidly during this period, and once-husky surpluses in the trade accounts turned negative in 1971. In fact, the terminal year of Roemer's study also was marked by a severe crisis in the international monetary system. This crisis ultimately led to the unsuccessful Smithsonian agreement, in which the dollar's value was lowered relative to most major world currencies. Since that time, the system has undergone a series of managed and unmanaged "floats," and the dollar's value has remained substantially below its pre-1971 level.

The question arises, therefore, whether the trade trends evident before 1971 have continued in subsequent years. Currency value changes of that year's magnitude might be expected to make Japanese exports less competitive and U.S. exports more competitive in the world marketplace. Supplementing the Roemer study with 1973 data, there are some slight indications that the U.S. position was improving or, perhaps more accurately, deteriorating less rapidly. The Japanese share of world markets continued to increase, but at a diminishing rate, in such industries as iron and steel and nonelectrical machinery. In one industry, textiles, the U.S. market share actually rose, while the Japanese position deteriorated between 1971 and 1973. The important automobile industry demonstrated continuing Japanese gains in market share, but not at the expense of U.S. producers, who maintained a relatively stationary position during that period.

U.S. Policy Problems in Pacific Basin Trade

In my view, the two areas of most immediate concern regarding U.S. trade policy in the Pacific Basin are, on the export side, the treatment of agricultural products and, on the import side, the attitude toward U.S. overseas subsidiaries established for export to this country, or the so-called export platform problem.

Recent years have witnessed an expansion of federal regulation of agricultural exports. To be sure, in earlier times, when price-support programs were in full operation, the federal government frequently disposed of its accumulated agricultural surpluses on the world market at prices below those being maintained domestically. But where "free" export markets existed, the government stayed clear. Now, however, with soaring world prices for wheat and feed grains, the Department of Agriculture is beginning to move toward increasing interference in the market process. Because of the great importance of agricultural exports to the Pacific Basin region, this development might well have serious impact on trade with this area.

The economic justification for export controls on agricultural products is simple enough. In a period of rising prices and worldwide food shortages, the administration can prevent increases in food prices at home only be restricting foreign demands from affecting the domestic marketplace. The idea of diverting overseas demand has great political appeal as well, because far more voters consume food in the United States than produce it. And, too, efforts to increase output and restrict demand in the agricultural sector have a better chance of success than in other sectors. Farming is the most competitive sector of the economy, and individual agricultural producers have few choices open to them in responding to the economic environment around them. Thus the control of major agricultural exports has both economic and political appeal to any national administration that is hard pressed to find solutions to an inflationary spiral.

Such blatant arguments for export regulation could hardly be expected from administration spokesmen, and it must be admitted that other more frequently voiced explanations also have merit. For example, we hear that restrictions on grain shipments to, say, the Soviet Union are meant to assure an "orderly" disposition of the crop between domestic and foreign buyers. With state-controlled purchasers entering the market to buy massive quantities of grain, day-to-day price fluctuations can be enormous and totally unpredictable. Moreover, monopolistic buyers can take advantage of unorganized suppliers to gain lower prices. These factors do argue for greater governmental intervention in international marketing of agricultural commodities.

Administration spokesmen have stated, however, that agricultural exports have no impact on U.S. food prices. This position is disingenuous, to say the least. Agricultural exports must have an effect on domestic prices for such products because exports alter the supply of goods available to satisfy local demands. Department of Agriculture analysts apparently mean that increased output should be sufficient to supply both foreign and domestic markets at prices no higher than in previous years. Given recent price movements in such commodities as corn, soybeans, and wheat, however, even this interpretation is difficult to defend.

The major argument for not restricting agricultural exports follows directly from the theory of comparative advantage that was reviewed briefly earlier. Compared with other economic sectors in this country, the farm sector is obviously efficient, and it produces a wide variety of outputs that are competitive in the world marketplace. It is in the interests of U.S. consumers to allow these products to flow to markets according to available prices. Such movements clearly will raise domestic food and fiber prices, as would be true for any export item enjoying increased demand. But the lesson of comparative advantage is that increased exports of efficiently produced commodities enable the United States to purchase other types of products made more efficiently elsewhere in the world. Obviously, such products would be cheaper for U.S. consumers than would be the case in the absence of import competition. In the great majority of cases it is simply not true that attempts to separate domestic from international markets are in the interests of the nation, whether taken as a group of consumers or producers. (Some economists might argue that agricultural export controls can be used for the purpose of redistributing income. Essentially, the farmer's losses are industrial workers' gains. However, if income redistribution is a goal—and it has not been explicitly mentioned—there are superior ways of accomplishing such an end.)

Of course, other changes also stem from a policy of export controls. Perhaps the most obvious one is that restrictions raise world prices, upset normal market relationships, and encourage buyers to seek more dependable—or at least more diversified—sources of supply. This phenomenon already has occurred in soybeans, with Brazil strongly entering world markets. In addition, some observers have suggested that a governmental export agency be established for major farm commodities. As we have seen, the idea has merit if the agency's purpose is to offset monopolistic buying organizations in the large consuming nations. Some analysts, however, apparently seek to create agricultural cartels as a bargaining device to oppose the OPEC oil cartel, presumably giving the government greater leverage in its quest for lower crude petroleum prices. This position represents such an obvious backward step in the U.S.'s traditional posture on both trade and development that one can only hope that it would be rejected out of hand.

While the policy treatment of agricultural exports is very important in U.S. trading relationships with the Pacific Basin area, much more attention has been given to imports from U.S. subsidiaries operating in some nations of that region. On one side of the issue are labor unions, which have attacked U.S. companies for "exporting" jobs. Unions have generally insisted that some form of direct investment control be instituted to prevent this type of activity. Moreover, recognizing that U.S.-developed technology might be used by foreign firms through licensing agreements, unions have also demanded tighter controls on such technology flows as a means of preserving jobs in this country. On the other side of the issue have been an assortment of business leaders and others claiming that "export platforms" simply recognize the facts of international production. In this view, the U.S. firm has the choice of investing in foreign subsidiaries and exporting to the United States or eventually being displaced in the domestic market by foreign competition. Businesses would also assert that export platforms are precisely the kind of investment needed to assist in the development of poorer countries. These nations can only gain from the additional employment provided by outside investors.

Economist Benjamin Cohen, however, has recently called this latter claim into question [3]. In a detailed study of export platforms in three Pacific Basin countries (Singapore, South Korea, and Taiwan), Cohen concludes, "subject to many qualifications, the economic benefits of foreign investment are negligible compared with the effects of local firms expanding their exports" [3, p. 13]. Note that he does not deny that economic benefits flow from private investment, but only that they are comparatively small. His rationale is that in most cases local firms already were producing particular export items prior to the foreign investment. If expansion of output for export were needed, it would have been more beneficial to the countries had the expansion occurred in local, as opposed to foreign-owned (i.e., U.S.-owned), firms. This conclusion, of course, begs the very important question whether the export growth would have taken place in the absence of outside companies. Interestingly, even the investing firms imply in their justification for building overseas plants that, in time, exactly that train of events would have been set in motion.

It seems fair to say that the rate of export expansion from these countries would have been markedly slowed without foreign investment—a point not explicitly considered in the Cohen cost-benefit analysis. The fact that U.S. firms undertook the foreign investment at all indicates that vertical integration within the companies was considered to be superior to arms-length dealing with foreign suppliers. Also, this preference for internalization of production probably would exist even if the technology were as well known as Cohen implies. Numerous other economies can flow from integration, ranging from closer monitoring of component quality to production scheduling. In addition, of course, the U.S. firm might be motivated to set up overseas production by the tax deferral provision on foreign income. For all these reasons, the growth of foreign exports of the type produced by U.S. export subsidiaries probably occurred much faster as a consequence of the U.S. investment.

Whether or not one agrees with Cohen's assumptions, however, there appears to be little argument that outside firms producing totally for export must yield some net benefit to the host nation. The question then becomes, Why should the United States allow the firms to invest abroad in export platforms? Businesses would respond to this question in two ways:

1. Direct investment yields economies of operation, and therefore lower prices, that would not be possible without control.
2. The type of production transferred would eventually be within the technological capacities of the exporting countries anyway. Therefore, if the

production is to be lost sooner or later, it is best that U.S.-controlled subsidiaries be the gainers.

From an economic point of view, the first response provides the only basis for supporting such investment activity. It is not, however, an adequate argument for continued tax deferral on foreign-based income from export platforms. Tax deferral is usually justified on the grounds that without it, U.S. foreign subsidiaries would be placed at a disadvantage relative to their primary competitors, foreign-owned companies, in foreign markets. Where the only market is the United States, however, the foreign subsidiary functions merely as an extension of domestic operations. Tax deferral then becomes an artificial means to enhance profits. Foreign investment with the tax advantage would be favored over domestic investment, even where all other costs were identical. There appears to be no persuasive reason, therefore, to continue tax deferral on export platform investments.

From a comparative advantage viewpoint, and aside from the tax problem, foreign investment in export platforms of the type thus far erected should be allowed. This conclusion would not be accepted enthusiastically by labor unions, because without question jobs are lost when production is transferred to overseas locations. But this is true of any trade-related unemployment, and the appropriate remedy should involve funded retraining and possibly relocation, rather than trade and investment barriers. The larger issue of the long-run impact on the U.S. economy of unrestricted foreign investment by U.S. firms, however, deserves far more study than economists and business scholars have given it.

Conclusions

Rapidly growing trade between the United States and other Pacific Basin nations has been mutually beneficial. Several formerly poor countries have used this trade as an engine for economic growth and are well on their way toward sustained increases in per capita incomes. The United States, on the other hand, has benefited from low-cost manufactured imports and from expanded markets for a wide variety of equipment and, especially, agricultural products. Although there is evidence of a long-term decline in U.S. worldwide market share, particularly with respect to Japan, more recent data demonstrate that exchange rate adjustments are, in part, reversing this trend. As economic development occurs in other parts of the world, however, market share losses are inevitable.

For two particular issues related to Pacific Basin trade—agricultural export policy and export platforms—it might be said that the most reasonable policy is essentially no policy. Farm export regulation should be limited to restraining severe price fluctuations and to negotiations with unusually large single pur-chasers such as the Soviet Union. Export platforms can be beneficial both to the host country and to the United States, although some evidence suggests that the benefits are frequently overstated. In any case, little is to be said for subsidizing export platforms through tax deferrals because the tax deferral merely provides U.S. subsidiaries an advantage over locally owned firms in the developing countries of the Pacific Basin.

References

1. Baldwin, R.E. "Determinants of the Commodity Structure of U.S. Trade." *American Economic Review* 61, no. 1 (March 1971), pp. 126-146.

2. Caves, R., and R. Jones. *World Trade and Payments: An Introduction.* Boston: Little, Brown, 1973.

3. Cohen, B.I. *Multinational Firms and Asian Exports.* New Haven, Conn.: Yale University Press, 1975.

4. Gruber, W., D. Mehta, and R. Vernon, "The R and D Factor in International Trade and International Investment of U.S. Industry." *Journal of Political Economy* (February 1967), pp. 20-37.

5. Heckscher, E. "The Effect of Foreign Trade on the Distribution of Income." *Economisk Tidskrift,* 1919. Reprinted in American Economic Association, *Readings in the Theory of International Trade,* edited by H. Ellis and L. Metzler. Philadelphia: Blakiston, 1949.

6. Keesing, D. "The Impact of Research and Development on U.S. Trade." *Journal of Political Economy* (February 1967), pp. 38-47.

7. Leontief, W. "Domestic Production and Foreign Trade: The American Capital Position Re-examined." *Proceedings of the American Philosophical Society,* 97 (1953). Reprinted in American Economic Association, *Readings in International Economics,* edited by R. Caves and H. Johnson. Homewood, Ill.: R.D. Irwin, 1968.

8. Leontief, W. "Factor Proportions and the Structure of American Trade: Further Theoretical and Empirical Analysis." *Review of Economics and Statistics* Vol. XXXVIII (November 1956), pp. 386-407.

9. Ohlin, B. *Interregional and International Trade.* Cambridge, Mass.: Harvard University Press, 1933; rev. ed., 1967.

10. Roemer, J.E. *U.S.-Japanese Competition in International Markets: A Study of the Trade-Investment Cycle in Modern Capitalism.* Berkeley: University of California Institute of International Studies, 1975.

11. Vanek, J. *The Natural Resource Content of United States Foreign Trade, 1870-1955.* Cambridge, Mass.: M.I.T. Press, 1963.

6

Industrial Development Strategies and Foreign Investment Policies of Southeast Asian and South Pacific Developing Countries

Thomas W. Allen

Basic Industrial Strategies

All developing countries in the Pacific Basin desire to control their own destinies. Such nationalism has involved the creation of regulations and control mechanisms to insulate the economy from foreign influences and to mobilize national capabilities for development. In recent years, however, its expression has become more intense with the elevating prominence of another dimension: the creation of mechanisms aimed at ensuring that ultimately, ownership of the means of production will be mainly in the hands of nationals.

Central to the concept of nationalism is the aim of national integration of the major political, economic, social, religious, and cultural units.[1] This is by no means a simple objective, especially for those with diverse, ethnic, and religious groups, and for those that need to ensure that many of the traditional characteristics of their society are preserved.

Second, all the countries have now pronounced aims that focus on social justice as well as on growth. Such was not the case in the past, although those in power paid lip service to the concept. The pursual of the growth objective was at the center of development policies. This led to the creation of an elitist class and ever-increasing concentrations of wealth in fewer hands (or in foreign hands, in the case of countries that did not have well-developed indigenous business sectors). The pressure to pay more than lip service to the concept of social justice is resulting in policies that focus more and more on ensuring that gains from growth are more evenly distributed either directly (e.g., encouraging industry to locate in rural areas) or indirectly (e.g., spending a greater proportion of government revenue in rural areas).

Third, there is a growing awareness of the need for self-reliance in many of the basic necessities of life: food, clothing, and shelter.[a] The desire for such insulation has become more apparent in recent periods of shortages—we could well see a growing list of items regarded as basic necessities to avoid the political repercussions of "economic ransom." The push for self-sufficiency in energy is one newer addition to the list.

---

[a]In the case of countries, such as Papua-New Guinea, that rely on external aid, financial self-reliance is also important.

51

The above triad—nationalism, socialism, and self-reliance—would seem to imply development along noncapitalistic lines,[b] but such is not the case. In all of the countries considered here, the brunt of development has been placed on the private sector. In most cases this has been by choice; in some cases, however, it has been by the desire of colonial powers. While nationalism has modified this stance to some extent, development policies have mainly focused on encouraging the continual, but controlled, development of the private sector.

Coupled with this is the recognition that foreign investment is needed, not as an end in itself, but as a means toward achieving development objectives. Capital, know-how, management, and market "packages" are the main factors that foreign investment contributes. However, there is the recognition that foreign investment must be controlled and directed to ensure that it remains a means to development and does not become an end in itself, which was the case in the past in many of the countries.

These three common elements are important in that they give an insight into the directions in which the independent Southeast Asian and Pacific countries are aiming. The policies toward industrialization and foreign investment in each country are structured with these points in mind.

Development Options

The pressures for development in each of the countries of the region are immense. Rapid population growth, land shortages in rural areas, increasing expectations and wants of the population, low and unequal living standards, and so forth are problems that policy-makers continually face. Short of revolution and a complete upheaval of the systems at work, the only course open to the countries is to supplement their resources and efforts with outside assistance.

The extent of development options open to the countries to overcome these problems within the framework of the development objectives varies from country to country. Population size and the extent of exploitable natural resources are perhaps the major determinations that affect the range of options open to a country. The information in Tables 6-1 and 6-2 indicates some options and the desired types of foreign investment.

Papua-New Guinea is an example of a low-population/high-resource-potential country. While it does have short-term employment and balance-of-payments problems, it also has various policy options to deal with these problems. It can choose, for example, to proceed with an all-out effort to develop its copper or timber resources; to utilize the hydroenergy potential of its major rivers; or to be more selective in the type of industries it wants to develop. While political considerations (the "next election syndrome") may cause some

---

[b]This triad is probably not applicable in the full sense to Singapore, whose survival depends on its internationalism.

Major Resources of the Southeast Asian and South Pacific Independent Developing Countries, 1973

(In Percent of Total Exports)

Country	Agriculture, Fishing	Forests	Mining, Gas, Oil
Fiji[a]	Sugar (62) Coconut Fish	—	Gold
Indonesia	Coffee (4) Palm oil (3) Tobacco (3) Tea (2)	Timber (18) Rubber (12) (Further potential for timber)	Oil (50) Tin (4) (Further potential for oils and minerals)
Korea, South	Fisheries (8)	Plywood (9)	—
Malaysia	Rubber (3) Palm oil (5) Prawns (2)	Sawed logs (13) Sawed timber (8) (Further potential for timber)	Tin, tin concentrates (12) Petroleum, petroleum products (5) (Further potential for petroleum)
Papua-New Guinea	Tuna, crayfish, prawns (4) Coffee beans (11) Cocoa beans (5)	Timber, logs, plywood (2) (Further potential)	Copper ores, concentrates (62) (Further potential)
Philippines	Sugar (21) Copra (7) Banana (2)	Logs, lumber (21) Timber, plywood (3)	Copper concentrates (14)
Singapore	—	—	Refining
Taiwan	General agriculture (7) Processed agricultural products (8)	—	Natural gas
Thailand	Rice (10) Rubber (4) (12) Maize (7) Tapioca (7)	—	Tin (5)
Western Samoa[a]	Copra (50) Bananas (7) Coffee, cocoa, spices (34)	—	—

Note: Further potential for agricultural and fishing development has not been noted as all countries, with the exception of Singapore, could develop their agricultural base further. The pattern for all countries changes dramatically with new discoveries, especially off shore, of oil and gas.
[a]Figures for 1968.

Table 6-2

Some Priority Manufacturing Industries for Foreign Investment in Southeast Asian and South Pacific Independent Developing Countries

Fiji	Processing of agricultural products such as fruit and vegetable preserving, peanut oil and butter, ginger oil, desiccated coconut, activated carbon, sugar refining, etc. Basic industries such as petroleum refining. Processing of wood products. Other manufacturing, almost of any type.
Indonesia	Export-oriented, labor-intensive industries; import replacement industries, and industries that further process raw materials.
Korea, South	Development of the machine and chemical industries (especially the heavy end), projects requiring small amounts of imported goods and services, and projects involving technological innovations.
Malaysia	Export-oriented, labor-intensive industries of high priority with some emphasis on import replacement. Priority products include those falling under the general heads of manufacture of food products; animal foodstuffs; wood products; rubber products, chemicals, and chemical products; hardware tools; industrial machinery and parts; transport equipment; components, accessories, spare parts, supplies and fittings of motor vehicles; electronic components/equipment; or electrical appliances, equipment, and components.
Papua-New Guinea	Main emphasis on processing agricultural and fishery products and related industries, such as farm machinery. Second in priority is further processing of timber. Low-priority, but still acceptable, basic industries such as cement, flour, and selected import replacement (with some export-oriented) industries. Little interest in imports in export-processing activities.
Philippines	Export-oriented, labor-intensive industries and those processing natural resources. The priority industries include forest products, fiber products, crop production, food processing, livestock and fishing, metallic and nonmetallic mineral products, chemical products, iron- or steel-based industries, hand tools, industry machinery, farm machinery, fabricated metal products, engines, electrical equipment, and transport equipment.
Singapore	Technology-oriented industries, upgrading present assembly-oriented operations. Emphasis on petrochemicals, machine tools, precision engineering, sophisticated electronics, office equipment, etc.
Taiwan	Export-oriented industries based on advanced technology that require larger inputs of skilled labor, such as electronics, petrochemical intermediates and end products, precision equipment and instruments, heavy electrical machinery, and shipbuilding.
Thailand	Export-oriented, labor-intensive industries. Little interest in import replacement or assembly operations accompanied by exports.
Western Samoa	Almost any type of manufacturing activity.

industries to be established purely because of employment considerations and other short-term problems, the long-term focus can be self-reliance and equal distribution of benefits. The lack of an indigenous private sector (and revenue constraints), however, will mean some compromise in its nationalistic objectives, at least until such a sector evolves.

If we take the Philippines, Thailand, and South Korea—countries with medium natural resource potential and fairly large populations—the development options are narrower. Employment and foreign exchange considerations are at the core of their development strategies. They have to utilize fully what resources they have, and they are forced to be less selective in the type of industries they establish. Their well-developed indigenous private sector, however, indicates that they do not have to place complete reliance on foreign investment, but they will welcome investment of most types, especially those of a labor-intensive and export-oriented nature, provided they meet the basic entry requirements laid down by the governments.

The options are narrower still for a country such as Singapore, which has little resource potential. While employment and balance of payments are not long-term problems there, to continue to grow Singapore must upgrade its skills and industry and become a key service and/or technology center—a task it is finding more and more difficult as it faces competition from other regional centers and notices the large multinational corporations' unwillingness to spin off research and development. Further, Singapore's very future will be questionable unless it remains international in character or becomes the hub of regional cooperation. Perhaps it could survive as a center with a "bit of everything" but it is doubtful whether such a passive role would benefit the aspirations of Singapore's leaders.

Indonesia, with high resource potential and high population, has wide development options, but they are somewhat limited by the need to employ a large, rapidly growing population. Balance-of-payments considerations, in the long term, are not so important.

The extent of development options will have a bearing on the industrial strategies adopted to achieve the goals of nationalism, socialism, and self-reliance. This should become more apparent throughout this chapter.

Present Policies Toward Foreign Investment

All the Pacific Basin countries use a wide range of policy tools in implementing their industrial strategies.[c] The traditional tools of foreign exchange controls,

---

[c]This section draws heavily from Thomas W. Allen, "Policies of ASEAN countries Towards Direct Foreign Investment." SEADAG Papers, No. 74.4 1974.

price regulation, credit lines, tariffs, and import restrictions all play roles. There is a strong tendency to treat foreign investment as an issue in itself, however, with specialized agencies being established for the purpose of implementing laws and regulations governing foreign investment. These agencies are now assessing more carefully the overall social and economic impact of foreign industrial projects, placing considerable emphasis on setting the ground rules for foreign involvement. This is important as it becomes apparent that many of those ground rules cover things such as access to foreign exchange and local capital, price regulation, tariffs and fiscal incentives, and so forth. This has meant that the conditions under which foreign enterprises establish are more clearly defined—as is the basis of their future operations—thus reducing future uncertainties considerably. The "contract" between the enterprise and the government could well spell out how all these items will be treated in the future vis-à-vis each particular project.

The transfer of controls to the entry stage of foreign investment has a number of significant implications. First, it forces the countries to look ahead and to plan their futures more carefully. By laying out conditions covering commitments both by the enterprise and by the government, the government reduces its future flexibility in the use of its various policy tools. For example, it may guarantee access to foreign exchange for the repayment of loans to an enterprise, giving it (the government) less flexibility in periods of balance-of-payments crises. Obviously, a government always can do what it wants in spite of the guarantees it may offer an enterprise, but if it does use this power, it risks the disfavor of potential investors. Thus the host government must more carefully determine the types of projects needed and the implications they have on the development parameters of the country.

Second, the uncertainties of the foreign enterprise are reduced. With the ground rules clear from the outset, the enterprise knows where it stands and can operate relatively unhindered without fear of continual policy changes. It might mean harder initial bargaining and uncertainties about whether a project would be established, but the uncertainties would be reduced once the project is established. Again, the extent to which this operational flexibility exists depends on the investors' confidence that the country's government would stick to its side of the bargain, but overall there does seem to be a more cordial relationship under entry-stage controls.

Major Laws Relating to Foreign Investment

Table 6-3 lists the major laws relating to foreign investment in the developing countries of the Southeast Asian and South Pacific region, along with the agencies given the responsibility of implementing those laws. While other laws affect foreign investment—such as exchange-control laws, tariff laws, land laws, and so forth—and policy objectives that are outlined in various development plans, the body of legislation governing the operations of foreign enterprises and investment incentives is contained in the laws listed in the table.

As set out, the laws are complicated in varying degrees. The Economic Expansion Act of Singapore, for example, is fairly simple and straightforward. The situation in the Philippines, on the other hand, is complicated with differential incentives for industries, varying limitations on foreign equity, and so on. Also, some laws that are theoretically simple and nonrestrictive are actually complex and somewhat restrictive in application; such is the case in Malaysia, for example. Thus in interpreting the laws, it is important to consider their application as well as the written word. Further, the laws should be construed in their environmental context.

The key element in all these laws is the control they provide over the inflow of foreign investment. All those with special acts relating to investment involve some form of registration process. While the benefits of foreign investment are appreciated (the provision of capital, entrepreneurship, and managerial know-how, technology and training facilities, export market access and experience, stimulation of the local business/industrial environment, bias toward industrial rationalization, taxpaying orientation, and so forth), the recipient countries want to ensure that these benefits are maximized and that various "malpractices" are minimized (excessive importing of raw materials, insufficient orientation toward export or unfair market sharing, uneconomic transfer pricing in dealing with overseas affiliates, failure to share equity with local entrepreneurs, inadequate employment and training of local personnel, lack of local research or adaption of technology to local needs, absence of local philanthropic activities and identity, and the like).[2] What the foregoing means, in sum, is that foreign investment is being subjected to closer scrutiny than in the past, although recipient countries realize that such scrutiny should not imply that foreign investment is not welcomed or encouraged. After all, a "joint venture" is involved, requiring an understanding between the host government and the investor.

Procedural patterns for project approval vary from country to country. Normally, a number of approvals are required for various purposes, involving company registration, land leases, forestry permits, local authority licenses, and so on, as well as registration with a central authority as a foreign enterprise. It can all be rather confusing for the investor unless the central authority also acts as a "clearing house" for approval or applications, or at least steers the investor to the appropriate authorities who issue such approvals. Some observers even suggest that the more the approvals require, the greater the scope for corruption.

Priority Areas of Investment

A number of countries have set certain industrial priorities, either in the form of a plan or through promotion efforts; these priorities reflect the industrial

Table 6-3

Major Laws Relating to Foreign Investment in the Southeast Asian and South Pacific Countries

	Major Laws	*Agency Responsible*
Fiji	No specific laws relating to foreign investment. Income tax exemptions given under the *Income Tax Ordinance and Amendments.*	No specific agency, except that those wishing to apply for income tax concessions submit applications to the Ministry for Commerce, Industry and Cooperatives. Appraisal with assistance of Ministry for Finance. For hotels, applications through the Ministry of Communications, Works and Tourism.
Indonesia	*Foreign Capital Investment Law, 1967* and other decrees designed to state the basic principles governing foreign private capital investment and both to encourage and regulate that kind of investment.	*Capital Investment Coordinating Board* and other governments
Korea, South	*Foreign Capital Inducement Law, 1966*, which includes a codification of the Foreign Encouragement Law (1960) and others, welcomes foreign investments, particularly in conjunction with Korean participation, the introduction of modern technology, and the development of resources.	*Ministry of the Economic Planning Board*, along with Foreign Capital Inducement Deliberation Committee and other ministries.
Malaysia	*Investment Incentives Act, 1966* (amended 1971), whose objective of channeling foreign investment into less familiar fields, and attracting foreign investment in new enterprises. Specific emphasis is given to export-oriented industries. (See also Income Tax Act, 1967.) (Note recent Industrial Coordination Act 1975 requiring all manufacturing companies with capital of M$100,000 and above or with 25 or more employees, to apply for a licence from the Ministry of Trade and Industry.)	*Federal Industrial Development Authority and Ministry of Trade and Industry*, along with Malaysia Industrial Development Finance Board, Malaysia Industrial Estates Berhod, and other government agencies and departments.

Table 6-3 (cont.)

	Major Laws	*Agency Responsible*
Papua-New Guinea	*National Investment and Development Act 1974*, to provide for the regulation, control, and promotion of investment (particularly foreign investment) in the interests of national development, and to set up the National Investment and Development Authority to administer the act.	*National Investment and Development Authority* and other departments.
Philippines	*R.A. 5186 Investment Incentives Act, 1967* (as amended by presidential decrees), to accelerate the sound development of the economy in consonance with the principles and objectives of economic nationalism; to achieve a planned, economically feasible and practical dispersal of industries under conditions that will encourage competition and discourage monopolies; and to channel investment into preferred areas. *R.A. 5455 Foreign Business Regulation Act, 1968* (as amended by the presidential decrees), to regulate foreign investment in all fields of activity in the Philippines and to prevent alien entry into fields adequately exploited by the Filipinos.	*Board of Investments,* involving also Department of Finance, Central Bank, Mariveles Free Trade Zone Authority, National Economic Development Authority, and other government agencies.
Singapore	*Economic Expansion Incentives (Relief from Income Tax) Act, 1967* (amended 1970), to embrace a free-enterprise system with growth maximization. The government's policy toward private investors—foreign and local—combines maximum assistance with liberal incentives.	*Economic Development Board,* along with Jurong Town Corporation, Ministry of Finance, and other government agencies.
Taiwan	Taiwan's incentive policy encourages investment to accelerate its economic development as evidenced by the promulgation of the *Statute for Encouragement of Investment, 1960*, which incorporates liberal tax concessions to new enterprises.	*Industrial Development and Investment Centre,* Overseas Chinese and Foreign Investment Commission, and other departments of the Ministry of Economic Affairs.

Table 6-3 (cont.)

	Major Laws	Agency Responsible
Thailand	*Announcement No. 227,* October 1972 (revised Promotion of Industrial Development Act of 1962), to promote investors whose businesses are of economic and social importance to the country. *Alien Business Law* (Announcement No. 281, 1972), to restrict majority-owned foreign enterprises in various fields of activity.	*Board of Investments*, involving also Ministry of Industry, Ministry of Interior, and other government agencies.
Western Samoa	No income tax exemptions given under the *Enterprise Incentives Act 1965* or its 1969 amendments.	*Department of Economic Development and Incentives Board*

strategy the particular country has adopted. In addition, most of the countries have specified certain areas of business activity that are reserved for nationals of the country or for the government itself, allowing no foreign investment in these fields. The conditions under which foreign investment is accepted, the availability of incentives, and the extent of foreign equity participation allowed are closely related to the priority areas in the countries, although the form in which such priorities are declared differs widely, ranging from a listing of specific products in the Philippines to a broad "high technology" categorization in Singapore.

Papua-New Guinea. Papua-New Guinea, for example, annually prepares a National Investment Priorities Schedule, which is revised at least once per year. The first schedule, published in April 1975, is in two parts. The first part lists the specific business activities in which new foreign investment proposals will be considered, along with the minimum terms and conditions, and guidelines for investment. Thus any new enterprise that wishes to set up facilities in Papua-New Guinea, or any existing foreign enterprise wishing to engage in new business activities, cannot do so unless it is approved by the government (on the recommendation of the National Investment and Development Authority) and the activities are listed on the priorities schedule.

The second part of the schedule specifies the business activities reserved for Papua-New Guineans. In these activities no new foreign investment is allowed (unless there are exceptional circumstances in a particular locality in the country), and existing foreign enterprises operating in these fields will be required to phase in local involvement.

While the first priorities schedule mainly reflected projects that were "in the pipeline" when the National Investment and Development Act came into effect, future schedules were being based on detailed industry sector programs. The aim is to avoid a "shopping list" approach to the schedule as has been apparent, for example, in the Philippines.

The Philippines. The annual priorities schedule prepared in the Philippines, the Incentive Priorities Plan, was first prepared in 1968. It has a different focus than does Papua-New Guinea's: it lists preferred areas for which incentives are available, and it is open to both foreign and domestic investors.[d] Such listing is on a product-by-product basis (for example, asbestos, nylon fibers, sorghum) with a specified, measured capacity for each representing local market potential—investors can register capacity in these fields until the measured capacity has been filled.

The preferred areas (there are approximately 100) are divided into "pioneer areas"—those that involve the production of goods not produced in the Philippines on a commercial scale or that use a technology new and untried in the Philippines—and "nonpioneer areas." The pioneer areas offer more liberal incentives and less restrictive conditions on foreign ownership and control. In determining the preferred areas, the criteria are the possibilities of import substitution, the extent of further processing of raw materials, and the possibility of exports, as well as the necessity for a project to be economically, technically, and financially sound, and to provide a high rate of return to the national economy.

In addition to the Investment Priorities Plan, the Philippines also prepares an Export Priorities Plan (first prepared in 1970), listing products and services for which incentives are available to existing as well as new entities engaged in exports, and a Tourism Priorities Plan (first prepared in 1973), listing services for which incentives are available to existing as well as new entities engaged in providing services to foreign tourists. Under certain conditions, foreign investors can register in these fields. Foreign investment is also allowed in other fields of activity outside these plans (without incentives), provided that such projects do not conflict with national objectives and other laws affecting the scope available for foreign involvement, that they are in areas not adequately exploited by Filipinos, and that they would provide tangible benefits to the Philippine economy.

The shopping list impression conveyed by the Investment Priorities Plan in the Philippines still reflects the import substitution phase, where incentives are offered to compensate for a distorted tariff structure and to attract investment into the listed fields.[e] This focus is now changing, and the Board of Investments

[d]In Papua-New Guinea, no taxation incentives are available to the enterprises wishing to engage in business activities listed in the schedule.

[e]In the 1968 Investment Priorities Plan, considerable reliance was placed on the private sector for determining priorities.

is attempting to prune the list, partly to avoid giving incentives to industries that do not really require them and thus to place more emphasis on industries that also have potential for export and for the further processing of raw materials.[f] The Export Priorities Plan supplements this change.

Malaysia. Malaysia has no fixed criteria for granting pioneer status, although local equity participation, market and employment prospects, and integration with existing industries are favorably considered in arriving at a decision about a particular application. However, special incentives and relaxed equity involvement are given for export-oriented investments and priority products. The review committee on investment incentives now recommends over fifty priority products, ranging from food canning to ball bearings.

Thailand. Thailand also prepares a list of "promoted" industries eligible for registration for incentives; it considerably restricts foreign investment in areas outside these activities. Labor intensity, potential foreign-exchange earnings or savings, extensive use of indigenous raw materials, and potential forward and backward linkages (as well as technical, financial, and economic viability) are among the criteria for choosing priority areas. While a strong element of import replacement is still apparent in the list of promoted activities (which includes fishing, processing of agricultural products, petrochemicals, mechanical and electrical components, textiles, and certain services), the desire to promote exports and upgrade existing processing is clear.

Singapore. Singapore has now also become selective in the projects it will encourage. It has a strong preference for those with a high technology content serving world markets, such as electronics. The Economic Development Board does not publish a list of such industries, although undoubtedly it has an indicative list for its own use and actively promotes investment in these fields through contact with relevant manufacturers throughout the world. Singapore has a number of foreign offices solely for the purpose of investment promotion.

Indonesia. Apart from restrictions on the extent of foreign investment in certain industries, Indonesia has not prepared any list of priority industries. With opportunities numerous in all fields of activity, the government has left it to the private sector to search out these opportunities and then apply for registration to obtain incentives and negotiate the conditions for the project. However, the recent reorganization of the Foreign Investment Board suggests that Indonesia also may start determining priorities on its own accord.

South Korea and Taiwan. South Korea does not have a priorities schedule, although it does publish a list of promising items to foreign investors. Any type

[f]The development of industry sector programs represents a new attempt in the Philippines to integrate industrial priorities more fully.

of industry, as long as it is conducive to the sound development of Korean industry, improves the balance of payments, and is not restricted, will be considered. Similarly, Taiwan has prepared a list of categories of productive enterprises that receive special treatment.

Fiji and Western Samoa. Fiji has a priorities list of industries, although proposals will be considered for projects not on this list. Western Samoa does not have any priority schedule, although its development plans do specify opportunities.

Thus while priorities are specified in varying degrees, all the countries seem to be concerned with establishing priorities either in a plan, and/or by specifying the characteristics of preferred projects. While priorities can be overdone, they do serve a number of purposes. For instance, they let the investor know what opportunities are open for negotiation, thus saving the time and expense a general search would require; they assist the countries to achieve more effective coordination of their plans and the activities of the various government instrumentalities; they ensure that a country has at least explored the opportunities available to help facilitate a more effective channeling of foreign investments into desirable fields and provide a basis for negotiating and determining conditions for their establishment; and they enable a country to determine whether incentives, tariff protection, finance, and the like are needed. Other advantages of having a system of priorities could also be listed, noting that the opportunity still exists for foreign investors to propose other fields they would like to enter. To the extent that this is the case, investment priority lists are more "indicative" than final; they are related to each country's overall industrial strategies.

Policies of Ownership and Control

All the Pacific Basin countries prefer joint ventures of foreign and domestic capital to fully owned foreign enterprises, although such a preference is enforced only in certain fields of activity. Even in areas where it is enforced (mainly in raw material and certain local-market-oriented projects), it is doubtful whether it causes considerable concern to the bulk of the foreign investors unless they are forced to accept minority interest and control where this is detrimental to the effective management of the enterprise or gives access to markets and specialized technology acquired by the foreign corporation at considerable costs.

Although local involvement is desired in the South Pacific countries, any attempt to have local participation is frustrated by the lack of a developed private sector and lack of federal funds. Thus the desire for joint ventures is not as strong at this stage, although phase-in programs may be required (provided that, in the future, local enterprises are available and the government has the funds). In Papua-New Guinea for example, only a minority equity (around 20 percent) is required in mineral projects, the government concentrating on taxation measures and other controls to ensure its fair share of the proceeds. Government options are built into timber projects, and phase-in programs may be required in other projects. In many instances the government appoints itself an intermediary by participating in a project with the ultimate aim of handing its share over to local citizens when the local private sector has developed to a stage when it can be involved. An Investment Corporation has been established with this as one of its aims.

Appendix 6A summarizes details of policies that relate to ownership and control of industrial enterprises. Since the table is self-explanatory, this discussion is limited to comments on a few significant points.

Only in the Philippines does the law itself specify the extent of foreign control in some of the areas open to foreign investment. In practice, however, all the countries have some form of restrictions with the exception of certain of the small South Pacific countries. In Malaysia, for example, companies that depend entirely on the local market for their sales are generally required to have at least 51-percent local equity; otherwise, equity participation is negotiable. A similar situation is found in Thailand and Indonesia. The interesting point is that most of the Southeast Asian countries have similar policies for new nonresource export-oriented activities; roughly, the greater the proportion of export, the greater the proportion of foreign equity participation allowed. Only in local market-oriented and resource-oriented projects do the countries become more stringent on foreign ownership and control; even for some of the projects in these fields, majority ownership and control by foreigners is accepted (at least for a period) if significant benefits to the economy, including technological transfer, can be shown to exist.

As implied by the foregoing, the continual comparison of the "restrictive" policies toward foreign ownership of, say, the Philippines, Malaysia, Indonesia, and Thailand with the "open" policies of Singapore is not valid. Singapore has no natural resources or local market of significance,[g] and it is only in these areas that the other countries are stringent on foreign ownership and control. Probably if Singapore were to have either of these factors, it would pursue policies similar to those of the other Southeast Asian countries. If we compare the policies toward export-oriented industries, there is very little difference among countries, except for the Philippines' requirement that local ownership and control be achieved within a thirty- to forty-five-year period (even longer in some cases), which is surely long enough in the eyes of all parties.[h] For the Southeast Asian countries with significant local markets and resources, foreign ownership and control requirements are also similar.

[g]For the local market Singapore does have, it has not found it worthwhile to be extremely stringent on local ownership and control, simply because it is insignificant as an attraction factor for investment. This attitude may change as more "intermediate" and service industries develop.

[h]Indonesia requires reapproval of projects after thirty years, presumably in the direction of greater local participation. All the countries encourage gradual local participation, where no restrictions exist.

A second point is that even when majority ownership and control are not permitted, the countries allow management contracts to be drawn up between the multinational company and the host country enterprise. This is quite common, and it allows the multinational corporation to have effective control over the management of the enterprise.

A final significant point is that many of the businesses in which foreign direct investment is restricted to under 50 percent of total equity in both Indonesia and Thailand are recent additions to the restricted list. In November 1972, for example, Thailand revised its Alien's Business Law to specify, among other things, certain areas where majority-owned foreign enterprises would not be allowed unless permitted by royal decree. Where they already existed, they were given two years to disinvest.

Operational Restraints on Foreign Enterprises

Thus far this chapter has outlined the areas open to foreign investment in the Southeast Asian and South Pacific developing countries, and indicated the ownership and control regulations affecting investment in these fields. Probably even more significant to the achievement of the countries' industrial goals, however, are the operating restraints placed on foreign investment: it is through the conditions placed on the operations of foreign enterprises that a country can ensure some form of control over their activities and derive maximum benefit from their presence.

The operational restraints range from restrictions on land ownership and the employment of foreign personnel to agreements relating to the phasing in of local content in the manufacturing operations. They can be grouped, for convenience, into three categories:

1. general restrictions, relating to such factors as employment of foreign nationals and exchange control
2. industry restrictions, relating to industry guidelines covering local content, the technology to be adopted, and so on
3. specific restrictions relating to the terms and conditions, in addition to the above, applying to a specific enterprise

Table 6-4 summarizes and compares the important general restrictions applicable to foreign-owned (and, in some cases, locally owned) firms in the Southeast Asia and South Pacific countries.

Investment Incentives and Guarantees

In an effort to overcome some of the natural and artificial barriers to investment in their countries, some governments offer some form of investment incentives

Table 6-4
Important General Restrictions on the Operations of Foreign-owned Firms in the Southeast Asian and South Pacific Countries

	Land Utilization for Industrial Purposes	Company Management[a]	Employment of Nationals	Exchange Controls– Remittances of Profit[b]	Exchange Controls– Remittances of Royalties[b]
Fiji	Some land freehold, but bulk on 99-year lease	Unrestricted	Unrestricted, but training programs	Unrestricted	Unrestricted
Indonesia	No foreign enterprise can own land. Foreigners may lease land for up to 30 years (can be extended for further 20 years at government's discretion).	Unrestricted	Employment of foreign nationals in managerial and technical positions that cannot yet be filled by nationals. Foreign enterprises required to organize and provide systematic training and educational facilities with aim of gradually replacing foreign emloyees with nationals.	Unrestricted	Unrestricted
Korea, South	Unrestricted, but note industrial estates	Unrestricted	Unrestricted, but training programs	Unrestricted	Unrestricted
Malaysia	Unrestricted. Lease on industrial estates and free trade zones.	Mgt. control usually required when Malaysian ownership also required. Mgt. contracts allowed.	Foreign companies required to maximize employment of nationals (especially Malays) and to plan for replacing expatriates by Malaysians. Training program required.	Unrestricted	Unrestricted
Papua-New Guinea	Leasehold	Unrestricted	Unrestricted, but training. programs except for reserved occupations	Unrestricted	Unrestricted
Philippines	Lease of public lands not to exceed 2500 acres per firm (applies also to local firms). Land to be owned only by companies with at least 60% Filipino equity. Lease industrial estates and free trade zones.	Mgt. control by Filipinos usually required when Filipino majority also required; mgt. contracts allowed	Firms receiving incentives not to employ aliens after first 5 years of operation. Within the 5-year period, alien employment in supervisory, technical, or advisory positions limited to 5% of firm's total such employ-	Generally unrestricted	May not exceed 50% of royalties earned during that year (not a permanent restriction).

			ment. For pioneer areas, period can be extended and restriction does not apply by category of employment. When majority foreign-owned, positions of president, treasurer, and gen. mgr. may be retained.		
Singapore	Appears unrestricted Lease on industrial estates.	Unrestricted	Employment of foreign nationals in technical and professional positions. Local workers must be trained.	Unrestricted	Unrestricted
Taiwan	Unrestricted, but note industrial estates	Unrestricted	Unrestricted, but training programs	Unrestricted	Unrestricted
Thailand	Foreign-owned and -controlled companies not allowed to own land. Countries with less than 50% foreign equity limited to 10 rai.[c] Promoted industries with approval allowed to own more if incorporated in country that has land ownership treaty with Thailand. Lease on industrial estates.	Thai mgt. control usually required when Thai majority ownership also required. Mgt. contracts allowed.	About 39 occupations restricted to Thai nationals. Work permits required. Thai workers must be trained.	Unrestricted except when Central Bank requires for balance-of-payments purposes.	Unrestricted
Western Samoa	Unrestricted	Unrestricted, but training program	Unrestricted	Unrestricted	Unrestricted

[a]Applies also to local enterprises.
[b]Where unrestricted, approval still required.
[c]1 rai = 1600 square meters.

Table 6-4 (cont.)

	Exchange Controls— Repatriation of Capital[b]	Debt/Equity Ratio Access to Local Finance	Access to Local Finance	Import Restrictions[a]
Fiji	Unrestricted	Normally 1:3	Limited to some extent	Limited
Indonesia	Allowed, but such repatriations not granted as long as exemption of concessions concerning taxes and other levies in effect	None specified	Unrestricted	Restrictions of varying degrees to protect domestic industries and conserve foreign exchange
Korea, South	At government discretion. Repatriation may be limited to 20% per annum beginning 2 years after start of operation	None specified	Unspecified	Restrictions of varying degrees to protect domestic industries and conserve foreign exchange
Malaysia	Unrestricted	None specified	Unrestricted	Restrictions of varying degrees to protect domestic industries and conserve foreign exchange
Papua-New Guinea	Unrestricted	None specified	Limited to some extent	Limited
Philippines	For export-oriented firms, annual repatriations may not exceed firm's yearly net foreign exchange earnings. For BOI-registered firms engaged in export or import substitution industries, repatriation limited to annual net foreign exchange earnings beginning 1 year after start of operations, or 3 annual dollar installments after 1 year of liquidation. For all other firms, repatriations limited to installments ranging from 5 years ($250,000 or less) to 9 years ($500,000 and above).	Normally limited to 70:30.	Restricted to some extent.	Restrictions of varying degrees to protect domestic industries and conserve foreign exchange

Country				
Singapore	Unrestricted	None specified	Unrestricted	Limited
Taiwan	At government discretion. Repatriation may be limited to 15% per annum beginning 3 years after start of operations.	None specified	Unspecified	Somewhat restricted to protect domestic industries and conserve foreign exchange
Thailand	Unrestricted, but capital freedom guaranteed only for investment capital derived by promoted person from for-	None specified	Unrestricted	Restrictions of varying degrees to protect domestic industries and conserve foreign exchange
Western Samoa	Unrestricted	None specified	Limited to some extent	Limited

aApplies also to local enterprises.
bWhere unrestricted, approval still required.
c1 rai = 1600 square miles.

Table 6-4 (cont.)

	Fixing of Royalties and Technical Fees[a]	Joining Local Trade Associations	Capital Issue Control[a]
Fiji	Subject to authorization	No compulsion	No laws
Indonesia	Subject to authorization	No compulsion	No laws
Korea, South	Subject to authorization	No compulsion	No laws, but number of shares issued at time of incorporation shall be more than 50% of authorized value
Malaysia	Left to negotiation between licensor and licensee	No compulsion	No laws, but Central Bank determines timing
Papau-New Guinea	Subject to authorization	No compulsion	No laws
Philippines	Subject to authorization	May be permitted	No laws
Singapore	Left to negotiation between licensor and licensee	No compulsion	No laws
Taiwan	Vary from 1% to 10% but subject to authorization	No compulsion	No laws, but number of shares issued at time of incorporation shall be more than 25% of authorized capital
Thailand	Left to negotiation between licensor and licensee	No compulsion	No laws
Western Samoa	Subject to authorization	No compulsion	No laws

[a]Applies also to local enterprises.
[b]Where unrestricted, approval still required.
[c]1 rai = 1600 square miles.

and guarantees. The natural barriers relate to the lack of workforce skills, undeveloped industrial support services and facilities, language and custom differences, and the like. The artificial barriers include (in some of the countries) distorted tariff and exchange-control structures and apparent economic and financial instabilities.

The basic guarantees are relatively straightforward and concern guarantees against nationalization and expropriation, freedom to repatriate income and capital, patent protection, and other measures to make the investor feel more at ease. It is difficult, if not impossible, of course, for any government to speak for future governments. Even the freedom to repatriate income and capital is generally qualified with phrases in the legislation such as "except in extreme cases of balance of payments strain where the Central Bank may limit the extent of repatriation for a short period." Investors, however, do look for guarantees along these lines and all the countries have made efforts to ensure that these are given. Table 6-5 summarizes the guarantees as they apply to each country.

The desirability and applicability of the various types of incentives has been the subject of considerable debate. Many commentators have argued that financial incentives in the form of taxation exemption are not important to enterprises in their investment decisions. Thus the developing countries are unnecessarily subsidizing industry or diverting their financial resources from more important attraction factors such as infrastructure and education facilities. Others argue that countries are competing for scarce capital, and so financial incentives are important.

Investment incentives in the countries mainly take the form of taxation incentives—exemptions from certain taxes (for example, import duties on capital equipment or income tax holidays for a five-year period) or certain deductions from the taxes to be paid (for example, deductions from income tax of labor-training expenses). Special incentives are also given to export industries. Nontax benefits include, for example, tariff protection and industrial sites.

The incentives are categorized as follows:[i]

1. income tax exemptions and deductions, and tax credits
2. import duties and tax exemptions and deductions
3. exemptions from other taxes
4. other benefits

Incentives can take a multitude of forms. In the Philippines a complicated pattern of deductions, exemptions, and tax credits is apparent. Although this setup requires more administrative control, it has been necessitated by many "anticipated" fiscal and monetary policies. On the other hand, the Singapore system, which relies on straight-out exemptions, administratively simplifies dealings with investors.

---

[i]It is too cumbersome to include the qualifications for each incentive in the various countries.

Table 6-5
Basic Guarantees to Foreign Enterprises in the Southeast Asian and South Pacific Countries

	Philippines	Thailand	Malaysia	Singapore	Indonesia	South Korea	Taiwan	Papua-New Guinea	Fiji	Western Samoa
1. Patent protection	Yes	No	Yes	Yes	Yes	Yes	Yes	n.a.	n.a.	Yes
2. Freedom from expropriation and requisition unless compensation	Yes[2]	No	No	No[11]	Yes	Yes	Yes[18]	Yes	Yes	Yes
3. Freedom from nationalization unless compensation	Yes	Yes	Yes[8]	No	Yes	Yes	Yes[18]	Yes	Yes	Yes
4. Guarantees of national treatment	No	Yes	No[9]	No	No[12]	Yes	Yes	n.a.	Yes	n.a.
5. Repatriation of investment and convertibility in foreign currency	Yes[3]	Yes[7]	Yes	Yes	Yes[13]	Yes[15]	Yes[19]	Yes	Yes	Yes
6. Remittance of earnings and convertibility in foreign currency	Yes	Yes[7]	Yes	Yes	Yes[14]	Yes[16]	Yes[20]	Yes	Yes	Yes
7. Remittance to meet payments of foreign loans and contracts and convertibility to foreign currencies	Yes	Yes[7]	Yes	Yes	Yes	Yes[17]	Yes	Yes[21]	Yes	Yes
8. Remittance of amount corresponding to depreciation of fixed capital assets	No	No	No	No	Yes	No	No	n.a.	n.a.	n.a.
9. Nondiscriminatory application of laws	No	Yes	Yes	Yes	Yes	Yes	Yes	Yes[22]	Yes	Yes
10. Employment of aliens (restrictions apply to local and foreign firms)	Yes[4]	Yes	Yes[10]	Yes	Yes	Yes	Yes	Yes	Yes	Yes

11. Company management by aliens (restrictions apply to local and foreign firms)	Yes[5]	Yes	Yes[10]	Yes	Yes	Yes	Yes	Yes
12. Access to all investment incentives	No[5] (40)	Yes	Yes	Yes	Yes	No	Yes	Yes
13. Access to all export incentives	No (40)	Yes	Yes	Yes	Yes	No	Yes	Yes
14. Access to loans from host government financial institutions	No	Yes	Yes	Yes	Yes	Yes[23]	Yes[25]	Yes
15. Access to loans from local private financial institutions	Yes	Yes	Yes	Yes	Yes	Yes	Yes	Yes
16. Access to awards for host government public work contracts	No (25)	Yes	Yes	Yes	Yes	Yes[24]	Yes	Yes
17. Access to awards for host government supply contracts	No[6] (40)	Yes	Yes	Yes	Yes	Yes	Yes	Yes
18. Freedom from government competition	No[5] (40)	n.a.	n.a.	Yes	n.a.	n.a.	n.a.	n.a.

1. For privileges not extended to wholly owned foreign firms, the figures in parentheses indicate the maximum percentage of foreign ownership permitted in order to be eligible for each privilege.
2. Freedom from expropriation is subject only to right of eminent dominion and convertibility in foreign currency. Freedom from requisition may be waived in case of war or national emergency and convertibility in foreign currency in cases where payments are received as compensation for requisitioned property.
3. See Table 6-4, and the earlier discussion on operational restraints.
4. Limited. Must ultimately be replaced by locals.
5. If pioneer preferred, yes.
6. This varies; for example, public works must be 70-percent Filipino or U.S. capital.

Table 6-5 (cont.)

7. Except in cases when required by the Central Bank for balance-of-payments purposes. Capital freedom is guaranteed only for that investment capital derived by the "promoted person" from a foreign country.
8. In 1966, however, the Malaysian government took over the cables of Overseas Telecommunication on a negotiated basis.
9. Guarantee (as regards nationalization) with the United States and Germany; open to other countries also.
10. Limited. Must ultimately be replaced by locals.
11. An investment guarantee agreement exists between the United States and Singapore with 100 percent political risk and guarantees against losses from expropriation, war, revolution, insurrection, non-convertibility of foreign currency, and 75 percent guarantees for political and business risk.
12. Guarantee valid for thirty years. Guarantee to American investors (bilateral agreement) against losses due to nationalization, war, and inconvertibility of currency.
13. Repatriation shall not be granted as long as the exemptions of concessions concerning taxes and other levies are still in effect.
14. Remittance of earnings or profits after subtraction of taxes.
15. Repatriation of investment up to 20 percent every year, after 2 years from the date the enterprise commences its business operations and convertibility into foreign currency. In the event of liquidation of the enterprise, total principal may be repatriated.
16. Remittance of profit dividends, justly accrued from the stocks or shares owned by foreign investors and convertibility into foreign exchange.
17. Remittance of: principal and interest under a cash loan contract; value of interest under a capital goods inducement contract; value of a technological inducement contract, and convertibility into foreign currency.
18. Freedom from expropriation or requisition within 20 years after commencement of business, if a foreign investor holds more than 51 percent of local capital and as long as such investor continues to hold at least 51 percent of total capital.
19. Yearly repatriation of 15 percent of total amount of invested capital 3 years after completion of approved investment plans and convertibility in foreign currency.
20. Remittances of net profit or accrued interest and convertibility in foreign currency.
21. Except for large projects, such as mining where approval may only be guaranteed for limited periods at a time.
22. Except for taxation concessions available only to Papua New Guineans.
23. Prefer, in most cases, for foreigners to bring in capital.
24. Except in case where Papua New Guinean enterprises given 10 percent advantage in costs in awarding of small government contracts.
25. Normally in line with ratio of local/foreign capital.

The Pacific Basin countries are more often using incentives to achieve their economic and social objectives rather than simply as straight attraction mechanisms for foreign investment. The Malaysian legislation structures incentives to encourage exports, the location of enterprises in less developed areas, and the input of local content in the manufacturing of priority products. Under the provisions of the special incentives for export-oriented industries, tax relief is allowed for periods ranging from four to seven years, compared with the three- to five-year relief period for other pioneer industries. Similarly, a company locating its factory in a less-developed area producing a priority product and having more than 50-percent local content can be granted a maximum tax relief period of eight years.

The Philippines incentive laws present a parallel situation with added incentives for exports, preferred industries, and the use of local raw materials and labor. Recent changes in the expansionary reinvestment allowance (which accounts for the bulk of the tax credits claimed by registered enterprises) have given fuller flexibility to the Board of Investments to use varying rates depending on labor intensity, exports, and regional dispersal.

Papua-New Guinea offers little in the way of incentives. It already has a low company tax rate (33 1/3 percent) and no commodity or other such taxes. It is fairly liberal in its deductions.

*Agreements with Other Countries Relevant to
Foreign Investment*

In closing the discussion of incentives and guarantees, it should be pointed out that a number of bilateral agreements have been concluded by the countries covering not only taxation agreements, but also general treaties to promote trade and investment. Two main types of general bilateral treaties are found: the comprehensive treaty of friendship including special provisions on the position of foreign investments; and the specialized treaty exclusively covering the promotion and protection of foreign investments.[3] The United States, Japan, and the United Kingdom, for example, have used the comprehensive treaty exclusively, while West Germany and Switzerland have used both but have been increasingly emphasizing the specialized treaty.

Relief from double taxation may be given "unilaterally by the capital exporting or the capital importing country, or through bilateral agreements. Such agreements either divide the field of taxation between the two countries, or provide for tax credits on double taxes incomes."[4] While there are few such agreements in the countries (with the agreements relating to income and profit taxes, generally providing that nonresidents will be taxed only on the income tax in another country), double taxation is not widespread since most countries unilaterally provide some relief.

Of particular importance is the fact that a number of countries have ratified the international agreements on Settlement of Industrial Disputes worked out by the United Nations, the World Bank, and others. This agreement came into force in 1966, and an International Chamber of Commerce handles trading disputes between foreign private companies and governments. Also noteworthy is the growing cooperation between some of the Asian countries in the investment field. An example is the complementation program currently being mooted. Although no agreement has yet been reached for any specific program, there appears to be great promise for cooperation on this basis.

Nationalism, Bureaucracy, and Regional Cooperation

Nationalism and Development

Nationalism is a fact often overlooked by economic commentators. One of its most significant developing expressions in the region is the desire for control over the means of production. To achieve this, laws and procedures have been devised to reserve certain business activities for the indigenous population, to restrict the entry of aliens into certain occupations, to require local participation in industrial projects and, in some instances, to expropriate alien property. New devices undoubtedly will evolve over the next decade to hasten this process.

The problem facing the region's developing countries, therefore, is to find some means of increasing control without causing much-needed foreign investment to shy away from setting up projects. While many investors welcome local participation in projects, their fear is that a government may nationalize or expropriate their property at any time. Compensation may be paid, but past experience has shown that it can take time, since arguments center around the amount of compensation. The procedures involved may also be costly.

Foreign investors are afraid that although a country may offer guarantees, nothing would prevent the country from reneging on these guarantees—one cannot "guarantee" what a future government will do. Interestingly, many companies, verbally supporting a democratic elective system of government, continually say in negotiations, "well, it's all right with the government, but what if it changes in the next election and the new government is more radical?" Unfortunately, in such a democratic elective system no administrators can guarantee for future governments. One wonders whether large foreign enterprises may indeed prefer to deal with one-party dictatorial governments!

Foreign enterprises can expect growing, rather than reducing, controls. To compensate, the host countries are evolving more rapid processing procedures to allow faster decisions, which will result not only from rationalized administrative procedures, but also from the creation of more definitive guidelines for investors.

Related to this trend is the changing form of agreements. In the past, emphasis was on "contracts," especially for large projects, wherein each item was subject to negotiation. Now countries are passing specific legislations that specify the requirements to be met (and the penalties, appeal mechanisms, etc., for not conforming to these requirements) before a proposal is considered. While this makes it easier for enterprises to know the requirements, it reduces their ability to write in safeguards for all requirements so common in contracts. Contracts may still be required, but under the legislation system, the enterprises are forced into agreement to have items out of terms and conditions (with strict penalties for nonconformity or no access to arbitration on certain matters) in a contract (with its inherent escape clauses), rather than the government having to negotiate each item.

The path to achieving nationalistic ideals, however, will not be smooth. The need to generate employment opportunities for an ever-growing workforce, the swelling of urban centers with people in search of nonexistent jobs and thus a massing of discontented persons in key localities, balance-of-payments problems, inflationary pressure, and so on, cause vacillations around the basic trend. In themselves, such vacillations cause foreign investors to find it difficult to distinguish the extent to which they are really welcome. Thus there are frustrations for both the government and the investors. The government is faced with the challenge of balancing the strength of the long-term desire for ownership and control of the productive assets with the need to counteract shorter term problems: i.e., it is a problem of identifying areas of foreign involvement and the controls to be placed on it. The investors are faced with the problems of gauging what the government really wants and whether the conditions for establishment reflect the country's short-term considerations or long-term nationalistic desires, which are likely to differ.

For the Pacific Basin countries, other external elements are to be considered. The dominance of China and the new regimes of Cambodia, Laos, and South Vietnam have caused a considerable reorientation of alignments. The Western world now has to compete for the region's favors, although it seems that Western investors have not yet realized that. The Southeast Asian countries, on the other hand, also realize that they have to build a strong economy based on nationalism to ensure that they do not breed internal discontent that could lead to even more powerful breakaway Communist elements within their own countries, elements who would have easier access to support from the outside Communist countries.

This is indeed a dilemma, but it can be solved with understanding. Golay et al. express it well:

Nationalists in South East Asia [and also in the South Pacific] are energetic and predictable in their efforts to ensure that economic development is national and not merely geographic. In seeking to enlarge their sovereignty, they are sophisticated and realistic and can be depended upon to take a skeptical view of threats to their independence whether from the capitalist West or Communist East. Because ex-colonial economic nationalism has been imperfectly perceived and inadequately appreciated, much of the potential effectiveness of past efforts on the part of the outside world to participate in economic development in South East Asia has been wasted. On the other hand, the gap in that part of the world establishes wide limits to the range of activities and projects that promise to contribute to economic development. There is so much to be done that surely the problems of developing institutions and techniques for effective participation that do not clash with the requirements of ex-colonial nationalism are capable of solution if approached with flexibility, initiative, and understanding.[5]

Nationalism, however, is not the only factor causing countries to look inward in certain areas. The increased volumes of trade and efforts of world bodies to induce countries to subscribe to the concept of specialization based on national advantages are viewed with certain misgivings by the Pacific Basin countries. Worldwide inflation, rising energy prices, shortages of food, and so on have moved the countries to push for self-sufficiency in key essentials and to broaden their own base of exportable items. This desire may run against outside advice (the experts argue that these are only short-term phenomena), but is a very real issue for national leaders facing discontent from a population, a large majority of whom have no conception of the outside world. It is almost impossible to explain to demonstrating crowds that inflation and shortages are not the government's fault but that the problem is worldwide.

Thus whether we like it or not, insulation will probably take place on an increasing scale.

Development and the Bureaucracy

The translation of ideologies into practical programs heavily depends on the bureaucracy's responsiveness. If the bureaucracy is not behind the ideologies expressed by the country, politicians' efforts to bring about changes can be forever frustrated. Even if they generally support the ideologies, there need only be a few weak links in the administrative chain to cause frustrations. Unless one has worked within a bureaucracy, it is hard to envisage the distance between the top decision-makers and the administrative field officers who have to implement the programs. At any one of a number of stages in this chain, programs can be delayed or changed without the top echelon's ever knowing what is really happening. The excuses of practical difficulties, reliance on some other department for a certain input, shortage of supplies and personnel, and so on are common in administrative vocabulary.

One of the problems arises from the fact that many administrators regard themselves as the guardians of the peoples' interests, which extends sometimes to believing this especially applies to politicians' whims. Such an attitude results not only from their own political convictions (and such persons would argue that they have none), but also from their own convictions that people do not understand the practical difficulties of implementing programs. Such "practical difficulties" are often the result of the administrator's own shortcomings, which include the inability to look for new ways of doing things, inexperience, or pure laziness.

For the foreign investor, such attitudes can cause frustrations: moving from department to department; inability to get a clear indication of government policies; having to make "service" payments; filling out numerous forms; delays in decisions being made; hearing different views from politicians and bureaucrats; and so on. The creation of "one-stop shops," such as the Boards of Investments, has reduced these frustrations considerably, but they still exist.

The preceding comments are not meant to convey the impression that all administrators can be classified this way or that all departments are so overbearing. However, it takes only a few in key positions in the system (these persons may not necessarily be at the top of the hierarchy) to thwart any real effort that others are making. With a growing bureaucracy in all the countries, this is going to be an increasing problem, but efforts are being made to streamline procedures and bring business-oriented technocrats into the administrative system.

One could present many observations about the administrative system of a country and probably evolve a more realistic development theory centered around institutions. Suffice it to say that bureaucracy is a fact of life and enterprises have to build allowances for its idiosyncracies into their decision frames.

Regional Cooperation

The drive for self-sufficiency and the desire for insulation from outside events have also manifested themselves in the search for regional cooperation. Realizing that such cooperation expands political, economic, and institutional horizons, countries have explored possibilities in this field that in some instances resulted in short-lived and controversial alliances.

The geographical boundaries of economic cooperation are overlapping. On the one hand, groupings have been mooted on a limited geographical basis, such as the ASEAN group and the South Pacific Islands group, and on a wider basis covering developed and developing countries in the Pacific Basin. Bilateral cooperation has also evolved.

ASEAN Economic Cooperation

To date, the Association of South East Asian Nations (ASEAN)—comprising Thailand, Indonesia, Malaysia, Singapore, and the Philippines—seems to be the most viable and promising of the groups. It is seen as a "response to political reality, within which the states of the region would work out their problems of development and stability in the absence of great power rivalry . . . a framework for the rationalization and coordination of projects and investment decisions within the region."[6] Most certainly the new attitude of the countries toward the People's Republic of China and the new governments in Cambodia, Laos, and South Vietnam add further impetus to finding common ground for cooperation among the ASEAN countries.

The economic arguments of cooperation rest on the advantages of bigger markets, economies of scale, and specialization. Potentially larger product/ activity mixes could be considered because of the breakdown of fragmented markets and the wider range of import replacement potentials and more specialized exports. A U.N. study team set up to explore the potentials however, realized that in the ASEAN context,

"though the extent of effective cooperation may increase significantly during the 1970s, there will not be as yet a preparedness to accept very close and complete integration in the form of a complete free trade area, a customs union or a common market. It may legitimately be assumed on the other hand, in the light of many economic and political forces working in favor of cooperation, that there will be a welcome for a limited trade liberalization scheme, covering a number of carefully selected commodities and a limited scheme for cooperation in the development of new industrial projects, supplemented by a number of other cooperative measures of a more direct character in the monetary and financial fields, in the provision of agricultural services, in shipping, in tourist facilities and in other similar forms."[7]

For industrial development, the U.N. team recommended three interrelated avenues for cooperation:

1. selective trade liberalization, negotiated on a product by product basis applied progressively on a wide scale;
2. a system of complementary agreements, involving specialization of different products, within an industry or related industries;
3. a system of "package deal" agreements, for the establishment of new large scale projects for a limited period in specific countries to avoid unnecessary duplication of capacities.

For each of these categories, a wide range of industries can be involved. In trade liberalization for example, focus could be on products such as garments, textiles, footwear and consumer durables; for complementarity agreements, the fields of automobiles, cosmetics and appliances are areas of promise; and for "package deals," steel ingots, fertilizers, newsprint etc. are possibilities. To implement such programs however, a spirit of cooperation is required. There are signs of such cooperation evolving (although initial moves have been on a bilateral basis) but it will be many years before the barriers of self-interest are broken down and effective cooperation even in limited fields is achieved.

In 1972 I interviewed a sample of multinational corporation executives to gauge their attitudes toward regional cooperation.[8] In ASEAN, although the companies acknowledged the benefits and the desirability of such a cooperation, they could not envisage its position in the next ten to fifteen years. They see the many problems facing the members, the most common to their mind being the determination of membership; disparities in economic, social, and political structures; and development of the ASEAN countries, strong competition among them, and the implications of administration. This does not mean, however, that the investors, especially the Japanese, would not consider beginning the process that would lead to its realization. Complementarity programs are a step to such possibility, and companies may have opportunities to integrate operations across countries. Large indivisible projects such as petrochemical complexes where economies of scale and/or proximity of activities is necessary, and large-scale divisible projects—such as car manufacture and assembly where economies of scale but not proximity is called for—are seen as major areas where complementation programs could be implemented.

The member countries themselves have been working hard to surmount these problems. Their respective governments have stepped up consultation with one another and with other regional bodies, such as the EEC.

Early in 1973 representatives of the regional government explored further the possibilities of achieving the goal of cooperation.[9] A permanent secretariat was formed to help create regional industries and entertain proposals of participation by multinational companies. However, local participation was emphasized, and the establishment of firms with equity shared among the members, with professional management, proposed. Generation of finance from domestic savings was also emphasized. Such emphasis notwithstanding, ASEAN recognizes the importance of the role the foreign investors would need to play if cooperation is to become a reality.

South Pacific Regional Economic Cooperation

Economic cooperation among the South Pacific countries is even more difficult. Not only do problems of transportation hinder effective trading among the island nations, but they are also hindered by their dependence on past or present colonial masters for trading purposes—a dependence that regional cooperation would tend to cut across.

In the face of these problems, the South Pacific countries have still persistently proclaimed the need to provide intraregional trade. The member countries of the South Pacific Forum (Fiji, Samoa, Papua-New Guinea) in particular have expressed strong desires along these lines, and a number of measures have been adopted to explore the possibilities. For example, a South Pacific Bureau of Economic Co-operation (SPEC) has been formed, and the United Nations has undertaken a Regional Transport Survey.

Regional cooperation in the South Pacific is in its early stages. Until the transportation question is solved and until the countries are willing to disassociate themselves from their dependence on their traditional markets, effective cooperation is not a reality. A start can be made through avenues such as ensuring similar standardization programs with an eventual view to regional manufacture, synchronization of policies and a firming of a common attitude toward development and the foreign investor, and a concerted effort toward ensuring continual dialogue (especially at the institutional level). However, there will be more lip service paid to cooperation than any determined effort to bring it into reality. Enough problems face the countries in their own internal development programs to cause regional cooperation to be of low priority in their development strategies.

Overview

One hopes for regional economic cooperation to be a reality, but in the immediate future it will be only on a limited scale. Geographical proximity alone is not enough of a basis to ensure its evolution: a common goal, an extent of development similar in each country, and a regional "nationalism" must evolve. Otherwise, programs for development at the regional level fall well below internal development programs for each country.

External influences are also important. Strong regional groups are often against the interests of surrounding countries and continually new groupings are suggested, normally on a much wider basis. Australia and New Zealand, for example, no doubt fear regional groupings in which they are not involved. China's influence also possibly has contributed more to conflict than cooperation in Asia.

However, a foreign investor with vision should keep the possibilities of regional cooperation in mind. It may be difficult for the countries to achieve, but the desire is there.

Other Issues

A treatise could be written on each of the above subjects as well as numerous others that come to mind on development strategies and foreign investment policies of the Southeast Asian and South Pacific countries. For example, the whole field of appropriate technology, the differing characteristics of projects established by enterprises of differing nationalities, and so on, are important issues that need deep consideration. The whole question of policing foreign investment projects to ensure that terms and conditions are being met needs close review in all the countries; the supervisory capacity is perhaps the area in which most of the countries are weakest. In addition, the implications of evolving appropriate technologies and the derivation of means of applying them needs to be examined. The differing characteristics of the ethnic groups within the region and the effect of their varying composition in each country on the form of development has also not received the attention in development literature that it should.

Notes

1. See F. Golay, R. Anspach, M. Pfanner & E. Ayal, *Underdevelopment and Economic Nationalism in South East Asia,* Cornell University Press, 1969.

2. See C. Draper, "Benefits Foreign Investment can Provide: An Issue," *Economic Cooperation Bulletin* 1 Economic Cooperation Center (January 1973):

3. See M. Sakurai, "Reviews of Laws and Practices Covering Foreign Investment in Developing Countries of the Region and Measures to Improve the Investment Climate in Them." (ECAFE: Asian Conference on Industrialization, September 1970), pp. 33-35.

4. Ibid., p. 27.

5. Golay et al., p. 469.

6. See Charles Draper, ed., "Essays in South East Asia Trade and Investment," *Economic Study No. 4,* ECOCEN, Bangkok 1973, p. 85.

7. Economic Cooperation for ASEAN (Report of a United Nations Team, 1973), p. 29.

8. For a fuller outline of this view, see T.W. Allen "Policies of ASEAN Countries Towards Direct Foreign Investment" SEADAG Papers, New York 1973, pp. 69-73.

9. See Draper.

Appendix 6A
Limitations on Foreign
Ownership and Control
of Enterprises in the
Southeast Asian and
South Pacific Countries

Fiji

Areas Closed to Foreign Investments
   Public utilities controlled by the government.
Areas Specifically Restricted in Proportion of Foreign Equity
   No areas specifically restricted.
Policy on Areas Open to Foreign Investment
   No specific requirements, though joint ventures preferred.

Indonesia

Areas Closed to Any Foreign Investment[a]
   Industries that are vital functions for defense, including arms and ammunitions, explosives, and war equipment. In the field of mining, foreign investment must take the form of "work-contracts." Sectors of trading and distribution businesses are also closed to foreign investors, particularly domestic retail trade and exporting and importing unless coupled with domestic manufacturing. From time to time the government issues regulations to restrict certain types of investment because the industry is "overcrowded" or could readily be exploited by Indonesians. Some forty industries in the light engineering field are on this "temporary" restricted list.

Policy on Other Areas Open to Foreign Investment
   Officially, foreigners are permitted to own and control 100 percent of a capital investment, but there is a general requirement that, at some suitable time, domestic capital will be brought into the venture (or if the arrangements under which the enterprise is put into operation involve government-established controls). An investment permit has a thirty-year maximum validity, but it may be renewed.

[a]The January 1974 amendments are not reflected in this table.

Malaysia

Areas Closed to Any Foreign Investment
Public utilities, domestic air transport, and certain military goods.

Areas Specifically Restricted in Proportion of Foreign Equity
No areas specifically restricted.

Policy on Other Areas Open to Foreign Investment
A high degree of flexibility exists, although companies that entirely depend on the Malaysian market for their sales are generally required to have at least 51-percent domestic participation in the equity. If fully export-oriented, up to 100-percent foreign ownership may be allowed. Companies whose export performance falls between these extremes can negotiate with the government and with Malaysia investors concerning the percentage of equity. In certain instances, flexibility also exists for high-technology products. Note that in petroleum, Malaysia has given Petronas, the state-owned oil company, the power to assume management control of all downstream petroleum activities (see Petroleum Development Amendment Act).

Philippines

Areas Closed to Any Foreign Investment
Permanent: Rural banks, mass media, retail trade, rice and corn (may be open in certain instances), and certain military goods.
Temporary: "Overcrowded industries" are closed to any new investment unless the product is to be exported or the location of the enterprise would promote regional dispersal. These products include room air conditioners, G.I. sheets, nails, pencils, radios, and matches. Forty industries are included on the overcrowded list.

Areas Specifically Restricted in Proportion of Foreign Equity
Banking institutions (70 percent)[b] except new banks established by consolidation of branches or agencies of foreign banks in the Philippines; saving and loan associations (60 percent); public utilities (60 percent); domestic air commerce and/or air transportation (60 percent); financing companies (60 percent); fishing vessels (61 percent +); marine mollusca and other fishing

[b]The figures in parentheses indicate the minimum local ownership control of equity capital. The + symbol after some of the percentages means that this amount can be Filipino or U.S. capital, a provision that applied until the expiration of the Laurel-Langley agreement in 1974.

activities (61 percent +); permits or leases for tapping or utilizing geo-thermal energy, natural gas, and methane gas (60 percent); natural resources (60 percent); certain educational institutions (60 percent); land (60 percent); and coastal trade (75 percent +). (Note that the Philippines is now increasing local participation requirements in natural resource and similar fields to 70 percent.)

For areas listed in the Annual Investment Priorities Plan (which can vary from year to year), the policy is as follows:

Pioneer Preferred Areas: Up to 100-percent foreign ownership and control may be allowed, but within thirty years it has to be reduced to 60-percent Filipino ownership and control (if exporting at least 70 percent of production, this is extended to forty years). These periods may be extended ten more years in special circumstances. Examples of present pioneer areas are copper metal, primary steel, asbestos, foundry coke, polypropylene, small gasoline engines, and interisland shipping.

Nonpioneer Preferred Areas: Up to 40-percent foreign ownership and control is allowed. However, if the measured capacity is not realized within three years after its first listing on the Investment Priorities Plan, the areas become "liberalized" and up to 100-percent foreign ownership and control is allowed, subject to conversion to 60-percent Filipino ownership and control within the time periods specified for pioneer preferred areas. Examples of present nonliberalized, nonpioneer preferred areas are palm oil, copper ore, glass containers, palay threshers, perlite, and feed yeast. Liberalized areas include barges and tugboats, coconut oil, fruit and vegetable processing, pumps, fishing boats, pulp, and paper.

For Areas Listed in the Export Priorities Plan as open for investment by new enterprises (List B), a similar pioneer/nonpioneer categorization to the investment priority plan exists. The ownership and control requirements are the same, except that foreign enterprises (that is, where foreign equity is above 40 percent) may register under the Export Priorities Plan even in the nonpioneer areas if they export at least 70 percent of production. Examples of present pioneer export industries are activated carbon, furs, rice bran oil, pliers and wrenches, and electronic parts and components. Examples of present nonpioneer export industries are (note there are no nonliberalized areas) essential oil, blockboard and blockboard cover, garments, footwear, processed vegetables, and food. (The 60-percent ownership and control requirement for the nonpioneer areas may be waived, and these may be treated as pioneer areas if regional complementarity is involved. Also, a 10-percent "public participation" in the equity of all enterprises receiving incentives is normally required.)

For Areas Listed in the Tourism Priorities Plan, up to 100-percent foreign ownership and control may be allowed, but within thirty years percentage has to be reduced to 60-percent Filipino ownership and control; this period may be extended ten more years in special circumstances.

For all other areas, up to 100-percent foreign ownership and control may be allowed, but when it is above 30 percent, such investment must be approved by the Board of Investments. Authority for such investment will be granted unless the proposed investment would:

1. conflict with existing constitutional provisions and laws for regulating the degree of required ownership by Philippine nationals in the enterprise
2. pose a clear and present danger of promoting monopolies or combinations in restraint of trade
3. be made in an enterprise engaged in a field adequately being exploited by Filipinos
4. conflict or be inconsistent with the Investment Priorities Plan in force at the time the investment is sought to be made
5. fail to contribute to the sound and balanced development of the national economy on a self-sustaining basis.

Singapore

Areas Closed to any Foreign Investment
Public utilities, domestic air transport, and certain military goods.

Areas Specifically Restricted in Proportion of Foreign Equity
No areas specifically restricted.

Policy on Other Areas Open to Foreign Investment
Generally, Sinagpore prefers local collaboration, but it is very flexible in its policy in this regard.

South Korea

Areas Closed to Foreign Investment
Special government control in military goods, telecommunications, power, railways, tungsten, coal mining, tobacco, ginseng, and salt industries. Foreign capital may be permitted on negotiated terms.

Areas Specifically Restricted in Proportion of Foreign Equity
No areas specifically restricted.

Policy on Areas Open to Foreign Investment

The official position is that joint ventures are desired, not necessarily majority locally owned—49 percent of foreign common equity is "preferred," however.

Taiwan

Areas Closed to Foreign Investment

Military goods, petroleum refining, telecommunications, power, railways, sugar, fertilizers, and alcoholic beverage industries owned or controlled by the government.

Areas Specifically Restricted in Proportion of Foreign Equity

No areas specifically restricted.

Policy on Areas Open to Foreign Investment

Joint ventures encouraged.

Thailand

Areas Closed to Any Foreign Investment

Public utilities, savings banks, rural banking, insurances, and certain military goods.

Areas Specifically Restricted in Proportion of Foreign Equity

Aliens doing business are subject to the Alien Business Law, which restricts the participation of non-Thai nationals in certain fields of business activity. These are classified in three categories:

Category A. This category includes business activities reserved for Thai nationals or enterprises that are majority-owned (that is, at least 51 percent) and controlled by Thais. Aliens engaged in activities in this category as of November 26, 1972, were given until November 26, 1974, to wind up their operations. Category A includes the agricultural areas of rice farming and salt farming; the commercial areas of internal trade of agricultural products and trade in real property; and the services of accountancy, law, architecture, advertising, brokerage, auctioneering, haircutting, hairdressing, beauty treatment, and building construction.

Category B. Existing foreign-owned and foreign-controlled business activities under this category that were operating in Thailand as of November 26, 1972, will be allowed to continue operations indefinitely. However, no new majority-owned foreign enterprise will be allowed to establish; that is, at least 51 percent Thai ownership and control will be required. The areas included in Category B are the agricultural areas of fruit and vegetable farming, livestock, forestry, and fishing; the manufacturing areas of rice milling, flour, sugar, beverages, ice, medicine, cold storage, wood processing, products from gold and other exotic minerals, lacquerwares, woodcarvings, matches, lime, cement and by-products, stone blasting and crushing, garments and shoes except for export, printing, newspaper publication, and silk products; the commercial areas of retailing (except those specified in Category C), sale of mining products and food and beverages (except those specified in Category C), and sale of antiques and works of art; the service areas of tour agencies, hotels, and businesses defined by law as service premises; photography and printing, laundry and tailoring; and internal transportation by land, water, and air.

Category C. As with Category B, existing foreign-owned and foreign-controlled businesses in Category C may continue to operate indefinitely. Further, the formation of new companies under foreign majority ownership and control may be allowed under certain conditions. However, for enterprises under this category (and Category B) existing as of November 26, 1972, production or sales in subsequent years were limited to 30 percent of the quantity produced or sold in 1972; for new enterprises under Category C the maximum growth is subject to negotiation. The areas included in Category C are the commercial areas of wholesaling (except those specified in Category A), export of all types of products, retailing of machines and tools, and sale of food and beverages for the promotion of tourism; the manufacturing and mining areas of animal feeds, vegetable oil, embroidered and knitted products, glass containers and light bulbs, crockery, writing and printing paper, rock salt mining and mining; all other services not specified under Category A and B; and other constructions except those specified in Category A.

Policy on Other Areas Open to Foreign Investment

Joint ventures are encouraged in all fields. However, in addition to Category C products, foreign-owned and -controlled enterprises may be allowed in the promoted areas that do not fall in categories A and B. These cover a wide range of fields including certain activities in agriculture, minerals, metals, ceramics, chemicals, mechanical and electrical equipment, construction materials, textiles, services, and other products. Incentives are available for these promoted activities.

Western Samoa

Areas Closed to Foreign Investment

No information available at time of writing.

Areas Specifically Restricted in Proportion of Foreign Equity
No areas specifically restricted.

Policy on Areas Open to Foreign Investment
No special requirements for local participation.

7

Host Country Policies and the Flow of Direct Foreign Investment in the ASEAN Countries

Steven W. Kohlhagen

A beginning student of international business, international economics, international politics, and international law might be pardoned for believing that the multinational corporation (MNC) is some sort of powerful man-made institution gone awry. The popular press and, more recently, many academic researchers accuse these corporations of preying on small, surprisingly weak, sovereign states by forcing themselves on their unwilling hosts, and draining them of their economic and social growth potential. We are led to believe that the MNC represents the limits of what can go wrong with the free enterprise system—large, powerful economic agents with unlimited flexibility, all but infinite access to resources, and no discipline from the classic restraints of market competition. They are characterized as maximizing profits that are corresponding losses to the host countries, who are either unwilling or unable to hold back the advance of these parasitic agents who rob them of their revenues, technologies, and resources that are so necessary for future development.

Multinational corporations are blamed for everything from corrupting public officials and increasing social tensions to pursuing corporate policies that have a negative impact on host and source countries alike. They are criticized for, among other things, not being responsible to host or source governments or employees, maximizing global profits, minimizing global tax liabilities, exploiting host country factors of production, abandoning source country factors of production, helping to create polarized societies in host countries, squeezing out local entrepreneurs and generating monopoly power, undermining national sovereignty, exacerbating international disparities in income distribution, siphoning off needed capital from host countries, diverting local savings from productive national ventures, restricting host country access to modern technology, failing to upgrade the local labor force, contributing to inflation, dominating key industrial sectors, and controlling host country technology, financial capital, and communications (see, e.g., Mason 1974a; Sloan 1974; Turner 1974; Barnet and Müller 1974).

On the one hand, critics of the MNC claim that international investments bring in outdated and obsolete technology. On the other hand, they claim that

I would like to thank Dion Reich for his conscientious assistance; Dick Conlon and Kathy Holman of Business International and Dick Buxbaum for their help; and the Institute of Business and Economic Research at the University of California, Berkeley, and the Regents of the University of California Fellowship Committee for their support.

such investments import techniques that are often too modern and inappropriate for development needs. Similarly, source countries accuse MNCs of setting up foreign subsidiaries abroad specifically to export goods back home; host countries accuse them of failing to develop export capabilities from foreign subsidiaries. Some say they destroy local initiative by hiring away labor from local competitors, and others say they bring in expatriates instead of hiring local labor.

One of the general policy conclusions often suggested by these analyses is that the multinationals should be controlled through international agreements undertaken by the source countries, host countries, and perhaps even the multinationals themselves (see, e.g., Ball 1967, Goldberg and Kindleberger 1970, and Rubin 1971). The specific nature of the controls or guidelines vary according to the particular critic's perception of which of the many threats posed by MNCs are the most serious and the extent to which that critic believes countries can work together to prevent further abuses of host country sovereignty or development potential.

Most of these criticisms overlook that the MNCs do not really force themselves on reluctant hosts. In fact, the variety of incentive schemes that have been designed to attract MNC investment into host country markets has been constrained only by the imaginations of policy-makers in host country governments. The fact of the matter is that the pattern and major characteristics of MNC investments have not been developed in spite of host country policies but to a large extent because of them.

In point of fact, advocates of control of MNCs should be encouraged by the extent to which host countries have already been quite successful in controlling international investment flows. Many of the abuses and costs of foreign investment have been caused precisely by the types of laws, policies, and incentives developed by host countries, and the manner in which they have been administered.

This chapter summarizes the past foreign investment policies of the ASEAN countries-Indonesia, Malaysia, the Philippines, Singapore, and Thailand—and the characteristics of the resulting foreign investment patterns in each country. It will be shown that the foreign investment policies of these five countries are at least partially responsible for many of the negative features of the subsequent investments. Finally, the chapter discusses implications for future investment, future policies, and future development in the ASEAN countries.

United States and Japanese Investment in Southeast Asia

This section summarizes the motivations, characteristics, and effects of foreign direct investment in Southeast Asia from the two principal sources: Japan and the United States. It also briefly views the reactions to the Japanese investment in light of the previously mentioned general criticisms.

Research efforts on United States and Japanese investments in Southeast Asia are spotty and fragmented both in scope and in quality. In fact, serious studies of United States investment in Southeast Asia are all but nonexistent.[a] Foreign direct investment from all sources in Southeast Asia has been increasing at a rapid rate due to expanding local markets, the existence of natural resources, cheap labor, a high relative rate of return, import substitution policies, and decreased opposition by local governments because of the reduced fear of foreign domination that resulted from the rise in the number of countries that are sources of investment (ECAFE 1971; Sherk 1973). Private flows account for about 30 percent of total resource flows, and the foreign share of the capital stock represents from 15 to 30 percent of the total capital stock (ECAFE 1971). There is an increasing trend away from the import substitution policies of the past and export promotion in these countries.

Hymer (1972) and Vernon (1972) have characterized U.S. investment abroad (including investment in the less-developed countries) as being oligopolistic (fifty firms account for 60 percent of the investment), very large, more capital-intensive than other host country investments but less capital-intensive than domestic U.S. investments, manufacturing-oriented, motivated by both offensive strategies (seeking new profits) and defensive strategies (protecting markets from future competition), and consisting mostly of wholly owned subsidiaries. Rhodes (1972) has observed that whereas the large corporations have continued to invest, the small companies had slowed down by the end of 1971; in addition, the attractiveness of the less-developed countries had declined somewhat due to political instability and their insistence on joint ventures (the less-developed countries accounted for 27 percent of investments in 1961 versus only 20 percent in 1971).

About 4 to 5 percent of U.S. foreign investments have been in Southeast Asia. The value of these investments doubled between 1964 and 1970, while the number of subsidiaries rose 30 percent between 1963 and 1967. These investments are similar to most other U.S. investments: usually capital-intensive, large oligopolistic firms involved in oil and mineral development (40 percent) or in technologically advanced fields (37 percent), usually wholly owned subsidiaries or at least majority equity arrangements (71 percent), and are often component production and assembly-type operations with significant exports back to the United States (ECAFE 1971; Sherk 1973; Vernon 1972). Allen (1973b) has noted that 40 percent of these investments are undertaken to secure, maintain, and develop overseas markets, while 32 percent are aimed at developing a low-cost export base. He adds that this latter motive—along with the ability to secure, maintain, and/or develop a regional base for complementation of activities—will dominate the motivation for future U.S. investment in this area.

---

[a]The most comprehensive work on United States investment is Allen (1973b). Sherk (1973) and ECAFE (1971) are the best studies available for purposes of comparison with Japanese investment in Southeast Asia. Kohlhagen (1974) reviews the literature on United States and Japanese investments in the Pacific Basin.

Japanese foreign investment enjoyed an annual growth rate of 36 percent between 1969 and 1973.[b] Despite this large increase in investments, Japan still makes smaller international investments (as a proportion of GNP) than other developed nations—1.6 percent as of March 1970, as compared to 20 percent for the United Kingdom, 7.5 percent for the United States, 5.2 percent for Canada, and 2.9 percent for Germany (Kitamura 1973). By the end of 1973 approximately 31 percent of all Japanese foreign investments were in mining and natural resource investments, 28 percent in manufacturing, 11 percent in commercial investments, and about 8 percent in financial and insurance concerns. Geographically, 23 percent were located in Asia, 24 percent in North America, 20 percent in Europe, 17 percent in Latin America, and the balance in Oceania and the Middle East (only about 2 percent were in Africa). In general, these investments are more labor-intensive than the U.S. investments. They are usually small, manufacturing firms affiliated with one of the large trading companies, willing to own a smaller proportion of the equity (one reason: their investments have a lower degree of capital sophistication), and they are more oriented toward the import substitution-type industries or industries where they are losing export markets (Sherk 1973).

Profitability figures are always difficult to interpret, but in Japan's case it seems that whereas foreign investment has not been an overwhelming profitable venture in the past, it has been steadily improving. Only half of Japanese investments showed a cumulative profit as of 1971 [only 60 percent showed a profit for 1971, and 74 percent showed a surplus by 1973; see Heller and Heller (1974)]. Southeast Asia and Africa were the most profitable areas (74 percent showed a profit in 1971). Two major reasons are normally given for the relatively low profitability: (1) most Japanese ventures are new; and (2) many of the investments are undertaken to provide raw materials or other inputs to the parent company rather than to earn profits. As Japanese ventures abroad mature, these profit figures should improve.

Two major factors have made the sudden surge of Japanese investment possible: (1) increasing liberalization of capital restrictions by the Japanese government; and (2) the existence of the large trading companies, without whose knowledge of foreign markets and opportunities many investments, especially those of small manufacturing firms, never could have been undertaken. The program of capital liberalization, pursued since the early 1960s, has been making considerable advances in the early 1970s due to external pressures on the Japanese government and the development of Southeast Asia.

Before capital liberalization, the Japanese government permitted Japanese investments abroad only to procure raw materials necessary for industrial expansion and to ensure necessary channels for exports. Similarly severe

[b]The most complete characterizations of Japanese foreign investment include MITI (1974a and 1974b), Miyoshi (1974), and Sherk (1973); investments in Southeast Asia are characterized in Allen (1973a) and Ozawa (1972).

restrictions were placed on foreign investments in Japan. But as it became clear that investments were merely being rechanneled into Southeast Asia and competing with Japanese exporting firms, that Western technology was becoming increasingly less available by licensing agreements, that the Japanese could not continue to run large balance-of-payments surpluses, and that export markets were being lost abroad, the Japanese government began relaxing its constraints on the flow of direct investment both into and out of Japan.

Generally, Japanese foreign investment can be characterized as being one of four types: natural resource—oriented, market-oriented, factor-oriented, and what we might call government control-oriented. Historically, the natural resource category has been crucial to the growth of the Japanese economy, accounting for nearly one-third of the investments in Asia and over 40 percent of all investments in the less-developed countries by the end of 1972 (Industrial Bank of Japan 1974). The policy of the Japanese government and business community has long been to ensure an orderly flow of raw materials to the growing Japanese economy.

The second factor determining investment flows has been the need to capture markets abroad or to protect existing export markets. This type of investment usually follows existing trade patterns and has often involved small-to medium-sized firms in light manufacturing industries setting up behind tariff barriers. The Japanese government has also encouraged this type of investment when it has been tied to export promotion, such as in the assembly of finished products from Japanese-produced parts. It has been increasing as a result of competitive pressures from the developing countries; in general, it yields a much higher payoff to the host country in terms of transfer of technology than do resource-oriented investments. Another spur to this investment flow is the reduced competitiveness of Japanese industry as a result of the revaluation of the yen.

The third type of foreign investment has been factor-oriented, which in the case of Japan is actually labor-oriented. The attractiveness of cheap foreign labor in Southeast Asia in the face of rising wages and a growing labor shortage in Japan has become a major factor in inducing many Japanese firms to move production facilities abroad. Many studies cited this motive as having become more important than securing and protecting foreign markets behind tariff walls. As the growth of the Japanese economy creates bottlenecks in the production process foreign investment will continue to be increasingly attractive.

Government control-oriented foreign investment involves two elements: the actions of foreign governments and the actions of the Japanese government. In the former category are such import-substitution attractions as tariff walls, tax concessions and holidays, and duty-free export zones. On the other hand, the Japanese business community has a very close relationship with the Japanese government, and policies dealing with the pattern of economic growth and foreign investment are determined through this working relationship. The capital liberalization program has accelerated due to external pressures and a relaxation of the need for controls on capital outflows when balance-of-payments surpluses reached large proportions. In addition, a large portion of capital outflows are in the form of government loans to Japanese firms. The most recent factor inducing Japanese direct investment has been stricter government pollution regulations on industry, a policy that will have the not surprising effect of driving some of the heavy manufacturing and chemical industries out of Japan and into other countries.

The most important factors determining the future patterns of Japanese foreign investment are the increasing liberalization of capital flow restrictions, the need for an orderly flow of natural resources to fuel economic growth, rising Japanese wages, domestic land and labor shortages, restrictions on pollutants and polluting industries, the increasing capabilities of Japanese managers, invitations from less-developed countries in the form of incentives and trade barriers, and the increasing maturity of Japanese firms and their subsequent need for oligopolistic defensive investment.

Projections based on these analyses indicate that Japanese investments will rise somewhere between sixfold in eight years to tenfold in ten years; investments in the developed countries will be made increasingly in commercial and tertiary activities, whereas manufacturing investments (especially among smaller firms) will dominate in the less-developed nations. Litvak and Maule (1970) point out that Japan will look increasingly to more stable markets (e.g., Canada and Australia) for raw materials and as a result of Japanese technological advancement will produce many products abroad that are not yet marketable in Japan. Roemer (1975) predicts the increasing importance of financial packages that include Japanese government loans in return for product-sharing agreements, especially in the field of natural resource procurement. Many have noted the increasing importance of oligopolistic elements in Japanese markets and the implications for patterns and motives of future investments, especially of the "defensive," market-oriented type.

The few studies that have discussed the effects of foreign investments in Southeast Asia (Hughes and Seng 1969; and Sherk 1973), have concluded that the benefits include increases in technological know-how, increases in the supply of resources for industrialization, an upgrading of the labor force, increases in production capabilities, increased contact with international markets (including capital markets), and increases in foreign exchange resources, management techniques, and employment. Listed among the costs of foreign investment are decreases in domestic research and development capacity, the stagnation of managerial skills, entrepreneurial skills, and local capital markets, an insufficient use of low-cost labor, a reduction in national sovereignty, an increase in cultural conflicts, decreased revenue due to tax concessions, some monopoly profits, the introduction of inferior products, a reduction in competition, and the fact that the best workers have been drawn away from indigenous firms.

Reaction to Japanese investments has been particularly harsh because they have accounted for an increasing proportion of the total in Southeast Asia, thus creating fears of foreign domination. This fear has been exacerbated by the fact that the Japanese are the most recent foreign investors and that the Japanese firms are predominantly industries that already exist in the host countries, so that they are in direct competition with local firms (Tsurumi 1974). They have been criticized for exploiting natural resources, not hiring local managers or technicians, using techniques that utilize low technology (Sebestyn 1972); wanting only to capture the host market and not exporting, insisting on continued tariff protection, using second-class personnel abroad, selling only inferior or second-hand machinery (Ong 1972); having too close an association with the local government in power, which is no doubt an extension of the government-business relationship in Japan (Itoh 1973); paying low wages, and not fulfilling their hosts' expectations that as fellow Asians they would not be mere profit-seekers but rather agents of economic development (Tsurumi 1974). It has even been noted that their knowledge of the local language has caused friction in Taiwan. Lin (1972) has observed that the Japanese companies have used Japanese managers, whereas out of necessity the U.S. companies have had to hire Chinese managers—a potentially severe source of conflict in the Japanese firms. Many of these criticisms are the same as those leveled at all MNCs.

A number of these problems can hardly be attributed to the existence of foreign investments. As the next section shows, it is often the industrialization policies of many of the host countries rather than the flow of foreign direct investment that has led to distortions in product and factor markets. Import substitution policies and accompanying tariff structures have brought about fragmented and oligopolistic markets, excess capacity, and distorted domestic markets (see especially Little, Scitovsky, and Scott 1970; Nartsupha 1970; Sadli 1972).

Policies Toward Direct Investment and the Resulting Flows in the ASEAN Countries

This section briefly summarizes both the characteristics of the foreign investment policies of each of the ASEAN countries and the investment and development patterns that have emerged.[c]

Indonesia

The Indonesian government is involved in business activity at all levels of the economy. It has actively sought foreign investment, creating an Agency for

[c]I am very grateful to Dick Conlon and Kathy Holman of Business International for providing back issues of their publication, *Investment, Licensing, and Trading Conditions Abroad.* Allen (1973c) includes a good review of current foreign investment laws in ASEAN countries.

Investment Coordination, signing investment guarantee agreements with source countries, and developing a set of policies designed to attract foreign investment. The environment for foreign investment is good, as profit remittances are freely allowed; there is little danger of nationalization; approval procedures have been streamlined; and there are abundant natural resources, cheap labor (although poor productivity), and a large potential market. Capital repatriation, however, is not allowed while tax advantages are being enjoyed, there has been poor infrastructure development, and the student riots against Japanese investments in 1974 have left some doubt about future policies.

Basic foreign investment incentives were increased in 1970 with the Foreign Capital Investment Law. Corporate tax rates were lowered, and the tax holiday was changed from a minimum of five years to a period of from two to six years with a reduction in tax liability for up to five subsequent years in some cases. Special incentives were offered for export earnings, import savings, government-specified priority industries, high-risk or heavy investment ventures, or location outside Java. To qualify for incentives, a venture must export a large proportion of output, use a minimum percentage of local labor or materials, bring in substantial capital or technology, add significantly to employment, increase infrastructure investment, or establish basic allowances and tax concessions on plant equipment expenditures. These incentives are also available for earnings on reinvested profits.

The tariff schedule is high (up to 400 percent) and very protective. Competitive imports and luxuries have all but prohibitive tariffs, whereas industrial goods essential to local industry have low tariffs. Exemptions from duties on basic equipment and supplies are granted to approved foreign investments, and whereas there is no guarantee of the ability to import needed raw materials and components, such imports are unlikely to be prevented.

Although there are significant export duties, foreign investors who subsequently export are eligible for even greater incentives, including a longer tax holiday, a more lenient interpretation of foreign investment regulations, and the possibility of rebates on import duties paid on raw materials and components.

About 30 percent of Japanese investments in Asia have been in Indonesia (only 12 percent since 1967); in terms of value, U.S. investments have been larger than Japanese investments, whereas the Japanese have more firms than the United States does.[d] Since investments are almost exclusively joint ventures, generally the Indonesian partner has been relegated to the role of marketer for the firm. Japanese investments have been 50 percent in mining, 30 percent in manufacturing, and 17 percent in agriculture. The market-oriented investments have been undertaken to avoid tariffs and import restrictions, indicating that their potential for expansion is uncertain.

Tsurumi (1973) notes that Japanese manufacturing firms have located in

[d]For studies of direct foreign investment in Indonesia, see Sadli (1972), Sebestyn (1972), Stikker and Hirono (1971), and Tsurumi (1973).

Indonesia to avoid tariff and other import barriers, and out of a fear of being pre-empted by their immediate Japanese competitors. He concludes that for foreign firms to realize their export potential, Indonesia will need to allow longer-term tax benefits, reduce restrictions on inputs, and remove export duties. Sadli (1972) observes that the tax holidays have been of little help in bringing in investment, but he suspects that a unilateral removal of these incentives would cost Indonesia needed investments. In addition, other incentives, coupled with the limited size of the domestic market, have brought about the classic condition of fragmented markets and too many large firms with excess capacity.

Malaysia

While the Malaysian government has remained receptive to foreign investment and, in fact, has continued to encourage it, it has more recently become more selective about the type, the percentage of foreign ownership, and the extent of government controls over subsequent activities. In the mid-1960s, the government began to emphasize local capital participation, and the 1968 Incentives Act (as amended and revised in 1971 and 1973) encourages firms to go public within five years. Despite increasing government interference in the private sector, there is little threat of nationalization or restrictions on capital repatriation or profit remittances.

The granting of pioneer status makes the venture eligible for a number of incentives, including tax holidays for five years or more. Between 1958 and 1968, pioneer status became more readily available, and the possible length of the tax holiday increased, but the possibility of deferred depreciation on capital equipment was dropped for pioneers. To be granted pioneer status under the current laws, a project must produce a priority product, be labor-intensive, export-oriented, based on local raw materials, capable of vertical or horizontal integration with existing Malaysian firms, or related to agriculture. Additional incentives are given to projects establishing in a development area, producing a priority product, meeting local content requirements, or producing primarily for export (including, of course, the introduction of the export processing zones).

Tariff protection and even the banning of competitive imports are also offered as incentives to many new industries. This use of protective tariffs is increasing in Malaysia, where up until recently, few tariffs had been as high as even 35 percent. Import duties and other taxes on machinery and raw materials have customarily been waived for approved industrial products. Other tax incentives include allowances for expenditures on plant equipment for non-pioneers and accelerated depreciation on equipment for registered exporters.

Direct foreign investment accounts for about 12 percent of total Malaysian investment (Stikker and Hirono 1971); the most recent foreign investments have been in light manufacturing, the processing of primary products, and petroleum and coal products. Investments in manufacturing industries are more important than their small number would indicate. The United States, the United Kingdom, Singapore, Japan, and Hong Kong are the principal sources of Malaysia's foreign investments. The primary factors attracting foreign investments have included Malaysia's long-term political stability, the abilities of Malaysian traders and businessmen, wage and price stability, and abundant natural resources. Whereas foreign direct investment has saved considerable foreign exchange by flowing into sectors previously serviced primarily by imports (i.e., modern consumption and intermediate industrial goods, and light manufacturing industries), it has also made significant contributions to the expansion of merchandise.

The Philippines

Since 1968 the Philippines has begun to replace the old import substitution policies with a complicated set of incentive schemes designed to bring about labor-intensive, export-oriented, high-domestic-content manufacturing investments with significant domestic equity interest. The local environment has improved considerably over the past twenty-five years with a favorable government attitude toward foreign investment, moderate taxes, liberal regulations on profit remittances and capital repatriation (considerably liberalized since the 1950s), and no threat of nationalization.

To qualify for incentives under the Investment Incentives Act of 1968, either a firm must be at least 60 percent owned by Philippine citizens, have the approval of the Board of Investments (BOI) by agreeing to list its shares on the Philippine stock exchange within ten years and be 60 percent Philippine-owned within twenty years, be in a field where more than 40-percent foreign ownership is allowed, and engage in a pioneer project where the capital or technology are unavailable domestically, or else it must be in a preferred area of investment where desirable production levels for local and export markets have not been achieved (as determined by the BOI). Investment incentives are available in different degrees, depending on whether the venture is automatically a preferred pioneer or a preferred nonpioneer, or whether the BOI must place it in one of these categories on a case-by-case basis. Preferred areas include import-replacing or export industries where 70 percent of value is local content or 50 percent of production is exported. Pioneer industries are those that produce goods not previously made in the Philippines or that use processes or designs new to the Philippines, and that use local raw materials where available.

Incentives include accelerated depreciation of fixed assets, tax credits for locally purchased equipment, partial exemption from national taxes, and tariff protection. Additional incentives available for exporting firms under the 1970

Export Incentives Act include a ten-year tax credit on taxes and duties paid on raw materials and semimanufactured goods used to produce goods for export, five-year reduced income tax, tariff and tax exemption on capital equipment imports, tax credit on local equipment purchases, and a five-year exemption from the export tax. In addition, there is a free export zone in Mariveles. There is a strong policy of protection of local industry, as tariff barriers are high (60 to 100 percent) and nontariff import restrictions are very strict, especially since 1970. More than any other ASEAN country, the Philippines has begun to explicitly encourage a high proportion of local ownership, high local content in production, and a strong export orientation in its foreign investments. This has been accomplished through the careful development of its foreign investment legislation and policies, within the context of an improving environment for foreign ventures.

Foreign investment in the Philippines is dominated by China and the United States (Itoh 1973; Mason 1970, 1973; Sebestyn 1972; Stikker and Hirono 1971; Virata 1972). It has been undertaken mostly to take advantage of the import substitution policies or to obtain raw materials (Japanese investment is almost exclusively in raw materials). There is an abundant supply of natural resources, a large well-educated labor force, and a well-developed commercial banking sector; however, there is also a short supply of skilled workers, inadequate infrastructure development, and waste and inefficiency in government planning. Because of the tariff structure and a lack of domestic capacity in needed intermediate goods, the import substitution policy has created excess capacity in finished assembly production and has caused a significant rise in imports of raw materials, machinery, and intermediate manufactured products by foreign firms. This drain on foreign exchange has recently forced a reemphasis toward export and intermediate goods production promotion policies.

Singapore

Singapore has been very aggressive in seeking foreign investment as part of its industrialization drive. The Economic Development Board was established in 1961 as a source of capital and as a vehicle for foreign investment promotion. The board provided both investment feasibility studies and technical consulting as part of its services. This policy of attracting foreign investment continued with the passage of the Economic Expansion Incentives Act in 1967, but labor-intensive and exporting industries were singled out as being especially desirable. By 1974 Singapore had become more selective, preferring investments that developed technological and management skills, created new export potential, increased labor skills, and broadened the industrial base through forward and backward linkages. Even with the increased selectivity, Singapore retained a very favorable climate for foreign investment with low taxes, minimal exchange controls, little if any threats of excessive government controls or nationalization, and ease of profit remittances and capital repatriation.

Exporting firms and those granted pioneer status (with at least S$1 million in fixed-capital investment) are exempt from corporate taxes for five years, and accelerated depreciation is allowed in the first year. Additional tax exemptions are allowed for capacity expansion if total production equipment is increased by at least 30 percent. To be granted pioneer status, a venture must produce a product not already manufactured in Singapore, or at least not yet produced sufficiently for local markets, or produce for export. (I.e., only a venture with the sole purpose of driving out existing local enterprises would fail to qualify for pioneer status).

Although there are only a few tariffs on goods imported into Singapore, they (along with existing import quotas) have usually been imposed to protect local manufacturing concerns. Raw materials and equipment are usually free of import barriers, and those that exist are usually removed for pioneer firms and those qualifying as export enterprises (to qualify, a firm must have at least S$100,000 of export sales, with at least 20 percent of its production for export). Other export incentives include a 90-percent exemption from corporate taxes on export earnings for at least fifteen years, with a further extension if the Minister of Finance deems it beneficial. In addition, there are two free port zones. Additional incentives are offered to ventures that provide training programs that increase local skills.

We may conclude that incentives in Singapore are generally offered to skill-intensive, export-oriented industries with high technology content, where these desirable qualities are measured by the amount of capital investment per worker, value added per worker, and the ratio of skilled workers to total workforce. Subsidized ventures are then usually highly capital-intensive or skill-intensive operations.

Much of the investment in Singapore has been due to the stable economic and political environment, the development of the best financial markets and commercial center in the region, a well-educated labor force and well-developed infrastructure, the locational advantage, a stable government that has encouraged industrialization and foreign investment flows, the need to forestall competition, and the protection that exists for domestic production facilities.[e] Tax breaks, in general, have *not* been an inducement, and they have deprived Singapore of needed revenue. Foreign (pioneer) firms tend to be larger, more capital-intensive, and more technology-based than domestic (nonpioneer) firms.

The industrial capacity of Japanese operations has been most affected by the size of the market. In fact, it has been economic and political events such as the creation of the Federation of Malaysia in 1962-1963, the severance of trade

[e]For studies of direct foreign investment in Singapore, see Hughes and Seng (1969) [including Hirono (1969) and Lindert (1969)], Ong (1972), Ozawa (1972), and Stikker and Hirono (1971).

relations with Indonesia, and the 1965 raising of trade barriers with Malaysia, rather than the changes in incentive schemes, that have had the primary impact on the number and capacity of Japanese investments (Hirono 1969). Protection and the threat of protective benefits for competitiors in the Southeast Asian market have been the primary factors in drawing United States investment into Singapore (Lindert 1969).

Japanese investments have accounted for 37 percent of all foreign manufacturing assets (although they have been declining due to wage increases), have been capital-intensive and technologically sophisticated, have been mostly joint ventures (most U.S. ventures have been wholly owned), and have often been reactions to competitive U.S. investments in Singapore (the high levels of protection have generated many oligopolistic markets). Most ventures are in light manufacturing, although a few are in heavy industry. The recent shift in emphasis from import substitution to export promotion policies has not come in time to prevent too many firms, each with excess capccity, from entering Singapore's industrial sector. In addition, there is still a growing import demand for raw materials and capital goods in much of the export industries.

Thailand

Thailand has increasingly broadened its foreign investment incentive schemes, increasing coverage in 1962, and then again in 1972 as a result of the balance-of-payments deterioration in 1969-1971. Emphasis is being shifted from import substitution to export promotion schemes and to a diversification of the sources of investment inflows away from Japanese domination. Although there is significant government control of industry in some sectors, there is no threat of nationalization to foreign investment. And whereas eventually there is no problem with either profit remittances or capital repatriation, the timing of the former and permission for the latter are both subject to government approval.

"Promotional" status is granted by the Board of Investment (BOI) under the Investment Promotion Law (1972) through a very broad set of criteria. The law gives preference to ventures that are export-oriented, located outside the Bangkok-Thonburi metropolitan areas, have a high local equity content (the BOI prefers at least 40 percent), use local components or raw materials, or are in industries where capacity for either local demand or export potential are still needed. Whereas the BOI has considerable room for discretion in granting "promotional" status, it is noteworthy that even these guidelines (especially those promoting exports) were not in effect until 1972.

Whereas the old law granted a five-year tax holiday from corporate taxes, the new law grants a three- to eight-year exemption (depending on location) with a further exemption from 50 percent of the tax liability for an additional five years. The corporate tax in Thailand is progressive and has been fairly low, reaching a maximum of 30 percent. Expenditures on plant equipment are also allowed as exclusion from taxes. In addition, import duties on machinery, equipment, and construction materials are waived for promoted industries (especially those exporting), while higher tariffs can either be placed on competing imports or be banned completely. Government policy is still quite explicit about keeping tariffs low on components and machinery while keeping them high on locally manufactured products.

Exports are now promoted extensively through exemption from the business tax for sales from exports, relief from import duties and business taxes on imported raw materials and components, and exemption from duties on imported equipment. Except for the rebate for customs duties paid on imported raw materials and components, these export incentives did not exist before the 1972 law.

Japanese investments have dominated foreign direct investments in Thailand to the point where the Thai government is concerned (Japanese firms account for 73 percent of all wholly owned subsidiaries and 43 percent of total investment as opposed to 18 percent for Taiwan and 10 percent for the United States).[f] The major attractions are the political stability, low wages, high-quality workforce, supply of natural resources, and the government's import substitution policies (these are partially offset by the underdeveloped capital markets and the lack of skilled labor). Most of the investment has been in light industrial sectors utilizing capital-intensive techniques, and it has brought needed industrial technology, managerial know-how, and managerial skills to the Thai economy. The import substitution policy has caused serious excess capacity more than in any other ASEAN country, while the low tariffs on intermediate goods and high tariffs on final goods have caused a high import content of export goods. This has meant that the import substitution policy has been partly self-defeating and that the industrialization effort has not had the positive impact on development efforts that it might have had. Consequently, a comprehensive program of export promotion is recognized as a fundamental need in Thailand.

Policies Toward Foreign Investment: An Appraisal

The preceding summaries outline the extent to which the ASEAN countries utilize a broad array of policies to attract foreign investment. The policies that have been developed are of the classical import substitution variety. They include protection and subsidies, and they result in the use of capital and capital-intensive techniques that have been discussed by many authors, including Allen (1973c) and Little, Scitovsky, and Scott (1970). More recently, these countries have embarked on policies of trying to attract more labor-intensive,

---

[f]For studies of direct foreign investment in Thailand, see Nartsupha (1970), Sebestyn (1972), Stikker and Hirono (1971), and Viravan (1972).

export-oriented investments[g] that are more integrated with the host economies and have a larger proportion of domestic ownership. That such investments have not been forthcoming in the past should not have been surprising in light of the types of subsidies that were offered and the types of distortions that existed in these economies.

The benefits to the Southeast Asian host countries of more labor-intensive and export-oriented enterprises are self-evident, but the desirable proportion of foreign ownership is still open to question (Mason 1974; Reuber 1974; SEADAG 1973; and Vernon 1972). Vernon has observed that there is less transfer of tangible and intangible resources in a joint venture than in a wholly owned subsidiary, making joint ventures less desirable on economic grounds. In addition, the so-called fade-out policies (where foreign ownership is scheduled to be eliminated or decline to a certain level) prevent some companies from undertaking investments or induce the least capable rather than the most capable firms to enter the market. Of course, the real or imagined noneconomic costs of foreign control of domestic enterprises must be weighed against these economic costs of joint ventures.

In a preliminary study, Reuber (1974) has concluded that the larger a foreign ownership in a domestic enterprise (holding export shares constant), the greater the financing from abroad and the less the purchases from local firms. However, there is substantially no effect on local hiring or the form of received earnings (if anything, there were less payments of fees and licenses). He concludes that if the proportion of foreign ownership has little effect on the firm's behavior, there is no reason to require joint ventures as the principal form of foreign investment. The preferred policy under these conditions would be to remove restrictions on foreign ownership and to try to obtain more of the gains for the host country (an admittedly difficult task with the existing level of competition among developing countries).

As part of their overall development (through industrialization) efforts, the ASEAN countries have erected a schedule of protective tariffs (highest in the case of Indonesia and lowest in the case of Singapore) to protect the industrial sector from foreign competition. To induce foreign firms to invest within this protective wall, each country has allowed raw materials (in some cases) and capital in the form of machinery, equipment, and components to be purchased duty free. In addition, each country allows accelerated depreciation, special tax exclusions, or tax credits for expenditures on plant and equipment (only the Philippines has special credits for *domestically* purchased equipment). Not surprisingly, the large industrial ventures created behind such tariff walls with subsidized capital and equipment have proved unable to reach significant export markets.

As Little, Scitovsky, and Scott (1970) show in their case studies, such

[g]Including the development of the export processing zones in Malaysia, the Philippines, and Singapore.

import substitution and subsidy schemes accompanied by high tariff walls most often lead to large, inefficient, industrial ventures operating at excess capacity with little if any export potential. If anything, such industrial development may lead to even *greater* demand for scarce foreign exchange, as demand for imported equipment, machinery, components, and raw materials replaces—and at times may even exceed—the earlier demand for the imported finished product.

Likewise, foreign investments have not expanded in a manner that has increased employment as much as had been hoped. Historically, some of the ASEAN countries have explicitly increased incentives as the size of capital or fixed assets increased, rather than as the impact on employment or linkages with the rest of the economy increased. As an example, even though Singapore offers incentives for a higher skill-intensive content in foreign ventures, it measures this concept by the capital that is used per unit of labor. Only comparatively recently have individual countries begun to offer special incentives for creating employment, upgrading skills, and transferring technology.

It is difficult to estimate the "equilibrium" exchange rate, but it is often claimed that overvalued exchange rates accompany protective import substitution policies such as those in the ASEAN countries. Signs of such overvalued exchange rates include the need to control imports and subsidize exports, accompanied by persistent trade balance deficits.

Among the ASEAN countries, only Malaysia has realized a persistent balance-of-trade surplus (Indonesia, as a result of its large petroleum exports, has had a balance-of-trade surplus for most of the past twenty years). Interestingly, Malaysia has also had the lowest protective tariff barriers and has had the most success (outside of the export zones in each country) with increases in export earnings as a result of foreign investment. The Malaysian case indicates that it is possible to attract foreign investment without inefficient protective tariffs, and also that foreign investors will seek export markets as long as they are not burdened by the tax of an overvalued exchange rate.

The advantage of an overvalued exchange rate is that it generates an excess demand for artifically inexpensive imports that may then be regulated by authorities, who may then keep out luxury goods (or at least earn high tariff revenues when they are imported) and goods competitive with domestic industry, and regulate imports of cheap machinery, equipment, and components.

Both domestic exporters and consumers pay for this subsidized use of cheap foreign capital. As a result of accompanying tariffs and nontariff barriers, consumers pay through higher domestic prices for both imported and domestically produced goods. Exporters (and potential exporters) pay because the overvalued currency acts as a tax on domestically produced goods offered for sale in foreign markets. Thus there is little wonder that after foreign ventures have been attracted to a growing domestic market in subsidized industries with subsidized (and perhaps inefficient) techniques, they are unable or unwilling to use the host country's production facilities as an export base for their output, which is not competitive in world markets.

Another serious problem has been caused by the loss of revenues from competitive tax incentive schemes levied by the Southeast Asian countries (ECAFE 1971; Hughes 1971; Hughes and Seng 1969; Sadli 1972; Stikker and Hirono 1971). Since all countries have legislated these tax schemes, they have no effect in attracting foreign investment and merely deprive the countries of needed revenues. Most corporations think that their profits are so small in the first few years of operation that the prospect of paying little or no corporate taxes is not as important as the stability of the environment, the accessibility to needed inputs, the availability of trained labor, the size and growth potential of the prospective market, or the behavior of their competitors. That countries continue to offer tax advantages in the form of holidays and credits is evidence of their own misconception of their bargaining position vis-à-vis the investing companies.

Host Country Policies and MNCs

Despite the criticisms of the MNCs' role in the development process, the evidence indicates that the investment pattern has been *exactly* what the host governments have legislated for in this "first round" of foreign investment flows. Labor-intensive, export-oriented ventures have been rare because foreign investment inducement schemes and laws, along with accompanying economic policies, have taxed export efforts and subsidized capital and capital-intensive projects. Contrary to popular opinion, the types of investments that have been made do not indicate that the host governments are weak or lack sovereignty. In fact, they testify to the ability of finance ministers and investment boards to bring in exactly the types of investments that their policies and economic incentives have called for.

The problem is not that international investors (in the form of MNCs) have acted as some powerful, uncontrollable economic and political force, poised to drain the politically and economically weaker developing countries of their needed resources in an all-encompassing drive for profits. Rather, the problem has been that the governments of the developing countries have been far too successful at developing schemes that attract suboptimal types of industries into economies distorted by suboptimal economic policies. Other policies and other distortions could have attracted other types of investments and could have led to distinctly different development paths.

The popular view of the host country and the foreign investor as two players in a zero-sum game is also partly responsible for the misconception of the roles played by each in the development process. It does not follow that what the MNC gains from an investment is the host country's loss (and even by some accounts, also the source country's loss). Actually, the very fact that host countries spend so much in resources in attempts to attract foreign investment may be the best estimate of the MNC's worth to the development effort.

In terms of responsibility for development efforts, it is the host government's responsibility to formulate policy and structure economic incentives in such a way that domestic goals (political, social, and economic) will be achieved. It is the MNC manager's responsibility to work within the environment that the host country provides in a way that will meet corporate goals without breaking either legal statutes or recognized moral codes. It is no more appropriate for foreign ventures to seek to specify, achieve, or maximize host country objectives than it is for host country officials to set and then help achieve corporate objectives for its foreign investors.

Possible Host Country Solutions

The specific form of a given direct foreign investment is determined by a bargaining process. The preceding discussion has implicitly assumed that host country policies are determined solely by government officials in consideration for the domestic economy's welfare. Recent charges of meddling in domestic politics by some MNCs (and bribery by many others) imply that policies may not in fact be made in isolation from the foreign investor's needs and goals. When policy is made by public officials with a vested interest in satisfying corporate, especially foreign, clients rather than in improving overall domestic welfare, the rewards system or the balance of power clearly needs to be changed.

As we have seen, some authors have suggested the possibility of controlling international corporations as a means of preventing such behavior. Alternatively, since none of these methods have received widespread acceptance or seem particularly pragmatic, host country governments might consider controlling themselves.

A policy of host country self-control is possible in two ways. First, one characteristic of most foreign investment laws is that they are couched in very general terms, with the specifics determined over time through a case-by-case negotiating process between the proposed investor and the various agencies, committees, and ministries charged with administering the law. Such flexible laws have obvious advantages to the host in that the emphasis on types and locations of investments as well as particular details of an individual project can be developed quickly within the context of current needs. The laws, however, are subject to a serious disadvantage in that they create an environment within which it becomes not only acceptable but necessary for prospective investors to seek favors from and influence with host country government officials. Flexible laws are advantageous in that they make negotiations possible, but as many host countries have learned (and subsequently complained), they may lead to disadvantageous agreements and certainly may cause foreign interests to have excessive inputs into policy-making.

An alternative to such flexibility is for host countries to develop very specific guidelines and laws with regard to the acceptance or rejection of foreign investment proposals. As long as planning is preferred to the free-market mechanism in development efforts, there will be a need for discretionary decisions and human judgment in investment allocation decisions.[h] But specific rather than general laws and guidelines should be used to minimize rather than maximize the interplay between potential investors and administrators. This reduction of such contact should go a long way toward reducing the need (and thus the potential) for bribery and influence-seeking by foreign investors among host country officials.

The second possibility for self-control is for host governments to work together to reverse the role of oligopolist and perfect competitor in the negotiating process. Whereas it is probably true that competitive tax incentive schemes by host governments have not increased the total amount of foreign investment or even changed its distribution among host countries, it is most certainly true that they have generated a direct wealth transfer from the host countries to the MNCs' stockholders in the form of lost tax revenues.

Host countries must work together to remove at least the competitive schemes that have had little if any allocative impact on direct investment flows. The reason that is most often given for the impossibility of this oft-repeated proposal is that the host governments are so diverse in their cultural, political, social, and economic backgrounds and that their bureaucracies are so weak that any agreements with respect to reducing tax incentives, suboptimal tariff structures, or implementing complementary agreement *even on a regional basis* are doomed to failure. But then these are also the very reasons why multilateral control of multinational corporations would fail. If host countries cannot agree to discontinue competitive policies toward direct investments, how could they be expected to agree on specific controls of corporate activities? If the temptation exists to break international investment policy agreements by giving preferential tax treatment, then the same temptation would exist to break international agreements on the control of MNCs.

If the host countries do ultimately lack any bargaining power, then the arguments about the MNC being a "power" capable of redistributing wealth away from the "have nots" and to the "haves" may well be true, but not through greed, nor through any fault of their own. Whereas the MNCs can be accused of using differential host country policies (toward both short-term and long-term capital flows) to their advantage, they can hardly be blamed for their existence.

The fault and the responsibility for host country welfare ultimately lies with the host country governments. They have shown themselves to be quite capable of structuring the form and characteristics of foreign direct investment through

---

[h]In fact, the technique for generating an excess demand for import licenses, investment licenses, and so forth, is to undervalue their price. Only by generating such excess demand can administrators exercise their powers of discretionary judgment in issuing scarce licenses.

their suboptimal and highly competitive policies of the 1950s and 1960s. Undoubtedly, the *economic effects* of the resulting investment flows have been beneficial on the whole. If the host countries are now unable to channel further flows in different directions so as to achieve alternate economic goals—in conjunction with their political and social programs—because of their overly competitive posture vis-à-vis each other, then it is hardly justifiable to blame the MNCs for failing to act in the hosts' best interests in every investment decision.

Even if each host country acts on its own, there is good reason to hope for success. By subsidizing the use of capital, guaranteeing domestic markets, and taxing exports in the past two decades, these countries have been very successful in attracting large capital-intensive ventures with much excess capacity and little ability to export. There is no reason to believe that they will not be equally successful in attracting more labor-intensive, export-oriented ventures in preferred industrial areas by pursuing positive policies that subsidize these activities. On the other hand, by pursuing negative policies such as excessive controls or even expropriation, host countries may succeed only in slowing the flow of investments (and the resulting benefits) that they so dearly desire.

As we have seen, the ASEAN countries have begun to shift their investment policies in a positive direction by directly subsidizing labor-training, technology-diffusing, well-integrated, and export-oriented projects as they change the focus of their investment inducement schemes. By continuing this trend and dismantling many of the old import substitution and capital-subsidizing policies, and by working together to increase the benefits from foreign investments rather than competing with each other to bid away the gains, the host countries of the world should be able to harness foreign investment as the distinctly positive force in economic and social development that it has the power to be.

References

Allen, Thomas W. 1973a. *Direct Investment of Japanese Enterprises in Southeast Asia.* The Economic Cooperation Centre for the Asian and Pacific Region. Bangkok.

———. 1973b. *Direct Investment of U.S. Enterprises in Southeast Asia.* The Economic Cooperation Centre for the Asian and Pacific Region.

———. 1973c. "Policies of ASEAN Countries Towards Direct Foreign Investments." New York: Southeast Asia Development Advisory Group of the Asia Society.

Ball, George. 1967. "Cosmocorp: The Importance of Being Stateless." *Columbia Journal of World Business* (November-December), pp. 25-30.

Barnet, Richard J., and Ronald E. Müller. 1974. *Global Reach: The Power of the Multinational Corporation.* New York: Simon and Schuster.

Business International. "Investment, Licensing, and Trading Conditions Abroad." Published periodically by country.

113

Economic Commission for Asia and the Far East (ECAFE). 1971. *Economic Survey of Asia and the Far East, 1970. Part One: The Role of Foreign Private Investment in Economic Development and Cooperation in the ECAFE Region.*

Goldberg, Paul M., and Charles Kindleberger. 1970. "Toward a GATT for Investment: A Proposal for Supervision of the International Corporation." *Law and Policy in International Business* (Summer).

Heller, H. Robert and Emily E. Heller, *Japanese Investment in the United States With a Case Study of the Hawaiian Experience*, New York, Praeger, 1974.

Hirono, Ryokichi, 1969. "Japanese Investment," in Hughes and Seng (eds.), *Foreign Investment and Industrialization in Singapore.* Madison: University of Wisconsin, pp. 86-111.

Hughes, Helen, and You Poh Seng, eds. 1969. *Foreign Investment and Industrialization in Singapore.* Madison: University of Wisconsin.

Hughes, Helen. 1971. "The Manufacturing Industry Sector," in *Southeast Asia's Economy in the 1970's*, Asian Development Bank, London: Longman Group Ltd.

Hymer, Stephen. 1972. "United States Investment Abroad," in Peter Drysdale ed. *Direct Foreign Investment in Asia and the Pacific,* Toronto: University of Toronto Press.

The Industrial Bank of Japan. 1974. "The Global Position of Japanese Industry and Its Transformation," *Quarterly Survey of Japanese Finance and Industry,* Vol. XXVI, No. 1-2 (January-June).

Itoh, Hiroshi. 1973. "Japan and Southeast Asia," *Solidarity,* (August) pp. 49-59.

Kitamura, Hiroshi. 1972. "Japan's Economic Policy Toward Southeast Asia," *Asian Affairs,* (February) pp. 47-57.

Kohlhagen, Steven W. 1974. "Direct Foreign Investment in the Pacific Basin," Conference on International Trade, Finance and Development of Pacific Basin Countries, National Bureau of Economic Research, Stanford, Calif. (December).

Lin, M.S. 1972. "Japanese Investment in Taiwan." In Robert Ballon and Eugene H. Lee, eds., *Foreign Investment and Japan.* Tokyo: Kodansha International, Ltd.

Lindert, Peter H. 1969. "United States Investment." In Helen Hughes and You Poh Seng, eds., *Foreign Investment and Industrialization in Singapore.* Madison: University of Wisconsin. Pp. 154-176.

Little, Ian, Tibor Scitovsky, and Maurice Scott. 1970. *Industry and Trade in Some Developing Countries.* London: Oxford University Press.

Litvak, Isaiah A., and Christopher J. Maule, eds. 1970. *Foreign Investment: The Experience of Host Countries.* New York: Praeger.

Mason, R.H. 1970. "Some Aspects of Technology Transfer: A Case Study Comparing U.S. Subsidiaries and Local Counterparts in the Philippines." *The Philippine Economic Journal* 9, No. 1:83-108.

_____. 1973. "Some Observations on the Choice of Technology by Multinational Firms in Developing Countries." *The Review of Economics and Statistics* (August):349-355.

_____. 1974a. "Conflicts Between Host Countries and the Multinational Enterprise." *California Management Review* (Fall):5-14.

_____. 1974b. "Strategies of Technology Acquisition: Direct Foreign Investment vs. Unpackaged Technology." Presented to SEADAG seminar on Multinational Corporations in Southeast Asia, Penang, Malaysia, June 24-26.

Ministry of International Trade and Industry. 1974a. "Japan's Economic Cooperation." *Japan Reporting* (June).

_____. 1974b. *Japan's Overseas Investments.* Background Information, B1-11. Tokyo.

Miyoshi, Masaya. 1974. "Japan's Direct Investments Overseas—Present State and Future Outlook." *Keidanren Review* 30 (July):5-10.

Nartsupha, Chatthip. 1970. *Foreign Trade, Foreign Finance and the Economic Development of Thailand, 1956-1965.* Bangkok: Prae Pittaya Ltd. Partnership.

Ong, Hui Chong. 1972. "Japanese Investment in Singapore." In Robert J. Ballon and Eugene H. Lee, eds., *Foreign Investment and Japan.* Tokyo: Kodansha International Ltd.

Ozawa, Terutomo. 1972. "Labor Resource Oriented Migration of Japanese Industries to Taiwan, Singapore, and South Korea." International Bank for Reconstruction and Development, Economics Staff Working Paper no. 134, August.

Reuber, Grant L. 1974. *Some Aspects of Private Direct Investments in Developing Countries.* New York: Southeast Asia Development Advisory Group.

Rhodes, John B. 1972. "Foreign Direct Investment by U.S. Corporations." *Columbia Journal of World Business* (July-August): 33-41.

Roemer, John. 1975. *United States-Japanese Competition: A Study of International Trade and Investment Rivalry.* Berkeley, Calif.: Institute of International Studies Monograph Series.

Rubin, Seymour. 1971. "Multinational Enterprise and National Sovereignty: A Skeptic's Analysis," *Law and Policy in International Business* 3, 1:

Sadli, Mohammad. 1972. "Foreign Investment in Developing Countries: Indonesia." In Peter Drysdale, ed., *Foreign Investment in Asia and the Pacific* Toronto: University of Toronto Press.

Sebestyn, Charles. 1972. *The Outward Urge: Japanese Investment Worldwide.* London: Economist Intelligence Unit Ltd., QER Special no. 11.

Sherk, Donald R. 1973. *Foreign Investment in Asia: Cooperation and Conflict Between the United States and Japan.* San Francisco: Federal Reserve Bank of San Francisco.

Sloan, Michael P. 1974. "When Transnational Corporations Sneeze, the World Catches Cold." *Business and Society Review* (Autumn):pp. 55-60.

Southeast Asia Development Advisory Group. 1973. *Ad Hoc Seminar on Multinational Corporations in Southeast Asia.* New York: SEADAG Reports.

Stikker, Dirk U., and Ryokichi Hirono. 1971. "The Impact of Foreign Private Investment." In *Southeast Asia's Economy in the 1970's.* London: Asian Development Bank, Longman Group Ltd.

Tsurumi, Yoshihiro. 1973. "Japanese Direct Investment in Indonesia: Toward New Indonesian Policies of Foreign Direct Investment." Cambridge, Mass.: Harvard Advisory Group, Harvard Business School, Multinational Enterprise Project.

_____. 1974. "Multinational Spread of Japanese Firms and Asian Neighbors Reactions." Paper presented to Yale University Conference on the Multinational Corporation as an Instrument of Development-Political Considerations.

Turner, Louis. 1974. "There's No Love Lost Between Multinational Companies and the Third World." *Business and Society Review* (Autumn):pp. 73-80.

Vernon, Raymond. 1972. "Restrictive Business Practices: The Operations of Multinational United States Enterprises in Developing Countries: Their Role in Trade and Development." New York: United Nations Conference on Trade and Development, United Nations.

Virata, Cesar. 1972. "Foreign Investment in Developing Countries: The Philippines." In Peter Drysdale, ed., *Foreign Investment in Asia and the Pacific* Toronto: University of Toronto Press.

Viravan, Amnuay. 1972. "Foreign Investment in Developing Countries: Thailand." In Peter Drysdale, ed., *Foreign Investment in Asia and the Pacific* Toronto: University of Toronto Press.

8 Technology Acquisition in the Pacific Basin: Direct Foreign Investment versus Unpackaged Technology

R. Hal Mason

When we think of international trade, whether in the Pacific Basin or elsewhere, the image that comes to mind is exchanging commodities—i.e., raw materials, machinery, textiles, consumer durables, and the like. We often forget that service items are in the trade accounts also. Among these service items are payments for technology. Indeed, one of the most rapidly growing sources of income to firms comes from the sale of rights to utilize proprietary technology. Of course, this is not the be all and end all of it: not all technological transfers are in the form of licenses or franchise agreements. Engineering and consulting firms sell techno-logical know-how for a fee. In some instances such transfers are accompanied by the transfer of hardware or physical capital, and in other instances they are not. Training programs and the provision of quality control engineers, management personnel, and the like involve the movement of people and may or may not involve transfers of physical capital or contractual access to patents, secret processes, or trademarks.

There is a substantial body of literature on technology transfer and the different devices that can be used to acquire technology. However, there have been but modest efforts to address the problem of unpackaging the technology.[a] Some observers believe that the cost of technology acquisition can be reduced if it can be divorced from direct foreign investment. This notion presupposes that the market for technology is highly imperfect and that firms owning the technology can obtain a higher rate of return via direct investment than they can by licensing or otherwise exploiting their know-how. It also presupposes that the needed technology or know-how can indeed be acquired, and at a price lower than that obtainable when technology is accompanied by direct foreign invest-ment. This chapter's objective is to examine the issues related to this hypothesis in light of the various methods available for the transfer of technology. It will also examine the circumstances where there are tradeoffs between reduced costs and an inability to obtain the desired technologies. This concept indeed is the central issue in the unpackaging process.

---

[a]The term *unpackaging* refers to the acquisition of the same or nearly identical technology normally transferred via direct foreign investment but now unaccompanied by the presence of foreign ownership or control of the operating assets.

Japan and the Unpackaging Strategy: A Lesson for Pacific Basin Countries?

Perhaps Japan has had the most notable experience with the acquisition of unpackaged technology: until recently, foreign ownership and control have been denied. Yet Japan has managed to acquire technologies on a major scale.[b] Historically, the Japanese have mounted an intensive effort to negotiate for technology whenever the domestic market could sustain a reasonably efficient-sized plant hiding behind protection. Japan's growth appears to have been tightly related to a balance between import substitution and export expansion sector by sector, where the export expansion follows rather closely on the heels of import substitution, implying that the strategy of acquiring technology was not one of indiscriminate protection and foreign investment but rather one of rationality, in the sense that it was concentrated in sectors where there was a high probability of becoming a net exporter in the longer run. It is also notable that Japan appears to have been able to adapt technologies to become more labor-intensive. In Japan's early period of industrialization, it appears that there was actual capital shallowing, in contrast to the rather rapid capital deepening taking place in the industrial sectors of developing countries today. Thus the Japanese acquisition process seems to have been accompanied by considerable adaptation of the technology to be more in keeping with Japan's abundance of labor.

We must recognize that Japan's strategy is probably not open to developing countries in the Pacific Basin today. For one thing, when Japan was learning how to acquire technology, the international firm was almost unheard of. Indeed, for Japan it was probably not a matter of unpackaging the technology but rather a matter of selecting an appropriate source and type of technology. Today's developing countries must deal in a different market that is certainly strongly influenced, if not dominated, by international firms—firms that usually prefer to own the operating assets through which the technology is applied. The question then becomes, Can developing countries adopt an unpackaging strategy, and if so, under what circumstances would such a strategy be most likely to succeed? Before this question is addressed, it might prove useful to review the various devices used to acquire technology.[c]

---

[b]It may also be true that, in many instances, the Japanese avoided the full costs of acquisition by ingeniously copying products and processes while skillfully skirting the problem of patent infringements. Japan has done a great deal of first-hand observation by sending teams of scientists (and others) abroad for training and field experience.

[c]We shall use the term *technology* in a very broad sense, to refer to that set of technical and managerial skills required to operate productive physical capital efficiently, produce the product, tie production into a marketing and distribution network, and adapt product, process, and marketing strategies to changing technical and market conditions. However, technology acquisition by developing countries usually refers to a bundle of know-how required to make physical capital and its embodied technology productive. Implicit in this definition is more than a mere neoclassical black box about which we make inferences by measuring simplistic values of inputs and outputs.

Methods of Acquiring Technology

Foreign firms may or may not be in a position to augment the recipient country's technological capacities, depending on the technological capabilities of indigenous firms. For the sake of argument, however, we shall assume that foreign firms do have access to technologies that are not available to local firms on the same terms; i.e., the local firm must purchase know-how, while the foreign firm can draw on an accumulated body of knowledge and ongoing research not readily available to local firms. The unpackaging process implies that the technology is not to be acquired via direct foreign investment where financial control is in the hands of the foreign firm. Thus the vehicles to be considered are:

1. licensing agreements
2. technical aid agreements
3. management contracts
4. turnkey plants
5. supply contracts
6. joint ventures with locally vested control
7. some combination of the above

Licensing Agreements

Licensing agreements almost universally specify the product to be produced, brand name or trademark to be used, patents and other proprietary rights to be protected, markets to be served, amount of remuneration to be paid to the licenser, how long the rights can be used, and conditions of renegotiation and/or termination of the contract by either party. They also may specify material and equipment requirements, the quality standards to be maintained, and the degree to which others are excluded from using these rights to serve the same market. In many respects, the license is limiting, especially with respect to the use of locally procured ingredients and the markets to be served. The licenser may be looking to the day when it may wish to enter the market. It also may seek to protect against a licensee's invasion of its own markets, particularly export markets. In this sense there is great motivation to keep the licensee heavily dependent on the licenser in such a way that the licensee has no more (if as much) leeway in its decisions than would a wholly owned or majority controlled subsidiary. One advantage of licensing is that the local firm has the flexibility to renegotiate or terminate its relationship and to work with more than one noncompetitive licenser. Also it is often true that licensing opens more avenues than does direct foreign investment, in the sense that some firms—particularly smaller and medium-sized firms—can supply technology but do not wish to invest. Thus from the country's point of view, licensing may offer a more competitive approach to the acquisition of know-how than would direct foreign investment, in which case only a tiny handful of firms might show an interest in market entry.

Technical Aid Agreements and Management Contracts

Technical aid agreements may prove to be the most effective device that can be used to unpackage technology. Along with management contracts, these agreements can be made quite specific as to the services foreign firms are to render. Also, if it is possible to specify precisely what is needed in the technology package, it can be opened to competitive bidding. This trait tends to be atypical of direct foreign investment and licensing agreements. Technical aid agreements can be tailored to specific needs and do run the gamut from turnkey plants—including the training of personnel—to the services of a quality control engineer.

Turnkey Plants

The turnkey plant may be a very sound method of obtaining embodied technology, but it may have to be accompanied by technical aid agreements and management contracts if disembodied technology is also an important ingredient in bringing about a successful transplant. (See pp. 122-125 for a discussion of embodied technology versus disembodied technology.)

Supply Contracts

Supply contracts offer a rather interesting possibility to countries rich in natural resources, for they can be used in several ways to stimulate technology transfer. For example, Dole Corporation has supply contracts for the production of pineapples in the Philippines. Dole introduced farmers to the technology of producing commercial quantities of pineapples of uniform grade and high quality. The farmers have learned the field culture of producing pineapples. In return, Dole has a reasonably assured supply of raw material in commercial quantity and of commercial quality.

Supply contracts can and do backfire. They are usually applied to commodities that are not highly differentiated, i.e., logs and lumber, agricultural commodities, minerals, and standardized manufactured components. Prices fluctuate widely, and consequently it is to the advantage of one or the other of the parties to not honor the contract. As a consequence, supply contracts come to have little meaning in many instances. Moreover, the countries themselves are quick to ask for renegotiation—particularly in these times of rising commodity prices. Thus supply contracts or raw materials concessions can no longer be considered long-term commitments. As a result, supply contracts have a limited usefulness as vehicles to stimulate technology transfer because the owners of technology cannot be confident about the terms of the exchange.

Joint Ventures

The joint venture can be expected to play a growing role as a transfer vehicle, mainly because the Pacific Basin countries themselves are insisting on local participation. However, as both Thomas Allen and Steven Kohlhagen note in chapters 6 and 7, the Southeast Asian countries have a relatively liberal application of their foreign investment laws. Yet there is little doubt that, in the longer run, they will exert pressure to reduce foreign control in most direct investments.

Joint ventures do not seem to be very interesting as a transfer vehicle except when the foreign firm is willing to transfer technology in exchange for an equity position in the venture. In that case it might heighten the foreign firm's incentive, since it now shares in the good (or bad) fortunes of the recipient firm. There has been the supposition that because they force foreign partners to rub shoulders with national partners, joint ventures may somehow miraculously bring about a transfer of high-level managerial and technical skills. They also may prolong the transfer process because of the time required to build mutual trust—witness the Japanese/General Motors joint venture that required two years before significant communication and mutual understanding were established.

So little is really known about joint ventures that it is premature to make judgments about their success or lack thereof. It would seem, however, that they can be used as an incentive to acquire technology from small- and medium-sized firms that might not otherwise participate in the technology transfer process. This is not the primary motivation for joint ventures at present, however. Rather, most are being used to achieve forced equity participation by nationals in the affairs of wholly owned subsidiaries of foreign-controlled firms. Also, with the exception of the Andean Pact countries, joint ventures are not being pressed vigorously in the manufacturing sector, where the large bulk of technology transfers are taking place. And even some members of the Andean group have backed away from strict adherence to the pact's foreign investment provisions.

In instances where technology is being acquired without foreign ownership, it appears that more than a single vehicle is being used. Licensing agreements are often accompanied by technical aid agreements and occasionally by management contracts. Turnkey plants may be accompanied by technical aid and management contracts. And any or all of these may result in joint ventures where equity participation is the specified method of payment.

As a final note, it should be recognized that there are other methods of obtaining technology and technical and managerial know-how. Training by direct observation and through formal programs have been key ingredients to the high-level performance of Japan's export drive. These methods do not necessarily involve foreign firms in major roles, although they can, depending on how the training is conducted. The Japanese have been prodigious consumers of short courses in technical and managerial subjects. Firms sponsor their employees to go to Europe and the United States to participate in group seminars on a wide range of subjects. These employees are then expected to come home and adapt what they have learned to the Japanese situation.

Japan also invites outside experts to offer training in the Japanese technical and management institutes. Perhaps more than any country, Japan has had an organized program of acquiring so-called free technology and managerial know-how. If this experience were copied, it would be very complementary to the unpackaging process. Moreover, acquiring this type of know-how need not involve large multinational firms, except that they may act as a laboratory or field site for direct observation and similar informal training. Greater exposure to these types of experiences could do much to educate local technicians and managers about alternative sources of supply of technology; accordingly, it could assist the Pacific Basin countries in their attempts to unpackage the technology, by improving the bargaining process in bilateral situations and by increasing the sources of supply so that bilateral situations become less essential to the acquisition process.

Embodied versus Disembodied Technology

It is important to recognize that industries (and projects) differ in the extent to which they call for embodied rather than disembodied technology.[d] The hypothesis is raised here that a strategy of reducing costs of acquisition will work much more effectively for industries in which embodied technology makes up a very large proportion of the technological package. It is here that unpackaging should work most effectively. Thus we might say that unpackaging is likely to work best in industries having the following characteristics:

1. the technology is not in a state of flux
2. the industry does not require significant scaling down of technology
3. there is no great need to adapt the technology significantly to use local materials and labor or to produce a product tailored only to local needs

[d]Embodied technology is largely incorporated into physical capital. It is in many respects an "off-the-shelf" item. Disembodied technology can be purchased and may be absolutely essential to the application of embodied technology, but the purchaser is much less sure of what he is getting.

4. the industry is not highly dependent on the marketing strengths of a few highly integrated international firms; i.e., if the product is not all sold domestically it can be sold on internationally competitive markets
5. there are alternative sources of supply for the technology; i.e., it is not so proprietary that it cannot be purchased via licensing or lump sum payments

Industries that have most of these characteristics are: basic inorganic and organic chemicals, chemical fertilizers, paints, agricultural commodities, ore concentrates and basic metals, textiles, paper-making, plywood and lumber products, and a variety of light manufactures including bicycles, certain leather goods and low-priced wearing apparel, small household appliances and electrical fixtures, wood milling, standard steel and aluminum shapes, and standard electronic and electrical components.

Sorting through the list of three-digit industries, one is hard put to find candidates that do not violate either one of the characteristics noted above or the factor proportions of developing countries. Perhaps the most critical problem for developing Pacific Basin countries that wish to develop export markets is presented by characteristic 4 in the list. Even in something so simple as shoes and wearing apparel, it is not the production technology that is constraining, but rather the marketing expertise and knowledge of changing consumer tastes and styles. It is not enough to purchase a set of lasts or patterns designed to U.S. specifications; one also must be prepared to change over quickly to new styles in a rapidly changing market. Thus marketing know-how becomes overriding, and the technology of production becomes secondary in importance. This is not to say that developing countries should avoid, say, shoe production, but just that they must recognize that the know-how most needed to serve export markets cannot be transferred readily. This does not imply that the technology cannot be unpackaged, but that when it is unpackaged, only a part of the essential technology can be acquired. The developing countries must rely on foreign sources to supply the missing links via licensing or other contractual arrangements.

Industries that appear to lack the major characteristics noted in the preceding list include: automobiles, heavy consumer appliances and electrical equipment, agricultural equipment, construction machinery, crude petroleum and its products going to international markets, complex chemical formulations, large-scale food processing operations and other highly differentiated consumer products where trademarks, advertising, and marketing skills are important. In all these fields it is not so much the complexity of the basic technology that provides a competitive advantage; rather, the complex organizing skills and/or market power cannot be readily unpackaged and allow firms to influence the terms of technology transfer strongly, not only with respect to what is to be transferred, but also with respect to which method will be used to accomplish transfer. And more often than not, those terms will specify direct foreign investment as the vehicle of transfer.

Several examples should suffice to illustrate the point. In the automobile industry, firms are perfectly willing to license local firms to assemble the final product as long as components can be imported. However, once countries insist on an increased level of local content, it is then necessary to build up upstream operations, i.e., local suppliers. Usually, the local licensee/assembler does not have the organizing skills and technical know-how to assist in the development of such suppliers. With the exception of the Fiat deals with Yugoslavia, Poland, and the Soviet Union, I can think of no instance in which the automotive firms have transferred their production technology in toto via licensing agreements and lump sum payments. It should be noted that the technical capacity of these three countries is well beyond what can be mustered in developing countries in the Pacific Basin or elsewhere. Moreover, the countries themselves are bearing the market risks with little expectation of serving any markets other than their own and little expectation that the product will be altered through annual style change, facelifts, and innovation. Even in these semi-advanced countries, the entire technology and organizing skills are not being acquired. What they have obtained is a turnkey plant *sans* the innovative know-how required to become internationally competitive on a continuing basis.

Large food processing firms are also reluctant to transfer know-how, except via direct investment. Del Monte, Heinz, and Dole have great expertise in organizing independent farmers to produce uniformly high-quality field and tree crops. This operational know-how, rather than the physical plant that processes the raw materials, provides them their monopolistic rents.[e] These firms can reduce the cost of acquiring raw materials and improve the quality and uniformity of those materials. A part of their advantage also lies in the differentiation of product via advertising and higher quality. While it might be feasible to unpackage this type of technology via licensing agreements and technical aid contracts, it is unlikely that the firms would readily do so given the variety of opportunities open to them to enter into direct foreign investments among the developing countries.

The desire of developing Pacific Basin countries for greater exportation and a sharing of ownership, even including majority local control, very well may fly in the face of obtaining the desired technology and types of investments most wanted. As Grant Reuber points out, policy has been shifting away from self-sufficiency and toward a heightened emphasis on international trade.[1] But accompanying this emphasis is implied acceptance of increased vertical integration because of the foreign firm's international marketing capabilities. Perhaps it is feasible to follow the policy of local ownership and purchased technology in developing export-oriented projects in fields where a large, well-organized, and competitive international market exists, as is the case with certain commodities

---

[e]As previously noted, the supply contract figures strongly into Dole's operations. Where the risks that supply contracts will not be honored are great, it is unlikely that such firms will be enthusiastic about technology transfer and the development of processing plants.

such as agricultural commodities and base metals. In these fields, international firms are much less dominant, and therefore marketing expertise is less important. This amounts to saying that at some points of the vertical chain, reasonable competition prevails, or that vertical integration has not become firmly established because the marketing skills required are not highly dominated by a few firms (as is true, for example, in petroleum products, rubber products, automobiles, and agricultural equipment).

Industries that are highly integrated vertically also may be persuaded by low-cost labor in the Basin's developing countries to establish specialized production facilities whose object is exportation to advanced country or other developing country markets.[f] The electronics industry is a good example of this process, through which labor-intensive assembly operations have been located in Taiwan, South Korea, Mexico, and a few other places. It is notable, however, that these moves toward specialization of labor-intensive production have also been accompanied by direct foreign investment, except where the technology is highly standardized. Because of rapid changes in technology and market requirements, it is doubtful that the technology can be readily unpackaged except in the most standardized items. It is interesting in this field that both Sony and Matsushita have chosen to get closer to the U.S. market by establishing assembly operations there, one by building a plant and the other by acquisition.[g]

The automobile industry is also attempting to change its *modus operandi* in some areas of the Pacific Basin. Both General Motors and Ford Motor Company are attempting to reorganize their methods of serving Southeast Asian markets. But both firms are using direct foreign investment to accomplish their ends. Again, the complex coordination of production facilities with markets becomes the critical ingredient to success, and it is doubtful that these companies would agree to technology transfers whereby licensees would produce components and still another set of licensees would take care of final assembly. Developing and serving large-scale markets is too hazardous a business to further compound the problem of coordination by having the product produced by a group of independent licensees scattered across several countries.

In summary, then, the unpackaging process would appear to be most nearly feasible in fields where technology is reasonably standardized and where the output will be used to serve the domestic market or competitive international markets. Products that call for the marketing expertise of international firms, where either a high degree of product differentiation is involved and/or the firms are highly integrated and few in number, are not subjected to the unpackaging process so easily.

---

[f]As analyzed in Chapter 5.

[g]Of course, appreciation of the Japanese yen may have had something to do with these events.

Relative Costs of Acquisition

The costs involved in acquiring technology may be viewed in various ways. However, it does seem that the prevailing view in most developing countries is that the costs of acquisition are higher than they need be and that a part of these costs derive from highly imperfect markets for technology, especially where the technology is part of a direct investment package. Yet the rates of net earnings plus licensing and other fees relative to total assets employed by U.S.-controlled subsidiaries seem not greatly different when comparing U.S. investments in Europe with those in Latin American. Licensing and franchising agreements appear to be rather standard regardless of industry and country of operation. Franchise agreements in the United States are similar to those in Latin America or Europe in terms of royalties paid, duration of contract, etc., but this certainly does not mean that markets are perfect. However, there appear to be some common practices. Whether these are traditional rules of thumb that have grown up over the years or whether they are the result of competitive forces, most licensees nevertheless confront similar conditions.[h] Of course, licensers do differ in terms of how seriously they work with licensees; hence the amount of "free" disembodied technology acquired can differ among licensees. But a wholly owned subsidiary/licensee probably has freer and more complete access to parent organization research and accumulated know-how than does an independent licensee. Moreover, as previously noted, firms will differ with respect to the types of technology they will transfer under the direct investment package as compared with the technologies they will transfer in unpackaged form. Thus two potential costs are involved in unpackaging: (1) the "free" disembodied technology that might be transferred to a subsidiary but not to an independent licensee; and (2) the cost of not being able to obtain the same technology that would be transferred to a wholly owned subsidiary/licensee but not to an independent licensee.

So far, no one to my knowledge has examined this problem very rigorously. My own casual observation in studying comparative samples of U.S. subsidiaries and locally owned independent licensees seems to suggest that subsidiaries obtain more help from the parent/licenser than do independent licensees. In this sense, licensing without direct investment involvement by foreign firms may be a costly way to acquire technology.

Japan has used the licensing strategy by penning over 18,000 licensing agreements to acquire foreign technology. But this has occurred over a number

---

[h]It is notable that several countries, particularly in Latin America, claim to have reduced licensing costs by placing ceilings on the percentage rates of payment allowed between licensees and licensers. This does not constitute *prima facie* evidence that the cost of acquiring technology has been reduced, for only the royalty rate has been reduced. This says nothing about the extent to which licensees now have access to licenser know-how. Nor does it say anything about other forms of payment such as technical aid agreements, changed transfer prices, and increased interest rates on loans between licenser and licensee. Numerous devices can be used to contravene restrictions on royalty payments.

of years during which Japan has simultaneously built up its capability to adapt the technology. So long as developing countries must rely on outsiders for the acquisition of this capability, licensing alone may not be the best alternative.

Strategies of Acquisition

Without substantially more research than has been done to date, we must use very fragmentary information to judge what types of situations might be approached most effectively through unpackaging. From the preceding comments I draw the following conclusions about the types of strategies the Pacific Basin developing countries might profitably follow as an interim measure.

1. If the project or desired expansion involves mainly embodied technology, the use of engineering consulting contracts, technical aid agreements, and management contracts should be strongly considered, and these services should be thrown open to competitive bidding.
2. In such projects, licensing should be avoided because there is little basis for infusing additional technology over time. Should there be a need for some re-equipping or process redesign decisions, technical aid agreements can be renegotiated and extended.
3. Where disembodied technology is important, the project is expected to serve only local market needs, and product differentiation, brand names, and proprietary process technology are unimportant, the technical aid agreement again can be used to acquire the needed expertise through expatriates employed on contract.
4. Even though there may be instances in which the technology is mainly embodied and stable, it may be necessary to accept licensing agreements if brand names and product differentiation characterize the products desired for local production.
5. Where the conditions of situation 4 prevail except that the technology is not stable, a combination of licensing and technical aid agreements may be required.
6. Depending on the bargaining power of the firm (its degree of monopoly power) and the market pressures for local production in situations 4 and 5, it may be necessary to accept direct foreign investment as an acquisition strategy.
7. Where international markets are important and there is strong vertical integration, direct foreign investment may be the only strategy open to acquisition.
8. Where complex organizing and coordinating skills are required for the venture's success, it may again be necessary to adopt a strategy of acquisition via direct foreign investment.

Application of the Framework to Developing
Pacific Basin Countries

It is interesting to compare two groups of countries and their approaches to direct foreign investment and the licensing of technology. The Andean Compact (ANCOM) countries (Chile, Peru, Ecuador, Colombia, Venezuela, and Bolivia) have taken one approach while the ASEAN countries (the Philippines, Indonesia, Singapore, Malaysia, and Thailand) have taken another. However, as Thomas Allen points out in chapter 6, the ASEAN countries are far from uniform in their approaches to the regulation and encouragement (or discouragement) of direct foreign investment. But in general, the individual ASEAN countries are more liberal than the ANCOM countries in their approaches to foreign investment. Moreover, all have spelled out priority industries with emphasis on those that are labor-intensive, export-oriented, or high-technology industries. Even in the Philippines and Thailand, which have the most stringent rules on foreign ownership in the ASEAN group, 100-percent ownership by foreigners is permissible. In the Philippines, foreign firms have up to forty years to reduce their ownership share to 40 percent. In Thailand, the high-technology industries are given the most lenient treatment, although joint ventures are preferred to wholly foreign-owned subsidiaries.

The ANCOM countries, at least on paper, are much less discriminating between high-technology and low-technology industries. Theirs is much more broadside approach to foreign ownership, in which all new foreign investments in manufacturing must spin off 51 percent of their equity to nationals within fifteen years. If they are to have access to the enlarged ANCOM market, existing investments would have to do the same. Interestingly, Chile, Peru, and, more recently, Ecuador have backed away from the provisions of Decision 24 within the pact, which established ownership regulations. Priorities appear to have shifted toward the high-technology industries, which are now receiving incentives and fewer strictures.

Licensing arrangements appear to reflect a recognition that certain types of technology are more valuable than other types as far as their contributions to development are concerned. For example, Chile, which has one of the strictest codes on royalties that specifies the maximum allowable payment, has established twenty-two product groupings with allowable royalty rates that increase largely with the degree of technical complexity of the product. Thus it appears that the Pacific Basin's developing countries do recognize some of the principles that have been suggested here. It also appears that the ASEAN countries have been more discriminating by delineating the industries where the technology can or should come in packaged form through direct foreign investment. The Andean group has taken a less selective, broadside approach requiring joint ventures and ultimately local control within a shorter period. Some of the ANCOM countries are backing away from this approach and are beginning to adopt the more sophisticated approach that is evident among the ASEAN countries.

It is apparent that the low-technology, stable industries are being foreclosed to foreigners or at least being given least favorable treatment. This suggests a recognition that the needed technologies can be acquired on competitive terms and that local firms can meet national needs equally as well as foreign firms could in these industries. One might call this selective nationalism.

As yet I do not see a full implementation of an unpackaging strategy, perhaps because the countries themselves have not been able to examine a sufficient number of alternative strategies. This may stem largely from a shortage of qualified personnel who are competent to evaluate various technology packages. Even the boards of investments are heavily overtaxed in terms of their ability to screen and evaluate new investment proposals. The region's developing countries recognize the need for technology and are attempting to reduce its cost. It would seem that within the limitations of their scarce resources to evaluate technology, the countries have opted for controlling ownership position and providing more permissive conditions in the priority industries. With some exceptions, these industries tend to meet the criteria outlined earlier in this chapter.

Conclusions

Industries differ significantly in their characteristics and hence the firms therein will differ with respect to the competitiveness with which they can or will make technology available. It is debatable whether the cost of technology transfers can be reduced by constraining the degree of ownership by foreign firms. But at least the developing Pacific Basin countries should examine their technology acquisition strategies closely with respect to the characteristics of the industries involved. A broadside approach to control of ownership structure and royalty rates, as attempted by the ANCOM countries, would not seem to be even a second-best strategy. Close attention should be directed to the types of technology most needed. If they can be obtained only via direct foreign investment, nationalism may have to yield if, indeed, there is an interest in obtaining technology on the best terms.

Note

1. Grant L. Reuber, *Some Aspects of Private Direct Investment in Developing Countries* (New York: SEADAG Papers, the Asia Society, 1974), p. 19.

Direct Foreign Investments and Investment Policies of Japanese Firms

Hans Schollhammer

Japan's International Business Strategies:
Historical Perspective

During the Tokugawa era (1603-1867) Japan was a closed, inward-looking economy because of the political rulers' conscious effort to restrict and discourage interchange with the outside world. With the Meiji Restoration in 1868, this policy was overturned. The new authorities recognized the importance of foreign trade, but Japan's opportunities for export, as a small, resource-poor country with limited technological know-how, were very restricted. During the late nineteenth century, much as today, the government played an active role in encouraging an export effort. Major emphasis was placed on developing export markets for tea, silk, and copper. With the gradual emergence of the so-called Zaibatsu companies (groupings of enterprises in various industries, bound together by fractional shareholdings in one another), by the turn of the century a light industry developed that provided a basis for an active pursuit of export opportunities for labor-intensive and inexpensive products such as toys, textile products, and porcelain. The quality of these products tended to be poor, and their only competitive advantage was their very low price. During the same period a uniquely Japanese business institution emerged that contributed in large measure to Japan's early international business involvement: the trading companies. The trading companies became the central element in the Zaibatsu conglomerates such as Mitsubishi and Mitsui, and they provided the impetus for Japan's early export drive by identifying suitable export products and by providing foreign market intelligence and export financing. The trading companies also served as an intermediary between the myriad small and medium sized firms who had no knowledge about export markets and foreign consumers.

By the end of World War II, Japan, a defeated nation whose large-scale production facilities were almost totally destroyed, had to reconstruct the economy and instill among its people a strong national consensus to achieve maximum economic growth. In the pursuit of these twin objectives, six strategies were emphasized:

1. close cooperation between the government authorities and the business community

131

2. a planned approach to the identification and development of key industries on a priority basis[a]
3. protection of the domestic producers from excessive foreign competition
4. acquisition of foreign technology to improve the Japanese manufacturers' international competitiveness
5. careful allocation of available foreign exchange in support of the stated priorities
6. strong encouragement of an intense export effort

These strategies worked remarkably well, and no other country has matched Japan's economic growth record during the three decades since World War II. Particularly impressive are Japan's export achievements. Since 1955 Japan's exports increased consistently at an annual rate of approximately 25 percent. Also, the percentage of Japan's gross domestic product that is exported has been rising steadily.

The figures in Table 9-1 indicate Japan's rapid economic growth, which was particularly marked among the various manufacturing industries whose average annual growth rate since the early 1950s was consistently around 15 percent. Among the fastest-growing manufacturing industries were shipbuilding, electrical and nonelectrical precision instruments, petroleum refining, chemicals, iron and steel, and automobiles. Some of Japan's more traditional industries such as textiles and paper production grew at a much slower rate, which signifies a

Table 9-1
Japan's GNP and Exports
(In Billion Yen)

Year	GNP	Exports	Exports as Percent of GNP
1948	1,962	93	4.74
1955	6,535	724	11.08
1960	15,214	1,715	11.27
1965	30,441	3,452	11.34
1970	70,731	8,273	11.70
1975	144,865	20,280	14.00
1976	164,470	23,838	14.49
1977	184,000 (est.)	27,000 (est.)	14.67 (est.)

Source: Various issues of *International Financial Statistics.*

---

[a]For example, during the early 1950s labor-intensive industries such as the textile industry, shipbuilding, steel production, and the fertilizer industry received close attention. During the early 1960s the emphasis shifted to capital- and technology-intensive industries such as petroleum refining, petrochemicals, electronics, and automobile production.

change in Japan's industrial structure in favor of high-technology, capital-intensive industries. For all Japan's high-growth industries, a rapid expansion of exports became a necessary precondition for further expansion. For example, during the 1960s 80 percent of the output of Japan's shipbuilding industry, 46 percent of the synthetic fiber output, 43 percent of the produced television sets, and 35 percent of the automobile production had to be exported.

Apart from a 75- to 80-percent self-sufficiency rate in foodstuffs, Japan has only very limited resources of raw materials and energy. As a consequence, it must import substantial quantities of raw and semiprocessed materials and export manufactured products to earn the foreign exchange for the necessary imports. Thus Japan's basic industry structure can be characterized as processing-oriented. The large volume of Japan's international trade (amounting to $55,783 million of exports and $57,863 million of imports in 1975) is handled to a large extent by a rather small number of so-called general trading companies, which have no counterparts anywhere else in the world. In 1970 the ten largest trading companies accounted for about 50 percent of Japan's exports and more than 60 percent of its imports.[1] About 70 percent of Japan's total exports go through the trading companies. Only about 30 percent of exports are sold directly by manufacturers, and these market mainly sophisticated industrial machinery such as automobiles, electronic and electrical equipment, cameras, and watches, which tend to require technical servicing at the point of sale.

Although the trading companies, with their network of branches and sales offices throughout the world, play a very significant role in Japan's international trade effort, they seem to have reached the limit of their effectiveness. Their sheer size causes them to be increasingly rigid in their business approach, and over the years they have developed too much of a "trader mentality" with emphasis on simply buying and selling (not servicing) and a rather short-term perspective. Above all, the trading company personnel have very limited technical and engineering expertise. As a consequence, trading companies are not very well suited to market technology-intensive products that generally require a technically oriented sales effort and extensive servicing. With the accelerating change in Japan's industrial structure toward technology- and capital-intensive industries, a growing number of Japanese manufacturing companies became directly involved in international trade. This reorientation made them more outward-looking and contributed strongly to their awareness of foreign investment opportunities.

During the second half of the 1960s Japanese manufacturing companies, for the first time, made sizable foreign direct investments in overseas operating facilities. Throughout the 1950s and the early 1960s the foreign direct investments of Japanese firms had been negligible. Similarly, foreign investments in Japan were severely restricted by the government, which relegated foreign investors to, at most, a role of minority partner in joint ventures with Japanese partners. During the mid-1960s the Japanese government grudgingly gave in to severe pressure to liberalize its tight restrictions against foreign investments. Although most of the legal restrictions against foreign investments in Japan had been reduced or eliminated by 1970, nonlegal entry barriers—such as the prevailing nationalistic sentiments in Japan and unfamiliarity with the Japanese management and marketing system—are still quite strong. In spite of these barriers, however, foreign investments in Japan increased at a high rate once the legal restrictions were liberalized. The inflow of foreign investments into Japan contributed to the local companies' awareness of foreign investment opportunities. The massive increase of Japanese foreign investments since the early 1970s is, however, a consequence of five developments:

1. a change in Japan's industrial structure from a labor-intensive to a capital- and technology-intensive orientation
2. a better knowledge of foreign markets among the Japanese manufacturing companies because of direct exporting and importing efforts rather than reliance on the trading companies as intermediaries
3. the imitation effect of foreign investors, especially a growing awareness of the internationalization of U.S.-based firms
4. rapidly rising wages and production costs in Japan
5. the revaluation of the yen and easy access to foreign exchange

In good Japanese fashion, the shift from an export orientation to an emphasis on investments during the late 1960s became a concerted effort involving a broad spectrum of companies, business associations, and the government. It initiated a development that has come to be called *kokusai-ka,* the internationalization of Japan.

Patterns of Japan's Foreign Direct Investments

The remarkable growth of Japan's foreign direct investments within only a few years is best highlighted by two figures: at the end of March 1965 the cumulative total of Japan's direct investments abroad amounted to only $789.8 million; at the end of March 1975 they had reached $12,660.0 million. During the past decade Japan's foreign direct investments increased sixteen-fold, a rate of growth unsurpassed by any other industrial country.[2] The growth of Japan's foreign investments has accelerated particularly since 1972, when the Japanese government eliminated most restrictions against these investments. In fact, two-thirds of Japan's foreign direct investments were made within only three years of 1972 to 1975. Table 9-2 summarizes the development and current state of Japan's foreign direct investments.

Table 9-2
Japan's Foreign Direct Investments

	1967		1970		1973		1975	
	$	%	$	%	$	%	$	%
Resource-oriented								
Agriculture, forestry, fisheries	37	2.5	80	2.2	229	2.2	280	2.2
Mining	443	30.5	1,132	31.6	3,061	29.8	3,527	27.9
Lumber and pulp	113	7.8	214	6.0	363	3.6	423	3.3
Subtotal	593	40.8	1,426	39.9	3,653	35.6	4,230	33.4
Labor- and market-oriented (manufacturing operations)								
Foodstuffs	27	1.9	52	1.5	167	1.6	231	1.8
Textiles	91	6.3	189	5.3	743	7.2	918	7.2
Chemicals	23	1.6	60	1.7	538	5.2	634	5.0
Iron and nonferrous metals	87	6.0	138	3.9	486	4.7	635	5.0
Machinery	38	2.6	68	1.9	217	2.1	307	2.4
Electrical machinery	22	1.5	73	2.0	328	3.2	426	3.4
Transport machinery	74	5.1	87	2.4	222	2.2	263	2.1
Miscellaneous manufactures	27	1.9	61	1.7	197	1.9	300	2.4
Subtotal	389	26.7	728	20.3	2,898	28.2	3,714	29.3
Services and finance								
Construction	25	1.7	38	1.1	67	0.7	84	0.7
Commerce	179	12.3	412	11.5	1,232	12.0	1,549	12.2
Banking and insurance	136	9.4	318	8.9	917	8.9	1,000	7.9
Miscellaneous	131	9.0	655	18.3	1,504	14.6	1,685	13.3
Subtotal	471	32.5	1,423	39.8	3,720	36.2	4,318	34.1
Branch operations	n.a.	—	n.a.	—	n.a.	—	404	3.2
Total	1,453	100	3,577	100	10,270	100	12,666	100

Source: Bank of Japan and Ministry of International Trade and Industry.

Resource-oriented Foreign Investments

A major motivating factor for Japan's overseas investments in recent years was the attempt to secure, within limits, the supply of basic resources such as ores, minerals, timber, petroleum, and agricultural resources. By 1975 more than one-third of Japan's foreign investments served this purpose, and it is expected that the share of Japan's resource-oriented foreign investments will rise farther in the future. This is not surprising if one considers the precarious resource limitations Japan is faced with, as Table 9-3 indicates. Since Japan is so highly dependent on foreign resources, the government has been providing very active support to Japanese firms' efforts to use foreign investments as a means to gain a certain degree of control over the supply of strategic raw materials. In addition, the Japanese government has initiated various development projects in which large Japanese companies are the main contractors and which serve similar aims as the resource-oriented investments. For example, since 1970 the Japanese government initiated a broad range of development projects in oil-producing countries of the Middle East (see Table 9-4).

These projects indicate one facet of Japan's international business strategy: a growing emphasis on Japan's ability to initiate and package large technology transfers and the delivery of complex technology-intensive systems. This strategy becomes particularly apparent in the case of the foreign operations of Japan's steel industry. Between 1965 and 1974 Japanese steel companies engaged in seventy-two joint venture projects abroad, three of which involved the establishment of integrated steel manufacturing facilities in Malaysia, Brazil, and Mexico. The rest of the projects were concerned with the development of facilities for rolling and galvanizing steel sheets and drawing steel pipes and wire rods. By 1975, thirty-four new venture projects by Japanese steel companies were in the planning stage.[3]

Table 9-3
Japan's Dependence on Foreign Supplies, 1973
(In Percent)

Overall dependence rate for agricultural products	27.0
Wheat	95.0
Sugar	80.0
Soybeans	80.0
Petroleum	99.7
Natural gas	52.8
Uranium	100.0
Coking Coal	83.9
Nickel	100.0
Aluminum	100.0
Iron Ore	99.2
Copper	91.1
Lead	77.1
Zinc	69.2

Source: Ministry of Foreign Affairs, *Waga Gaiko No Kinkyo (Our Diplomacy These Days)*, 1975, Tokyo.

Note: Dependence rate = $\dfrac{\text{demand} - \text{domestic supply}}{\text{demand}}$

Table 9-4

Development Projects in Six Persian Gulf Countries Initiated by the Japanese Government

Country	Project	Cost	Main Contractor
Iran	Petrochemical center	$2.6 million	Mitsui & Co.
	Oil refinery	Unknown	Mitsui & Co.
Iraq	Chemical fertilizer plant	$1.0 million	Mitsubishi Group
	Petrochemical center	$3.1 million	Ishikawajima-Harima
	Oil refinery	Unknown	Toyo Menka Kaisha
	LPG plant	$1.0 million	Mitsubishi Group
Kuwait	Buaxite development	Unknown	Not yet decided
Qatar	Steel mill	$1.0 million	Kobe Steel, Ltd.
Saudi Arabia	Petrochemical center	$1.0 million	Mitsubishi Group
	Oil refinery	Unknown	Mitsibishi Group
	Steel mill	Unknown	Nippon Steel Corp.
	Mineral resources development	Unknown	Nippon Mining Co.
United Arab Emirates	Desert vegetation	Unknown	Komatsu, Ltd.
	Natural gas production	Unknown	Japan Line, Ltd.
	Steel mill	Unknown	Kawasaki Steel Corp.

Source: The Middle East Economic Research Institute

Some of Japan's resource-oriented foreign investments also reduce pollution-intensive operations in Japan. The foreign ventures of the Japanese steel industry are a case in point. Japan has virtually no iron ore deposits and negligible coking coals. Yet since the end of World War II, it has become one of the largest steel producers in the world. The steel industry is highly polluting, and in recent years the Japanese government has adopted very stringent regulations against environmental pollution. In response, Japanese companies started to establish pollution-intensive operations in other countries where the required antipollution standards are not yet as stringent as Japan's. Many of the resource-oriented foreign investments of Japanese companies thus serve multiple objectives, such as securing the supply of basic raw materials for Japan's industry, helping developing countries in their development effort, reducing pollution-intensive operations in Japan, taking advantage of lower wage costs abroad, and so on.

Labor- and Market-oriented Foreign Investments

Labor- and market-oriented foreign investments currently account for less than 30 percent of Japan's total foreign investments. In contrast, 45 percent of the U.S., 56 percent of the British, and 65 percent of the German foreign direct investments fall into this category. These investments encompass essentially all foreign manufacturing operations. One of their major aims is to improve the investing company's production efficiency, for example, by taking advantage of lower wage costs abroad or by defending and/or improving an already established market position that has been supplied by exports but that may become more difficult to maintain because of import restrictions imposed by the host government.

Among the manufacturing industries, Japan's textile industry accounts for the largest share, i.e., slightly more than 7 percent of Japan's foreign investments. Just before World War II the Japanese textile industry employed one-third of the industrial labor force, and it accounted for 40 percent of the total manufactured output and 55 percent of Japan's exports. Not surprisingly, after the war Japan again placed heavy emphasis on the redevelopment of its textile industry. Since 1953, however, Japan's textile industry grew at a lower rate than the Japanese economy as a whole; to improve their production efficiency, most textile companies started to establish production facilities abroad. Ninety percent of these investments were in developing countries of Southeast Asia such as Korea, Taiwan, Thailand, Hong Kong, and Indonesia. The two main reasons for the textile companies' foreign investments were (1) lower production costs abroad because of lower wages and lower costs for plant sites; and (2) the attempt to overcome the host countries' import restrictions against Japanese textiles.

One of the manufacturing industries with sizable foreign investments is Japan's electrical/electronics industry. As Table 9-5 shows, this industry grew in all industrialized countries at a remarkable rate, but nowhere as fast as in Japan.

As in the textile industry, most of the foreign investments in the electronics industry were made in developing countries of Southeast Asia. As of March 1975 about 50 percent of these investments were made in Taiwan and South Korea; in addition, Hong Kong, Singapore, Thailand, and Malaysia each accounted for about 5 percent. The motivations for these investments were practically the same as in the case of the textile industry: low wage rates in the host countries and the need to overcome import restrictions.

Table 9-5
Output and Growth of the Electronics Industry

	Japan	West Germany	France	U.K.	Italy	U.S.A.
1967	$ 3,969M	$2,376M	$1,833M	$1,930M	$ 839M	$27,827M
1974	$16,410M	$7,547M	$4,120M	$4,174M	$1,595M	$38,098M
Average annual growth rate (%)	22.5	18.0	12.3	11.6	9.6	4.6

Finance- and Service-oriented Foreign Investments

From 1948 to 1965 a significant proportion of Japan's foreign investments were made by the large general trading companies such as Mitsubishi, Mitsui, Sumitomo, and C. Itoh to establish a marketing network in support of their international trading activities. Most of these investments were made to establish sales offices, warehouses, and service centers. With the growth of Japan's foreign exchange surpluses since 1965 and the gradual expansion of foreign manufacturing, Japan's banks became very active in setting up banking operations overseas. There now exists a rather extensive network of Japanese banking subsidiaries in the United States, particularly in California and New York; in Europe, especially in England and Germany; and in Hong Kong and most other Southeast Asian countries. Similarly, the expansion of Japanese tourism abroad has led Japanese firms to establish or acquire a string of hotels in the United States (mainly in Hawaii and California), Taiwan, the Philippines, and Hong Kong. In addition, in recent years Japanese firms have made sizable investments in foreign real estate, most of which are also counted in this category. By the end of 1974, 35.8 percent of Japan's foreign investments could be characterized as finance- and service-oriented. The relative importance of these investments is expected to decline to less than 25 percent by 1985, however.

The Regional Distribution of Japan's Foreign Investments

An analysis of the regional distribution of Japan's foreign investments shows interesting patterns. In contrast to the investments of other industrialized countries, the majority of Japan's overseas investments have been made in developing countries. As Table 9-6 shows, about 25 percent of Japan's total foreign direct investments have been made in Asian countries, about 24 percent in the United States and Canada, 20 percent in Central and South America, and 17 percent in Europe. In addition, the Middle East and Australia/New Zealand each account for about 6 percent, and Africa accounts for only about 2 percent. The individual countries with the most sizable Japanese investments are the United States, the United Kingdom, Brazil, Indonesia, Saudi Arabia, Kuwait, and Australia.

It is not surprising that the majority of Japan's investments in Africa, Oceania, and the Middle East can be characterized as resource-oriented; i.e., they have been made to secure a supply of essential resources such as minerals, ores, and petroleum. As far as the investments in Asian and Latin American countries are concerned, more than 50 percent went for the establishment of manufacturing facilities. This situation reflects very clearly that Japanese enterprises prefer low-wage countries for their foreign manufacturing operations. Almost

Table 9-6
Regional Distribution of Japan's Foreign Investments, March 1975

	Asia		North America		Central and South America		Europe		Middle East		Oceania		Africa	
	$M	%	$M	%	$M	%	$M	%	$M	%	$M	%	$M	%
Resource-oriented	1051	33.66	584	19.40	652	25.97	855	39.11	378	48.46	497	66.45	213	68.93
Labor- and market-oriented (manufacturing operations)	1475	47.25	471	15.64	1255	50.00	214	9.79	106	13.59	142	18.98	51	16.51
Services and finance	561	17.97	1916	63.63	599	23.87	1073	49.09	19	24.46	106	14.17	44	14.24
Branch operations	35	1.12	40	1.33	4	0.16	44	2.01	277	35.51	3	0.40	1	0.32
Total	3122	100.00	3011	100.00	2510	100.00	2186	100.00	780	100.00	748	100.00	309	100.00
Investment by area, as percent of total foreign investment ($12,666M)	24.65		23.77		13.82		17.26		6.16		5.90		2.44	

Source: MITI.

two-thirds of Japan's investments in North America and half its investments in Europe are in the finance and service sectors, i.e., banking, insurance, sales/ service organizations, construction, and hotels and other real estate ventures.

Thus the major motivating factors for Japan's recent foreign investments were to secure the supply of vital resources from abroad, to take advantage of relatively low wage rates in certain developing countries for labor-intensive manufacturing operations, and to gain or protect a market position in major industrialized countries. On the surface, this situation is not very different from the foreign investment motives of European- and U.S.-based multinationals. A more detailed analysis of the factors affecting locational decisions of U.S., European, and Japanese multinational firms reveals, however, significant differences, as shown in Figure 9-1.[b]

For Japanese multinational firms, supply considerations and the availability and cost of production are the single most important factor category affecting the locational choice for a foreign investment. In contrast, locational decisions of U.S. firms are strongly affected by the perception of the political risk situation. As compared with U.S. and European firms, Japanese multinationals seem to let themselves be less encumbered by legal difficulties, bureaucratic red tape, and environmental adversities posed by potential host countries. Japanese firms also seem to be more cost-conscious, and they tend to have a greater aversion to competitive rivalry than do U.S.- and European-based multinationals. On the latter issue, Ballon observes that "Japanese business has very little self-confidence once it looks for an establishment outside Japan."[4] After all, exports can be directed from inside Japan; investments are altogether different. The consequence, then, is that to the surprise of outsiders, Japanese corporations display a definite preference for joint ventures (with local partners or cooperation with a Japanese competitor) rather than for wholly owned subsidiaries. The well-known preference of Japanese companies for joint ventures in the international arena is not only a reflection of a lack of self-confidence, as Ballon suggests, but a result of the Japanese firms' expectation to make most of their return in foreign investments through exports and imports. For instance, Clark points out that "provided the share of the Japanese investor in the [overseas] project is sufficient to give him control over the project's purchasing and/or sales policies, he hopes through trade gains to draw a return for his contribution to the venture."[5]

Japanese Investments in Pacific Basin Countries

More than 60 percent of Japan's foreign investments are concentrated in countries bordering on the Pacific Basin. A country-by-country analysis of these

[b]These "profiles" are based on information provided by ninety-five U.S.-based, forty-five European-based, and twenty-eight Japan-based multinational firms. For further details, see Hans Schollhammer, *Locational Strategies of Multinational Firms* (Los Angeles: Center for International Business), 1974.

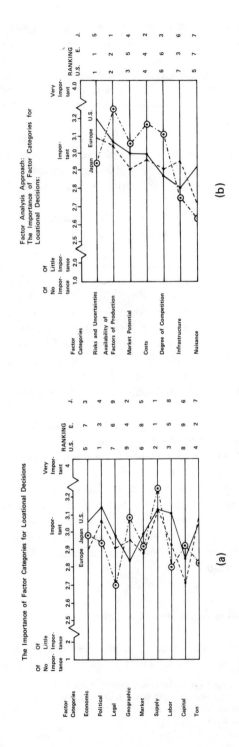

Source: Hans Schollhammer, *Locational Strategies of Multinational Firms* (Los Angeles: Center for International Business, 1974).

Figure 9-1. The Importance of Factor Categories Affecting Locational Decisions of U.S.-, European-, and Japan-based Multinational Firms

investments would be beyond this chapter's scope. However, a discussion of Japan's investments in some of the Pacific Basin countries should shed light on typical patterns of Japan's international investment strategies.

Thailand

A large proportion of Japan's foreign investments have been made in developing countries of Southeast Asia; but in no other country of this region do Japanese investments play such a dominant role as they do in Thailand. Between 1960 and 1973 the total cumulative value of foreign investments in Thailand came to 2878 million baht, and Japanese enterprises accounted for 37.3 percent (1074 million baht) of these investments. United States investments in Thailand amounted to 467 million baht (16.2 percent), followed by Taiwan with 15.4 percent and all European countries combined accounting for 14.5 percent.

As Table 9-7 shows, investments by Japanese enterprises, with their technological know-how and management, loom very large in a few important industrial sectors, especially the automotive, textile, chemical and glass industries.

Although Japanese interests control only about 21 percent of the invested equity capital in the textile industry, all major Thai firms have Japanese participation and are largely managed by Japanese expatriate executives (see Table 9-8).

Because of their conspicuousness, Japanese investments and managers in

Table 9-7
Equity Participation by Nationality in Various Industrial Sectors of Thailand, 1960-1973
(In Percent)

	Thai	Japanese	U.S.A.	Others
Automotive vehicles and spare parts	59.2	29.6	5.2	6.0
Textile and fiber products	65.5	20.5	1.2	12.8
Chemical industry	61.6	17.6	2.7	17.8
Glass sheets and optical glass	66.6	15.4	–	18.0
Rubber and plastic products	57.2	9.1	13.6	20.1
Electrical appliances	56.7	9.1	17.7	16.5
Petroleum and petro-chemical products	43.4	8.8	19.5	28.3
Metal and mineral products	64.3	6.8	12.8	16.1
Agricultural products and fishery	65.1	5.6	23.2	6.1

Source: Board of Investment of Thailand.

Table 9-8
Japanese Management Participation in Thailand's Major Textile Firms

	Number of Directors		Nationality of Management	
	Thai	Japanese	Manager	Deputy
Pangkok Nylon	6	5	J	T
Capital Kanebo Textile	6	5	T	T
Erawan Textile	4	5	J	J
Luckytex, Thailand	2	2	T	J
Peony Blanket Industrial	0	6	J	J
Siam Synthetic Textile Industry	5	6	J	T
Siam Synthetic Weaving	4	4	T	n.a.
Teijin Polyester (Thailand)	5	5	J	J
Thai Teijin Textiles	5	5	T	J
Thai Toray Textile Mills	4	5	J	J
Toray Nylon Thai	4	5	J	T
Thai Yazakimahugana	2	2	J	J
Thai Karubo	3	4	J	J

Source: Chamber of Commerce, Bangkok.

Thailand have become the target of hostile, xenophobic outbreaks, which were particularly intense during Japanese Prime Minister Tanaka's visit in January 1974. Various analyses that followed these events brought to light accusations and complaints that essentially centered on two sets of issues. (1) Investments by Japanese firms dominate important sectors of the Thai economy, but it was thought that their contribution to the overall economic development of Thailand was less than expected; i.e., they were viewed as basically exploitive. (2) The large number of Japanese expatriate managers in Thailand are considered to exhibit an exaggerated sense of superiority that limits their interpersonal relationships with the locals. In addition, the Japanese managers' persistent demands for a high work discipline and for considering company interests more important than the employees' personal interests, the Japanese managers' lack of adjustment to the local way of life, and the perception that Japanese-controlled ventures made little effort to put Thais in managerial positions have all contributed to the general discontent with foreign investments in Thailand. As a result of these widely held views, and also because of the changes in the political realities in Southeast Asia, Thailand's receptiveness for foreign investments has declined since 1974, and the inflow of new Japanese investments has dropped significantly.

Singapore

Among the Association of Southeast Asian Nations (ASEAN), Singapore has been most successful in its industrialization process. Between 1965 and 1974, Singapore's GNP at factor cost grew at an average annual rate of more than 16 percent, with the manufacturing sector growing at an average annual rate of almost 22 percent. Foreign investments played a significant role in achieving this high rate of economic growth, with Japanese investments accounting for about 12 percent of Singapore's total foreign investments in the manufacturing sector (see Table 9-9).

Although Japan's investments in Singapore accounted for only 12 percent of the foreign investments, their growth rate in recent years has been spectacular. Whereas from 1965 to 1969 Japanese investments in Singapore grew at a modest annual rate of only about 5 percent, in 1970 they increased by 89 percent, in 1971 by 59 percent, in 1972 by 73 percent, in 1973 by 35 percent. In 1974 Sumitomo proposed the development of a large-scale petrochemical complex in Singapore; when it is completed, Japan will probably be the largest foreign investor in Singapore. The main determinants for Japan's rapidly increasing investments in Singapore are the strategic location of this city-state with respect to world shipping lines, relatively low wage rates, a disciplined workforce and few ownership and environmental restrictions.

During the 1970s Japan became Singapore's largest trading partner; during 1974 its exports to Singapore amounted to S$3670 million, but its imports from Singapore came to only S$1610. This large and persistent trade imbalance in Japan's favor has led many Japanese companies to invest in import-substituting ventures (manufacturing mainly consumer durables) to protect their market position there.

The Philippines

In 1971 Japanese investments in the Philippines accounted for only 1.1 percent of the foreign investments there (as compared with the U.S. share of 79.2 percent). The limited Japanese investments were in mining (iron and copper ore), forestry, the assembly of consumer durables (e.g., automobiles, refrigerators, air conditioning equipment), and in sales/service organizations in support of Japan's exports to the Philippines. Between 1971 and 1975 the foreign investments in the Philippines rose from a level of US$889 million to approximately $1193 million, with Japan accounting for about 20 percent of these new foreign investments. About one-third of the Japanese investments went into finance- and service-oriented segments of the Philippine economy, particularly

Table 9-9
Level of Foreign Investments in Singapore's Manufacturing Industry, 1974

	Millions of S$	Percent
Total foreign investments	3054	100
U.S.A.	1082	35.4
U.K.	424	13.9
Netherlands	420	13.8
Japan	354	11.6

Source: Economic Development Board of Singapore.

into banking and the acquisition of hotels for the accomodation of Japanese tourists. About 28 percent of the Japanese investments in the Philippines went into manufacturing operations, and the remaining 40 percent into resource-oriented ventures, mainly the establishment of an iron-ore sintering plant, the acquisition of agricultural land, and food processing. Table 9-10 summarizes the foreign investment situation in the Philippines and Japan's contribution to it.

Malaysia

Since the Investment Incentive Act of 1968, Malaysia has made a major effort to attract foreign investors. By the end of 1973 the total foreign investments in Malaysia amounted to $488 million. With investments of $48.7 million (10 percent of the total), Japan was Malaysia's fourth largest foreign investor behind Singapore (28.7 percent), the United States (18.8 percent), and the United Kingdom (18.7 percent). It is remarkable that more than two-thirds of Japan's investments in Malaysia are in manufacturing and processing, mainly the processing of timber and pulp, the processing of minerals, and the manufacture of electrical applicances. About 30 percent of Japan's investments in Malaysia can be characterized as resource-oriented, and the remaining 5 percent as finance- and service-oriented. Ninety percent of the Japanese operations in Malaysia are in the form of joint ventures; only 10 percent are wholly owned by Japanese interests.

North America

As of March 1975 Japan's foreign investments in Asia and in North America were of about equal magnitude. Japan's total foreign investments amounted to $12,666 million, $3122 million (or 25 percent) of which was invested in various Asian countries and $3011 million (or 24 percent) of which was invested in the

Table 9-10
Foreign Investments in the Philippines

	Total Foreign Investments, Dec. 1970 (US$)	New Foreign Investments, 1971-1975 (US$)	Japanese Investments, 1971-1975 (US$)	Japanese Investments, as % of Foreign Investments (1971-1975)
Agriculture	0.89	5.06	1.62	32
Mining	128.86	22.83	1.96	8
Manufacturing	512.78	114.96	33.07	28
Commerce and banking	95.09	148.03	18.80	12
Other	151.07	12.28	2.67	21
Total	888.69	303.16	58.12	19

United States and Canada. Table 9-11 shows, however, considerable differences in Japan's investment strategies in these two areas.

Almost two-thirds of Japan's investments in North America are in support of Japan's international trade (sales offices, service centers, hotels) and a rapidly growing banking network. Investments for the purpose of securing resources account for about 20 percent of Japan's investments in North America; manufacturing operations account for only about 15 percent. This shows that Japan's overseas manufacturing operations are largely in labor-intensive industries, industries for which Japanese enterprises prefer, naturally, low-wage countries such as Taiwan, Hong Kong, Thailand, and South Korea. The manufacturing operations of Japanese enterprises in North America essentially protect a market position that had previously been developed through exports, or gain rapid access to advanced technologies. A sizable proportion of Japan's investments in North America has been made only since 1971, and many of these investments can be characterized as "opportunistic" or in imitation of a Japanese competitor rather than reflecting a well planned strategy.

Some Evaluative Conclusions

Since the late 1960s the "internationalization of Japanese enterprises" became a national endeavor. With the typical commitment that characterizes many Japanese efforts, a great many Japanese business firms have begun to transform their operations from a basically national orientation with extensive export interests to an international orientation with a rapidly growing network of operating facilities abroad. The Japanese government actively supported this transformation; as a consequence, Japan's foreign investments, which amounted

Table 9-11

Composition of Japan's Foreign Investments in Asia and North America, March 1975

(In Percent)

	Asia	*North America*
Resource-oriented	33.66	19.40
Labor- and market-oriented	47.25	15.64
Trading, services, and finance	17.97	63.63
Branch operations	1.12	1.33
Total	100.00	100.00

to only about $1 billion in 1965, had reached a level of more than $12.6 billion by mid-1975. It is expected that Japan's foreign investments will continue to expand rapidly during the next ten years; in fact, according to some estimates, they will reach approximately $95 billion by 1985. As in recent years, the largest proportion of Japan's foreign investments will be resource-oriented, i.e., for the purpose of securing vital raw materials and energy resources for Japan's industry. By 1985 resource-oriented foreign investments may well account for about 45 percent of Japan's total foreign investments. The share of Japan's foreign manufacturing operations is likely to grow also, accounting for probably 35 percent of Japan's foreign investments in 1985. This means that the relative share of Japan's finance- and service-oriented foreign investments will shrink to about 20 percent (as compared with about 35 percent in 1975).

In recent years Japanese enterprises have been investing predominantly in the developing countries of Asia and Latin America. A major aim of their effort was to secure basic material resources and to develop off-shore production sites in countries where labor costs are relatively low and where pollution regulations are rather lenient. In fact, quite a few Japanese companies in pollution-intensive industries have started to erect new facilities in countries where antipollution regulations are not as stringent as they are in Japan.

Japan's share of manufacturing operations, in its total foreign investment situation, is considerably lower than that of other industrialized countries. In addition, a large proportion of foreign manufacturing investments are centered in light industries such as textiles, electrical appliances, and consumer durables. Moreover, to a large extent Japanese foreign manufacturing investments are made for the assembling of parts and accessories shipped from Japan that require relatively low initial investments abroad.

Regardless of their national origin, the management style of the large majority of multinational firms is "ethnocentric," i.e., strongly affected by and patterned after the sociocultural idiosyncrasies of the home country. This observation seems valid for a significant segment of the U.S.-based multinational firms, but it is much more apparent as far as Japanese firms are concerned. The Japanese manager abroad tends not to be a "manager-at-large"; rather, he is essentially an employee of the home office charged with "coordination" and a continuous responsibility of monitoring developments in and around the foreign subsidiary. Japanese expatriate managers seem to have particular difficulties in adjusting their management style to local preferences. In some cases this can be a virtue, although in most cases the drawbacks tend to outweigh the benefits of an ethnocentric management approach. In the aftermath of the hostilities that former Prime Minister Tanaka encountered during his visit to various Southeast Asian countries, the five major Japanese management federations proposed a set of guidelines for the management of Japanese foreign operations, such as: (1) promoting business activities based on mutual trust; (2) advancing the employment and promotion of local personnel to management positions; (3) transferring authority from the home office to the staff of the foreign operation; (4) cooperating with the host country's industries; and (5) adapting to the host country's social customs.[6] The actual implementation of these guidelines remains a challenge, but as Japanese multinational firms gain more experience in managing their foreign operations, they might well make a concerted effort to make them a reality.

Notes

1. Morishisa Emory, "The Japanese General Trading Company," in C. Fred Bergsten, ed., *Toward a New World Trade Policy: The Maidenhead Papers* (Lexington, Mass.: Lexington Books, D.C. Heath and Company, 1973), p. 131.

2. Toshiwo Doko, "Japanese Enterprise and International Citizenship," in E.C. Bursk and G.E. Bradley, eds., *The Management of International Corporate Citizenship* (Washington, D.C.: International Management and Development Institute, 1976), p. 51.

3. Japan Iron and Steel Federation, *Status and Future Prospects of Japanese Steel Industry's Overseas Joint Venture Activities*, Tokyo, September 1974.

4. J. Ballon, "Japan's Investment Overseas," *Aussenwirtschaft* nos. 3 and 4 (1973):148-149.

5. G. Clark, "An Analysis of Japanese Direct Investment Overseas in Postwar Years," *The Developing Economies* 9, 1 (March 1971):61.

6. "Localization Strategy of Japanese Multinational Enterprises," *MERI's Monthly Circular* (September 1974):7.

10 Doing Business with the People's Republic of China
Byron Miller

In 1972 I was involved in negotiating a contract between the Chinese govern-ment and the Boeing Company for the purchase of several aircraft by the Chinese. These negotiations were somewhat of a trailblazer, both for Boeing in terms of setting a precedent for other U.S. firms who would follow in doing business with China, and to a certain extent for the Chinese in that—to the best of my knowledge—these were the first negotiations between them and a major Western business firm.

Making Initial Contact

We at Boeing worked for well over a year in places such as Tokyo, Hong Kong, and Karachi in attempting to make direct contact with the Chinese. We finally wrote a letter to the National Machinery Import and Export Corporation, which resulted in an invitation to the Canton Trade Fair. This trade fair was held in April of 1972, some two months after President Nixon's visit. After about ten days of hectic preparations, we took off with a team of four for China. None of us had had any business contact with the Chinese whatsoever, so we elected to take as much material as possible for what we thought would be a fact-finding trip. We took some 900 pounds of data with us. We had nine movie films covering various aspects of all our aircraft—the 707, 727, 737, and 747. We also took slides (and our own slide projector, transformer, and movie projector because we did not know just what sort of facilities the Chinese would have available), and just about as much information in brochure form as we thought possible.

After our first arrival in Peking we were met by the senior officials of the National Machinery Import and Export Corporation, which does all the buying and selling of more or less technical items, running the gamut from aircraft, buses, and railway equipment to avionics and electronics.

A small, seemingly insignificant item reveals an interesting difference in the negotiating techniques of our two countries. Although we were introduced by name to our Chinese friends and presented them with our calling cards (printed in both English and Chinese), the Chinese themselves generally resisted identi-fying themselves. We were told to write only to the Machinery Corporation, and not to attempt to use personal names in any of our contacts with them.

Consequently, we were never successful in obtaining an organizational chart of either the Machinery Corporation or the airlines, Civil Aviation General Administration of China (CAGAC). In other words, it seemed to be the official rule for the Chinese to deal as a group rather than on an individual basis. In practice, however, we did notice a strong desire on their part to establish more personal relationships with us and to rely on building a rapport and trust based on the experience in these business negotiations. So, as we viewed it, we were still dealing with the mysterious and somewhat contradictory East.

Business and Ideology

On our first contacts with our Chinese counterparts, they were obviously sizing up how they could approach us. Of course they were at all times courteous and quite proper, and they never lost an opportunity to express the opinion that business dealings could be successfully concluded between Americans and Chinese and that the successful consummation of business would lead to improved relations between the governments of both of our countries. And while it was never discussed, we could not miss the careful omission of mention of the U.S. government in statements such as "we know that the American people are friends of the Chinese people." This was unmistakably in keeping with their belief that the peoples of the world would get along just fine if it were not for their oppressors, whoever they might be. We encountered this subtle propagandizing approach during most of our social occasions.

It was apparent in our first set of meetings that the main objective of the Chinese was just to get to know the Boeing Company better, to become more acquainted with its product line, and to learn more about the general technical details of its aircraft. It appears that they wanted to create, first of all, a friendly atmosphere for discussions and tried to establish themselves as individuals with whom we could work. Our discussions lasted about two weeks. We presented material and information to them and subsequently they requested proposals on our aircraft—all of our aircraft. This necessitated my return to Seattle to get firm price and delivery proposals on each aircraft. In the meantime, in Peking, our two engineering representatives continued detailed technical discussions on the aircraft's performance parameters and systems.

Problems with the U.S. Government

Our ability to make a firm proposal was somewhat hindered by the need for an export license to be issued by the U.S. government. Such a license requires information that the Chinese were not ready to divulge at that time. But what's more, they told us that they could not be involved in any contract subject to

U.S. government approval since the two governments did not recognize one another. During my absence from Peking, however, something very important happened. We had been informed that the Machinery Corporation was interested in purchasing the 707. At least we knew what we were selling—or rather, what the Chinese were considering buying. They did not, however, indicate to us how many aircraft they were interested in or whether they were to be cargo aircraft, passenger aircraft, or combination aircraft. As a result we entered into further technical discussions while at the same time trying to conduct some basic contractual negotiations. But we still had to cope with the problem of the export license and the number of aircraft they wanted. (Incidentally, the export license is required for any export sale a U.S. business makes to any country in the world.)

The Chinese evidently thought that this disclosure would detract from their bargaining position, and thus they were loath to furnish the information. Yet we could not get an export license without divulging that information to our government. We had already spent three and a half weeks going through the contract several times, and we had some idea that they were interested in both the 707 cargo and passenger aircraft. But still we had a lot of questions that had to be answered in the United States, both in Seattle and in Washington, D.C. The Chinese wanted changes in the aircraft they were interested in, but we did not know how to price these additional cost items because we did not know how many aircraft to base these changes on. Also we still did not know our own government's position regarding an export license, which also had to be based on the number of aircraft.

Breaking the Ice

At this point we took our hearts in our hands and announced that we had to leave early the next day. This announcement, fortunately, broke the ice. We were invited on another sightseeing trip to the Great Wall. The trip was actually a very carefully staged working session. During our drive to the Great Wall, I found myself wedged between the two Chinese negotiators in the back seat of one of the cars. Finally, the chief Chinese negotiator said, "Okay, if you need this information in order to get the export license from your government, we will tell you the number of aircraft we are interested in." And for the first time, some two and a half months after our initial contact, the Chinese announced that they wanted to buy ten aircraft, provided, of course, that the price was right. Upon our return to the United States we explained the discussions that we had to the Department of Commerce and the urgency connected with getting an export license issued as soon as possible. Such a license is usually given only after a contract has been signed, and our request required cutting a lot of red tape in Washington. However, after we explained the chicken-and-egg nature of this deal, and after the Department of Commerce had coordinated with various other departments—most significantly the Department of Defense and the National Security Council—we did finally obtain the necessary approval, which enabled us to return to Peking for what turned out to be our most extensive visit.

Finalizing the Contract

Within two weeks we were able to conclude the configuration definition of the aircraft successfully, and our engineers packed their bags and went home. This left the finalization of the contract, even though we had already covered the details at least three to four times and then gone over them again another five or six times. We repeatedly got into matters of such detail on all the articles of our purchase agreement. Unfortunately, I cannot go into all the specifics of the various articles because of a contractual confidentiality clause. However, I may be able to give you a general feeling for the atmosphere in which these negotiations took place.

I believe our experience could apply, to some extent, to almost any type of commodity and to any party, whether buyer or seller. As I have indicated, the Chinese negotiations were quite rigorous and tough and probably the most difficult and painstaking that I have ever been involved in. After some six weeks of discussions we really had not agreed on a single article in the contract. Instead we had discussed mainly what the Chinese call "matters of principle." It was only in the last three weeks that we were finally able to agree on actual terms and language. To emphasize the point, let me quote our counsel, who was involved in our negotiations for almost four months. After we returned to Seattle and he was sending us the final documents, he stated in a memo, "I want to say that it was an absolutely grand experience to participate in negotiating this contract on behalf of the Company. In fact, it was such a fine experience that I will do everything I can to insure that some other deserving person has an opportunity to replace me in any further negotiations with the Chinese. Unfortunately, I have discovered since my return that I will not be available for future negotiations since I will be taking a three-year, high priority assignment to the garnishment desk."

Administering the Contract

It is easy to laugh about these things afterward, but there certainly is a considerable amount of pressure when a contract involves $125 million. But I would say that a person who goes to China to negotiate mainly has to be able to be patient, keep cool, and stand by his principles. In sum, I would say that the contract as it finally read was very fair. There is a great deal of difference between the Western and Far Eastern approaches to business. The negotiations were probably as frustrating to the Chinese as they were to us at times. But these different concepts can be reconciled. All in all, the Chinese are very reasonable business partners.

It may be of interest that although the aircraft are being flown today by CAGAC, the contract was signed between the Boeing Company and the Machinery Corporation. The majority of our contacts and discussions were with the Machinery Corporation although at times the Machinery Corporation would ask the CAGAC people to join technical discussions.

The Chinese do not believe in lawyers, which they made abundantly clear on many occasions. Yet their chief negotiator was probably one of the best lawyers I have ever dealt with. And although they give this chief negotiator some other title, he has a tremendous knowledge of contract law and really strikes a hard bargain. The Chinese, especially procurement agencies such as the Machinery Corporation, take a great deal of pride in being able to negotiate a good contract. Many times it is more significant to them to win a point in a clause than to be concerned about the actual impact of that particular clause on the contract or a term in the contract, as if it were important to make the contract consistent with what they have done before. It is as if the procurement agency negotiators are being graded on the basis of what they are able to accomplish on particular articles of the contract rather than the larger picture of, say, overall benefits that might inure to the party.

At a very early stage the Chinese suggested that they wanted a very simple contract. They said it should be short and broad in its perspectives so that it would be reasonably vague, and so that things that might arise later could be handled through friendly negotiations. As we negotiated, we found that where detail was necessary to give them more protection, they were all in favor of complexity. As was indicated earlier, we reviewed the contractual language many, many times; the finalized contract consisted of 125 pages. We did believe, however, that the Chinese would put great store in Boeing's subsequent performance in this case. We thought that the contract would probably be put into a file and not looked at as long as the two parties got along well and the product was of good quality and was delivered per schedule. We expected the Chinese to be sticklers for conformity to the specifications because they are quite conscious of quality control. We added a substantial inspection document to our purchase agreement and found them to be rigorous in their inspection of the aircraft prior to final technical acceptance.

We encountered some delay in the final technical acceptance of the first few aircraft because of different attitudes about what we call aircraft cosmetics as compared to, say, structural integrity. We have always successfully worked out our differences without too much difficulty. Interestingly enough, we delivered the last seven aircraft with hardly an inspection by the Chinese. Once they had established their point and had indicated to what level they wanted us to perform, the Chinese achieved what they had wanted and smooth deliveries commenced thereon.

We had hoped that after consummation of the contract we would be able to establish more of a rapport with the CAGAC people and maybe get involved in some salesmanship, to get an indication of how they are doing in terms of their experience in flying the aircraft and so forth. We have had a very, very limited amount of contact with the airline itself, even though we had a service representative there for more than two and a half years. In fact, we pulled our service representative out of Peking and the Tokyo representative now covers that area. It is very difficult to establish contact and develop a rapport with the end user. All businesses are still faced with the middleman in the form of one of some thirteen corporations in various industries.

In sum, I would like to say that it is quite easy to strike up a fairly comfortable relationship immediately with a Chinese counterpart. The climb over the Great Wall is not all that difficult. As individuals, the people on the other side are not all that difficult to deal with or so different from ourselves. And recognition might be the most significant part of our Chinese sale—the one part that should have the greater impact on the future between U.S. businesses and the Chinese corporations.

11 Methods, Channels, and Financing of Purchases in the Pacific Basin

Harvey E. McCoy

The impressive growth in industrial activity in the Pacific Basin during the past decade—coupled with an abundant labor supply, low labor rates, and relatively high productivity ratios—has made it an attractive source area and market for a broad variety of industrial and consumer goods.

This chapter focuses on the design and development of purchasing channels in the Pacific Basin and provides an overview of some of the mechanics of international trade that would be employed in the financing and shipment of the goods to the United States. However, because of the diversity of cultural, political, and economic influences inherent in the Pacific Basin, this report of necessity must deal with fundamentals rather than with specific trade practices and governmental regulations, which vary within each market.

Traditional Distribution Channels

Traditionally, most Pacific Basin manufacturers have distributed goods through local trading companies to third parties such as importers and overseas traders, rather than selling them directly to the ultimate consumer. The reasons for this practice—which dates back to the earliest records of commerce in the area—are numerous and beyond this chapter's scope. To the extent that the trading companies influence the current situation, however, some comment is in order.

In some countries the use of these trading companies was simply a matter of political ideology: the belief that it was essential to the control of their economy and trade balances to require all exports to be channeled through state-operated or state-controlled trading firms. This requirement still exists today in several of the developing nations, and in the People's Republic of China, where all trade is handled by the State Trading Corporation. In other Pacific Basin states, due to language barriers, lack of knowledge of international trade practices and the demands of overseas markets, and financial limitations, many manufacturers came to rely on the trading companies' expertise and financial strength for the marketing of their products. Frequently, the relationship between the manufacturer and the trading company transcended the normal buyer-seller relationship, with the manufacturer relying on the trading company for guidance in product design and specification, for raw material procurement, for financing of work in process, and finally for handling all export procedures and shipment.

157

With the passage of time, the role of many manufacturers was reduced to little more than that of a subcontractor, responding to the demands of the trading companies who dominated the sales and distribution channels to overseas markets. Approximately 75 percent of all exports from the Pacific Basin during 1973 were handled by trading companies.

Changing Distribution Patterns

While it cannot be denied that the trading companies' activities contributed substantially to the industrial development and expansion of exports in the Pacific Basin, it is also recognized that this traditional method of distribution, from manufacturer to trading company, to importer, to overseas distributor or wholesaler, left much to be desired from both economic and operational standpoints. In addition to incurring the penalty of multilayered distribution costs, the manufacturer was deprived of direct market contact and had no sound basis for determining the acceptance of his products, his competitive position, or his market share. Moreover, with the demand for his products completely under the control of a trading company—which all too frequently also handled competing products—the manufacturer could not predict continuity of demand or develop long-term trade relationships. Also, with the emergence of more sophisticated consumer and industrial products, it became obvious that the trading firms and their intermediary channels were incapable of providing technical sales services or after-sale service and replacement part availability as required. Consequently, many larger manufacturers who have attained some degree of financial stability are no longer content to leave the marketing and distribution of their products to a trading company and third party and are actively seeking avenues to enter overseas markets more directly.

This trend toward more direct distribution, which is growing in free enterprise countries, presents a timely opportunity for U.S. companies that are interested in establishing direct purchasing arrangements in the Pacific Basin.

Organizing for Direct Purchasing

While many approaches might be taken to establish direct purchasing arrangements in the Pacific Basin, factors of anticipated volume and complexity and breadth of product line would dictate the most favorable approach.

The first, and simplest, approach is the retention of a commission agent who is already on the scene and has experience or familiarity with the industries and products of interest. For companies with limited volume and relatively simple product lines, this approach offers the most practical and economical contact with the market, and it avoids company involvement with foreign law and trade practices.

A second and possibly more favorable approach is to place a company employee in the area as a full-time representative. As one who is familiar with the company's needs and objectives, an experienced employee would be better able to communicate with the home office and give direction to company buying programs. Moreover, conflict of interest situations that frequently develop with a commission agent would be avoided with a full-time employee-representative. However, this approach would entail all the expense and formalities required to transfer the employee and his family to the overseas location, plus the need to provide him with some sort of office space and an indigenous employee to assist with language interpretation. Thus the third approach—the establishment of a branch buying office—would be the most productive.

In this third approach, the branch does not transact business for its own account but rather acts as a liaison between the suppliers and its home company. Its employees' activities would include source and product development, receipt and transmittal of samples and price quotations, processing and transmittal of purchase contracts on behalf of and in the name of the company, production follow-up, quality control, assignment of letters of credit, approval of shipping documents, and arranging for the services of freight forwarders and customs brokers to assure the timely and orderly shipment of the goods. In short, the branch office handles all the liaison functions connected with the purchasing activity—except the actual purchase transaction, which is consummated by a contract of purchase between the supplier and the home company.

The branch office is reimbursed by its home company for its expense and earns no income in the host country. Thus if it properly limits its activities to liaison functions and does not engage in commercial transactions, it will not be subject to taxation in most countries. In countries where taxes are imposed on branches engaged in purchasing liaison activity, they are minimal and usually based on some small percentage of the expenses the branch incurs.

Most Pacific Basin countries are eager to expand their exports and recognize the advantages of more direct trade relations with branch buying offices within their borders. In most cases they make rapid response to requests for visas for personnel and approvals for branch registration. Even though registration is not a requirement in all Pacific Basin countries, it is an important formality that should not be overlooked. It provides not only a legal basis for the induction funds, the hiring of personnel, and the acquisition of property in the name of the branch (office space, equipment, telephones, cars, etc.) but also status and recognition for the company and its employees. This status and recognition is a matter of particular significance in the development of business contacts and associations in the Pacific Basin.

Registering a branch buying office is relatively simple in most Pacific Basin countries. The usual requirements are: proof of corporate identity, appointment of a legal resident representative empowered to receive notice and act in behalf of the company, and the filing of an advance report detailing the branch's proposed activities. In countries having more stringent foreign-exchange control laws, a schedule of anticipated receipt and disbursement of funds is also required.

Of course, the cost of establishing and operating a branch buying office will vary with location and how much personnel is required to provide the desired services. Based on a comparison of landed costs with the prevailing wholesale prices on a broad variety of imported goods, it has been determined that an effective branch can easily be justified on the basis of the annual purchases of approximately $2 million at factory cost.

Developing Sources of Supply

For companies interested in establishing direct purchasing arrangements in the Pacific Basin, initial contact with potential suppliers are easily arranged. In addition to channels provided by U.S. embassies, consulates, and chambers of commerce, most countries maintain state-supported and state-controlled export promotion organizations that are eager to arrange introductions and factory visits. Typical of these are the Japanese External Trade Organization (JETRO), the Korean Overseas Trade Association (KOTRA), and the Taiwan Board of Trade. These organizations operate trade centers with exhibits of locally manufactured goods and are staffed with knowledgeable bilingual residents who are usually reliable sources of information on local manufacturers and trade practices. Through their overseas activities and exposure to foreign markets, they have acquired some understanding of the purchaser's needs and can be very helpful in screening potential suppliers.

In addition to the above, U.S. branch banks and service firms can provide advice and introductions. For example, in Japan there are currently over twenty-five U.S. banks, nine accounting firms, twenty-one industrial and management consultants, thirteen law firms, and numerous firms representing the insurance and transportation industries. All are closely affiliated with the U.S. Chamber of Commerce and are valuable sources for information and contact with the market.

The matter of proper source selection becomes increasingly important in establishing purchasing arrangements in foreign markets. Apart from the customary considerations of sound management, finanacial stability, adequate facilities, and a good "track record" in the local market, the following are some examples of additional factors that should be considered.

1. Does the manufacturer have an adequate quality control program capable of assuring that the product shipped will meet corporate standards? Tolerances in workmanship, appearance, performance, and fit vary with the definition of quality in many markets. Therefore what could be considered acceptable

quality by the source might not be acceptable in U.S. markets. Problems of quality, or what might be considered product defect by U.S. standards, can be difficult to resolve after the goods have been paid for and shipped approximately 9000 miles.

2. Does the supplier have the knowledge and capability for packaging the product for overseas shipment, and the facilities to assort and hold the goods to permit orderly and economical shipment? Many small- to medium-sized manufacturers are accustomed to shipping and receiving payment for their goods as they are produced, a practice that might not be compatible with the overseas purchaser's needs.

3. Is the product line subject to U.S. quota regulations or local government restraint? If so, is the supplier's stature with trade associations and governmental agencies strong enough to assure adequate quota availability and/or export licensing to permit the production and shipment of the required quantities on a continuing basis?

4. Does the product line fall under a category subject to U.S. product safety, packaging, or labeling regulations? If so, does the supplier have an understanding of these regulations and the capability for compliance? On products produced in the United States compliance is the manufacturer's responsibility, whereas the purchaser must accept this responsibility with imported goods.

The foregoing list mentions only a few of the problems that could be encountered in overseas purchasing programs: problems that will vary with product line and the locality of purchase but that can be avoided with proper planning and source selection.

The advantages of establishing direct purchasing relations with Pacific Basin manufacturers are obvious, and this approach to the market should receive priority in the selection of all sources of supply. It is only through direct contact that mutually beneficial relationships, capable of coping with economic cycles and the ever-changing needs of the marketplace, can be developed. This fact is substantiated by the increasing number of large U.S. chain stores and manufacturers who have opened branch buying offices in the area.

The International Contract

The single most important document in international trade is the purchase contract. Properly conceived and prepared, not only does it constitute a legal written agreement covering all aspects of the purchase, but it also provides the basis for the issuance of all subsequent documentation required for the financing and shipment of the goods. Because of the complexities of foreign trade terms and language interpretation, the contract must be drawn in precise language and must be amplified when necessary to assure complete understanding about product specification and the obligations of both seller and purchaser. The following are some examples of the more important clauses of a purchase contract and the detail in which they should be covered to assure a satisfactory transaction.

Description of the Goods. In addition to a complete written description of the product, specifications, patterns, and samples should be provided to establish standards of conformity. Also, the type of labeling, packaging, and case markings should be specified, and samples or drawings should be provided.

Quantity Purchased. The unit of measure should be clearly stated and defined when necessary. For example, generic terms such as dozen, gross, hundred-weight, or ton are not commonly used or understood in many countries, and misunderstandings can occur if they are not properly defined. Where possible, the quantity should be stated in the unit of measure of the country of export to avoid confusion. Also, since it is not always possible for the manufacturer to produce and ship the exact quantity purchased, a tolerance for the overshipment or undershipment of the contract quantity should be specified under this clause.

Pricing. It is important to state clearly the currency of the price in which payment will be made, and the unit of measure to which it applies. Pricing terms such as F.O.B., C.I.F., etc., should be amplified to specify the precise point of delivery to establish responsibility for the payment of export licenses, forwarder's fee, and local shipping charges.

Delivery. The transit time from many Pacific Basin ports to the United States can vary from two to as much as six weeks depending on the port of entry and the route. To assure arrival of goods by a desired date, the precise time and place of shipment, the carrier, and the port of discharge should be specified. Also, agreement about whether split shipments will be permitted should be included in this clause.

Insurance. While the responsibility for providing marine and war risk insurance is usually determined by the price terms F.O.B., C.I.F., etc., it is sound business practice also to specify this responsibility and the amount of coverage to be provided in the purchase contract.

Terms of Payment. This clause should specify in detail the method of payment and under what conditions payment will be made. Brief statements such as "net cash against documents" are inadequate and can lead to serious problems of faulty payment documentation. A more appropriate statement would read "by irrevocable letter of credit available by sight draft drawn on the XYZ Bank of

New York when accompanied by the following documents." The documents specified would normally include a clean bill of lading, commercial invoice, and customs invoice. This clause should also specify the number of copies of the documents that will be required and how they should be distributed.

Other Clauses. In addition to the preceding clauses, the contract should include certain contingency clauses that would provide for contract cancellation for nonperformance or undue delay in shipment, arbitration in the event of a dispute on product quality, and indemnification from patent or product liability suit.

The function of the purchase contract, aside from its legal aspects, is to clearly communicate the rights and obligations of the buyer and the seller. To the extent that this communication is accomplished by the various clauses in the contract, potential problems will be eliminated and more satisfactory business relations will become possible.

Financing Purchases in the Pacific Basin

The most common—and undoubtedly the most advantageous—method for financing purchases in the Pacific Basin area is by letter of credit issued by a U.S. bank. Most U.S. banks have branches or correspondent arrangements throughout the area and are familiar with prevailing trade practices and foreign currency exchange regulations.

Basically, a letter of credit represents a contractual agreement between the purchaser and his bank, whereby the bank issues a letter to the seller guaranteeing to make payment, on behalf of the purchaser, upon receipt of documents confirming that the terms of sale have been met and that the goods have been shipped.

In practice, the purchaser arranges for a line of credit with his bank, designates the beneficiary of the letter of credit, and stipulates the documents that the seller must provide as proof of compliance with the terms of the purchase contract. The usual documental requirements are the commercial invoice, the customs invoice, the certification of insurance, and the proper bills of lading. The bank then issues the letter of credit in accordance with the foregoing and sends it to its overseas branch or correspondent for transmittal to the seller. When the goods have been shipped, the seller presents a draft and the documents with the letter of credit to a bank in the country of export. If the bank is satisfied that the documents are complete and have been prepared in conformity to the letter of credit, it negotiates the draft and makes payment to the seller in the currency of the country at the current rate of exchange. Afterward, the bank remits the dollars received from the U.S. bank to its country's foreign exchange control. Copies of the draft and all documents are forwarded to the U.S. bank and to the purchaser in accordance with the instructions contained in the letter of credit.

This method of financing affords the purchaser the greatest degree of protection because payment will not be made until the correspondent bank has examined the documents and determined that all requirements of the letter of credit have been met. By the same token, letter of credit financing is the preferred method of payment for Pacific Basin manufacturers because it relieves them of all credit risk. In addition, in some countries an irrevocable letter of credit provides the basis for obtaining short-term financing at very favorable rates and also can be used as a hedge against currency exchange fluctuations.

Two variations to the standard letter of credit can facilitate a branch buying office's day-to-day operations. The first variation is the assignable letter of credit, which would name the branch as beneficiary with the right to assign portions of the credit to various suppliers as purchases are made. This obviates the bank's need to issue separate letters of credit to cover each individual purchase. The second variation is the revolving letter of credit, which can also be made assignable. It provides for a certain amount of credit to cover purchases made during a specific period, and the automatic reinstatement of the same amount of credit at the expiration of that period. This process can be continued for periods as long as one year, and it is especially helpful in financing products being purchased on a continuing basis.

While letters of credit can be issued in the currency of most Pacific Basin countries, the bulk of U.S. purchases made in the area are in U.S. dollars and are covered with a dollar letter of credit. The primary reason for this practice—aside from the desire to avoid payment of interest costs incurred in the conversion of foreign currencies to dollars—is to avoid the risk of exchange loss. During the past five years, drastic fluctuations have occurred in the exchange rates of many foreign currencies, which would have severely penalized U.S. purchasers if their contracts and letters of credit had not been drawn in dollars.

U.S. Customs Regulations

With the exception of articles designated as contraband, and products that fall under quota restriction, most foreign goods can be freely imported to the United States with proper documentation and payment of duties prescribed by the U.S. Customs Service.

When a shipment arrives, the purchaser or his agent is required to file with the customs officials a copy of the bill of lading signed by the carrier, and a certified copy of the customs invoice. The bill of lading, endorsed by the purchaser or his agent, provides proof of ownership of the goods. The customs invoice provides the customs collector with the information needed for assessing duty and compiling statistics on U.S. foreign trade.

The rates of duty on individual products are established by the U.S. Congress and are published in tariff schedules distributed to all ports of entry (copies are available from the U.S. Government Printing Office). There are two bases for the assessment of duties: specific duty rates that are assessed by quantity, weight, or measure, without regard to value; and *ad valorem* duties that are assessed as a certain percent of the product's dutiable value. On some products, a combination of these two rates represents the total assessment.

The dutiable value of the goods is not necessarily the price that the purchaser paid for them. It is primarily based on the foreign value or export value, which is defined as the price at which such or similar merchandise is freely offered for sale for home consumption to all purchasers in the country of export, including the cost required to place the merchandise in condition and packed ready for shipment to the United States.

The procedures involved in making customs entry and securing release of the goods for onward delivery in the United States is highly specialized and requires a thorough knowledge of customs law and regulations. Therefore most importers use the services of a licensed customs house broker who acts in their behalf in filing all required documents and all matters pertaining to customs clearance. Fees for this service are considerably less than they would be for an individual purchaser to maintain a staff to file documents and deal directly with the customs collector.

Before the purchaser is allowed to take delivery of his goods, he or his agent is required to file a bond with the customs department that obligates him to comply with all laws governing imports and the payment of the assessed duty. The customs house broker can arrange for these bonds, which are usually general term bonds based on the estimated value of expected imports for the following twelve-month period.

After the entry has been made and estimated duties have been paid, the customs officer issues a permit releasing the goods to the purchaser. The entry is still subject to appraisement, however, and if the appraiser should determine that the dutiable value of the goods is higher than the entered value, the importer will be assessed additional duty based on the appraised value. If the importer does not agree with the appraisal, he has the right of appeal to the U.S. Customs Court. After the matter has been adjudicated and final duties have been paid, the entry is considered to have been liquidated, and the customs files are closed.

Generally, U.S. customs procedures are simpler and U.S. duties are lower than in most Pacific Basin countries. Customs officials located in U.S. embassies and consulates all over the world are available to assist firms interested in importing goods to the United States.

Purchasing from the People's Republic of China

Purchasing from the People's Republic of China is not a private matter between the manufacturer and the purchaser; rather, it represents a transaction between the purchaser and the Chinese government. All exports are handled by specified state trading corporations, which have complete responsibility for all negotiations on specifications, pricing, deliveries, terms of payment, and selection of the manufacturer who will produce the goods. In most cases, the purchaser has no opportunity to meet with the manufacturer or visit the factory where the goods will be produced.

To purchase Chinese products, contact must be made by letter to the State Trading Corporation in Peking or its agency in Hong Kong. The letter should provide details of the purchaser's business and reasons for wanting to purchase Chinese goods, and it should indicate the products, quantities, and desired delivery date. If the Chinese are interested and have the goods available, the purchaser will be invited to attend the next Chinese Export Commodities Fair to consummate the purchase. These trade fairs are held in Kwangchow (Canton) in the spring and fall of each year. Usually three to five days of negotiations are required to finalize specifications, prices, and delivery schedules.

Prices will be quoted on a C.I.F. basis to ports called on by Chinese or Chinese chartered ships, or on a C.I.F. basis to Hong Kong, where the purchaser must arrange for onward shipment. The required method of payment is by sight draft drawn under a confirmed and irrevocable letter of credit established by a bank acceptable to the Bank of China. Letters of credit must reach the Chinese at least fifteen days before the month of shipment. They are required to contain clauses permitting a plus-or-minus 5-percent allowance of the credit and the quantity to be shipped.

Since China's export program is determined annually by the State Planning Commission and is based solely on the need to develop foreign exchange, great variations in product availability and pricing occur from year to year. In some cases, a previously available product will suddenly no longer be available, or the quantities available will be drastically curtailed. Obviously, these fluctuations pose real problems for purchasers who require continuity and cannot conduct their business on a spot-market basis. While this situation is expected to improve with the country's further economic development, at present the potential for establishing meaningful purchase arrangements with China are extremely limited.

12

The Development of Markets and Marketing in the Pacific Basin

Noel Capon

This chapter is for the practicing business executive who is considering international expansion of his operations, notably into Pacific Basin countries. It examines some critical basic data about Pacific Basin countries as target markets. These data about Pacific Basin countries are presented and organized to highlight product, price, distribution, and promotion decisions. And since companies venturing abroad are likely to consider more than one market entry, the results of studies attempting to group sets of countries into similar environmental clusters are presented.

Environmental Variables in the Pacific Basin

The data presented here are of a type that managers should have before they collect data on the particular products and markets with which they are concerned. From the data, the manager can form an impression of the nature of the Pacific Basin countries, which serve as potential markets.

Table 12-1 describes the Pacific Basin countries in terms of basic demographic data. Most striking is the large disparity in population, ranging from a massive 800 million in China to just over one-half million in Fiji. Fourteen of the thirty-two countries have populations of less than 10 million, thirteen are between 10 million and 100 million, while five—China, Indonesia, Japan, the United States, and the Soviet Union—have populations of over 100 million. The relative land areas also are extremely disparate: the Soviet Union has a land mass two times greater than Canada, China, and the United States, its nearest rivals in size. At the other end of the scale, the city-states of Singapore and Hong Kong are extremely small, Hong Kong being fifty times smaller than the next smallest country of over 1 million population, Costa Rica. Population figures have important implications for size of foreign markets, while the population density figures give some idea of how spread out those markets are. On this measure, Australia and Canada are extremely spread out, while Singapore and Hong Kong have exceptionally high population densities—roughly fifteen times the population of the next highest country, Japan. A better measure of market disparity would include data on urbanization, but population density provides a first approximation.

More extensive population data is presented in Table 12-2, where birth rates

Table 12-1
Basic Demographic Data for Pacific Basin Countries, 1972

	Population (Millions)	Land Area (Km)	Population Density (Number per Km²)
Australia	12.96	7,687.0	1.7
Cambodia	7.64	181.0	42.0
Canada	21.48	9,976.0	2.2
Chile	10.04	757.0	13.3
China	800.00	9,597.0	83.4
Colombia	22.50	113.9	198.0
Costa Rica	1.84	50.7	36.3
Ecuador	6.51	28.4	229.0
El Salvador	3.55	21.4	166.0
Fiji	0.54	18.3	29.5
Guatemala	5.41	109.0	49.6
Honduras	2.69	113.0	23.8
Hong Kong	4.08	10.0	4,080.0
Indonesia	121.63	1,491.0	81.5
Japan	106.96	372.0	288.0
Korea, North	14.70	120.0	123.0
Korea, South	22.04	98.0	225.0
Malaysia	10.43	528.0	19.8
Mexico	52.64	1,973.0	26.7
New Zealand	2.91	269.0	10.8
Nicaragua	1.99	130.0	15.3
Panama	1.52	75.6	24.0
Papua-New Guinea	2.18	461.0	4.7
Peru	14.46	1,285.0	11.3
Philippines	39.04	300.0	130.0
Singapore	2.15	0.6	4,667.0
Taiwan	15.29	36.0	471.0
Thailand	36.23	514.0	70.5
U.S.A	208.84	9,363.0	22.3
USSR	241.72	22,402.0	10.8
Vietnam, North	15.90	158.0	101.0
Vietnam, South	20.00	173.0	116.0

and overall infant mortality rates are presented in addition to the raw 1972 population figures. Birth rates range from less than 2 percent in Canada, Japan, the United States, and the Soviet Union, to 4 percent in sixteen of the thirty-two countries. In the overall mortality rate figures, Indonesia has the highest rate, which is almost four times greater than the smallest rates, in Hong

Kong and Singapore. Infant mortality rate figures also vary widely, with a factor of ten between the highest and lowest countries. Combinations of the birth, mortality, and population figures give the population growth statistics. These range from a low of 0.6 percent in the United States to a massive 3.8 percent in Costa Rica. Additional figures give life expectancies. The data in these two tables are extremely basic but nevertheless critically important for the aspiring international marketer, who needs to understand the basic determinants of the potential market, its population, and the shifts that are taking place there. Learning the age distribution, indicators of which are birth and death rates, can give an idea of the consumer needs that might exist. When all these data are combined with per capita income figures (see p. 172), the marketer can start to understand not only what consumer needs and wants might exist but also the probable ability of consumers in those countries to purchase goods and services to satisfy those needs.

Table 12-3 gives gross domestic product (GDP), population, and GDP per capita figures for countries with available data. The United States is clearly the wealthiest country on a GDP basis, four times larger than second-place Japan. Canada is the only other country with a GDP greater than $100 billion, and eighteen of the remaining twenty-three have GDPs of less than $10 billion. Thus in terms of potential markets, this broad view suggests that many U.S. firms may wish to exploit their home markets fully before venturing into the much smaller Pacific Basin markets.

Much of the difference in the GDP figures is, however, accounted for by the population differences. When the GDP figures are divided by population to form GDP per capita data, a few of the extreme differences between the United States and the other countries are somewhat diminished. Seven countries have GDP per capita greater than $1000, and four of these are greater than half of that of the United States, which leads with a figure in excess of $5500. Only Indonesia falls below $100; of the remainder, five are between $500 and $1000, and thirteen fall between $100 and $500.

Growth rates of GDP, population, and GDP per capita vary from country to country. Notably, the United States has the lowest GDP growth rate in the ten-year period, although of course it started from the highest base. The growth rates in GDP represent the economic progress made by the less-developed countries, although in absolute terms they represent a fraction of what the United States achieved. As previously indicated, marked variations in population increase have occurred, and high population increases have reduced the growth in per capita GDP, an effect that is most striking for the countries with higher population rate increases.

Economic Structure

Table 12-4 presents data that describe the economic structures of the Pacific Basin countries for 1963 and 1972. The economic activity is broken down into

Table 12-2
Basic Population Information for Pacific Basin Countries

	Population, 1972 (millions)	Birth Rate (% per annum)	Death Rate, Overall (% per annum)	Death Rate, Infant (% per annum)	Population Growth (% per annum)	Year Measured	Life Expectancy at Birth	Year Measured
Australia	12.96	2.1	0.85	1.7	1.9	1972	71	1960-62
Cambodia	5.72	4.5	1.60	12.7	2.9	1965-70	62	1970-75
Canada	21.48	1.6	0.74	1.7	1.6	1972	72	1963-67
Chile	8.83	3.0	0.94	7.8	2.0	1970	63	1969-70
China	800.00	3.3	1.50	3.4	1.8	1965-70	50	1965-70
Colombia	22.50	4.5	1.06	7.0	3.4	1965-70	45	1950-52
Costa Rica	1.84	4.5	0.76	5.7	3.8	1965-70	63	1962-64
Ecuador	6.51	4.5	1.10	7.9	3.4	1965-70	52	1961-63
El Salvador	3.55	4.1	0.86	5.3	3.2	1972	58	1965-70
Fiji	0.54	3.5	0.53	2.6	3.0	1965-70	68	1965-70
Guatemala	5.41	4.2	1.40	8.3	2.8	1971	49	1963-65
Honduras	2.69	4.9	1.70	3.9	3.2	1965-70	49	1965-70
Hong Kong	4.08	1.9	0.52	1.8	1.4	1972	70	1968
Indonesia	121.63	4.8	1.90	12.5	2.9	1965-70	47	1960
Japan	106.96	1.9	0.66	1.2	1.3	1971	71	1968
Korea, North	14.70	3.9	1.10	–	2.8	1965-70	57	1965-70
Korea, South	22.04	3.6	1.10	–	2.5	1965-70	62	1966
Malaysia	10.43	4.0	1.10	3.3	2.9	1965-70	60	1965-70
Mexico	52.64	4.3	0.89	6.1	3.4	1965-70	62	1965-70
New Guinea	2.18	4.2	1.80	–	2.4	1965-70	47	1965-70
New Zealand	2.91	2.2	0.85	1.7	1.5	1972	71	1960-68
Nicaragua	1.99	4.6	1.70	4.5	3.0	1965-70	49	1965-70
Panama	1.52	4.1	0.90	3.4	3.2	1965-70	59	1960-61

Papua-New Guinea	14.46	4.2	1.10	7.3	3.1	1965-70	59	1960-65
Philippines	39.04	4.5	1.20	6.2	3.3	1965-70	51	1966-69
Singapore	2.15	2.3	0.54	1.9	1.8	1965-70	68	1965-70
Taiwan	15.29	–	–	2.2	–	–	68	1960
Thailand	36.23	4.3	1.00	2.3	3.2	1965-70	56	1960
U.S.A.	208.89	1.6	0.90	1.9	0.6	1971	71	1971
USSR	241.72	1.8	0.90	2.4	1.0	1972	70	1968-69
Vietnam, North	15.9	3.8	1.60	4.3	2.1	1965-70	50	1965-70
Vietnam, South	20	3.8	1.60	4.3	2.1	1965-70	50	1965-70

Table 12-3
Basic Economic Indicators for Pacific Basin Countries

	Current Values, 1972			Real Rate of Growth per Annum, 1963-1972		
	GDP (1000 million US$)	Population (millions)	GDP/capita (US$)	GDP (%)	Population (%)	GDP/capita (%)
Australia	47	12.96	3626	5.02[a]	1.9	3.03
Cambodia	–	5.72	–	–	2.2	–
Canada	104.97	21.48	4887	5.58	1.6	3.89
Chile	8.07	8.83	914	4.57[a]	1.8	2.3
China	–	800[d]	–	–	1.8	–
Colombia	8.41	22.5	374	5.65	3.2	2.33
Costa Rica	1.16	1.84	630	4.89[a]	3.2	1.74
Ecuador	2.8	6.51	320	12.95[e]	3.4	9.24[e]
El Salvador	1.16	3.55	325	1.0	–	–
Fiji	247.3[f]	0.54	458[f]	7.11[a]	2.5	4.73
Guatemala	2.16	5.41	400	5.51	2.9	2.6
Honduras	0.81	2.69	301	4.84	3.1	1.66
Hong Kong	4.49	4.08	1102	11.2[c,e]	2	9.01[c,e]
Indonesia	10.94	121.63	90	4.91	2	1.95
Japan	294.4	106.96	2752	10.47	1.1	9.21
Korea, North	–	14.7	–	–	2.8	–
Korea, South	9.83	22.04	446	9.80	2.3	7.39
Malaysia	4.02	10.43	385	–	2.9	–
Mexico	41.09	52.64	781	7.60[b]	3.5	4.04
New Zealand	8.23	2.91	2828	8.7[e]	1.5	7.09
Nicaragua	0.99	1.99	495	5.86	3.1	2.14
Panama	1.31	1.52	863	7.62[a]	3.0	4.48
Papua-New Guinea	–	2.18	–	–	2.5	–
Peru	7.52	14.46	520	5.31	3.1	2.17
Philippines	8.48	39.04	217	4.71	3	1.37
Singapore	2.8	2.15	1302	12.09[e]	2	9.89[e]
Taiwan	5.69[g]	15.29	372	14[e]	2	11.17[e]
Thailand	7.7	36.23	213	7.39	3.1	4.61
U.S.A.	1159	208.84	5549	4.21	1.1	3.13
USSR	58[f,h]	241.72	240[f,h]	6.1	1.1	4.9
Vietnam, North	–	15.9	–	–	2.3	–
Vietnam, South	1127	20.0	–	–	2.5	–

[a]1963-1971 [f]Million local currency units
[b]1963-1970 [g]Net domestic product
[c]1966-1972 [h]Net National Product
[d]1974
[e]Not adjusted for inflation

eleven standard classifications, which enable us to identify the structure of the economy in 1972 and to identify structural shifts that have occurred in the ten years since 1963.

Highlights of the table include the vast disparities among countries in the percentage of the economy in the agricultural sector, from a low 3 percent for the United States to a high of 41 percent for Indonesia. Together with the structural changes, these disparities have striking and important implications for potential markets for U.S. companies. In the ten years since 1963, South Korea has shifted from over 42 percent in the agricultural sector to 28 percent, a drop of 14 percentage points. Indonesia has dropped from over 51 percent to 41 percent, while some of the more developed countries—in particular, Australia and Japan—have halved agriculture's importance. Increases may be observed in the extractive category (II) and the physical production categories (III, IV, and V) for some countries, although just as many countries show reductions in physical production sectors. Countries showing little or no increase in the physical production sectors typically show increases in the service industries (categories VI-IX), suggesting that even though physical production may be a relatively constant percentage of GDP, underlying structural changes at a finer level than this table shows may be taking place.

The changes that have occurred in this ten-year period are really quite striking, and they suggest that the Pacific Basin countries' requirements in terms of goods and services are changing at a substantial pace. The aspiring international marketer interested in the Pacific Basin must be abreast both of the size and the shifts of the sectors noted in Table 12-4 and in the underlying processes that give rise to these figures. By a detailed analysis of the underlying causes, potential opportunities may be isolated and explored.

Foreign Trade and Investment

Tables 12-5 and 12-6 offer data on the external trade relations of the Pacific Basin countries. Table 12-5 displays import and export figures for goods and services, and net direct investment figures. Almost all countries show increases in their foreign trade figures, although actual increases vary widely. Once again, the developed countries—the United States, Canada, and Japan—show the largest absolute increases, but not the highest percentage increases. The largest percentage increases are for Ecuador, Japan, South Korea, Singapore, and Taiwan, although most countries show over 100-percent increases in all categories over the six-year period. The Central American countries of Honduras, Nicaragua, and Panama, together with Peru, show the smallest increases.

Net direct investment figures also vary a great deal. Net investment decreased for Canada, Chile, Columbia, Honduras, and Nicaragua, while the absolute negative figures for Japan represent net positive foreign investment. Increases in investment are more common than decreases, although some of the large percentage increases are figured from a very low base. Such investment

Table 12-4

Percent Gross Domestic Product of Pacific Basin Countries, by Type of Economic Activity, 1963 and 1972

(In Current Prices)

	Year	I Agriculture, Forestry, Fishing	II Mining, Quarrying	III Manufacturing	IV Electricity, Gas, Water	V Construction	VI Wholesale, Retail Restaurant, Hotel	VII Transportation, Storage, Communication	VIII Finance, Insurance, Real Estate	IX Community, Social Personal Service	X Government	XI Import Duties
Australia[b]	1963	12.9	1.6	25.4	3.1	6.9	12.8	7.2	9.1	6.4	7.0	—
	1971	6.4	2.8	23.6	3.1	7.6	11.9	7.6	11.5	7.5	10.0	—
Canada	1963	6.0	3.5	23.2	2.4	4.9	11.0	7.8	10.0	6.7	11.5	12.3
	1972	3.7	3.1	20.4	2.5	5.5	10.7	7.6	10.0	8.2	14.6	13.2
Chile	1963	9.5	9.2	25.0	1.2	5.4	22.5	4.5	7.4	10.9	4.4	—
	1972	6.7	6.4	26.3	0.99	5.1	22.7	5.3	5.7	13.9	7.0	—
Colombia	1963	29.0	2.8	20.8	1.0	3.8	13.8	6.8	8.9	7.3	6.2	—
	1972	26.8	1.3	19.7	1.5	4.8	16.6	6.1	9.3	7.3	6.5	—
Costa Rica[b]	1963	25.3	← 17.5 →		1.3	5.3	16.6	3.8	11.4	9.6	9.2	—
	1971	21.9	← 19.3 →		1.8	5.2	16.7	4.2	9.8	9.4	11.6	—
Ecuador	1963	34.2	2.1	14.5	1.3	3.4	10.2	3.7	8.7	13.2	—	—
	1972	22.2	2.7	16.0	1.1	4.9	11.8	5.9	9.4	7.4	7.6	—
El Salvador	1963	10.3	—	17.2	8.9	4.9	4.9	27.1	19.2	5.9	1.5	—
	1972	4.2	—	22.6	5.9	4.8	3.8	29.1	13.5	11.2	4.8	—
Fiji[a]	1968	27.4	1.3	12.6	1.0	6.5	16.1	6.0	—	14.3	—	—
	1972	19.2	1.1	11.3	1.4	5.2	20.4	6.4	11.2	1.1	9.2	11.3
Guatemala	1963	30.1	0.1	13.4	0.9	1.6	27.0	4.8	10.5	5.8	4.9	—
	1972	27.9	0.1	15.8	1.3	1.7	28.0	5.9	8.7	5.6	4.6	—
Honduras	1963	40.6	1.6	9.9	0.6	3.8	11.2	5.6	9.1	6.5	3.1	—
	1972	33.3	1.9	12.5	1.4	4.5	11.1	5.6	9.5	7.5	3.2	—
Indonesia[a]	1968	51.4	4.7	8.5	0.4	2.1	16.8	2.6	2.4	6.0	5.0	—
	1972	40.9	8.4	9.2	0.4	3.5	20.1	4.1	3.2	4.2	5.8	—

	Year	1	2	3	4	5	6	7	8	9	10	11	12
Japan	1963	10.7	1.2	33.8	2.5	6.3	16.6	8.6		9.5	11.3	3.3	—
	1972	5.8	0.7	33.0	1.9	7.5	17.4	8.0		12.4	13.7	3.6	—
Korea, South	1963	42.4	1.7	15.1	1.0	3.0	12.9	4.1		6.2	6.2	5.8	1.4
	1972	28.2	0.9	23.3	1.8	4.6	17.3	5.7		4.4	6.8	5.1	1.5
Malaysia[a,b]	1968	32.3	5.5	11.4	2.6	4.0	15.0	4.7		6.7	11.4	6.4	—
	1971	30.5	5.8	13.9	2.5	4.1	13.9	4.2		6.5	11.3	7.0	—
Mexico	1963	14.9	5.0	19.6	1.2	4.1	33.7	3.2		8.7	4.8	5.3	—
	1972	10.7	4.6	23.5	1.9	4.6	31.9	3.4		← 14.3 →		6.1	—
Nicaragua	1963	24.0	1.5	17.9	1.3	2.8	21.7	5.5		9.9	9.1	6.2	—
	1972	26.2	0.4	19.0	1.9	3.0	20.0	5.1		7.8	10.2	6.2	—
Panama	1963	20.8	0.3	14.5	2.0	5.8	9.6	4.8		9.3	22.5	2.7	—
	1972	16.5	2.6	15.2	3.3	6.8	7.5	6.7		10.3	20.0	2.6	—
Papua-New Guinea[a,b]	1965	40.4	0.4	← 4.3 →		15.4	6.2	5.4		4.2	14.1	7.2	2.7
	1971	34.0	2.9	6.3	0.7	14.7	6.7	6.2		4.3	10.4	10.8	
Peru[a]	1968	18.3	9.0	20.0	1.2	4.7	↓		38.6	↑	↑	8.1	—
	1972	15.9	7.7	21.2	1.3	6.5	↓		39.3	↑	↑	8.0	—
Philippines	1963	28.3	1.0	16.4	0.5	3.1	9.5	3.0		7.6	9.1	6.5	7.7
	1972	30.2	1.8	15.4	0.4	2.4	7.6	2.7		7.4	7.5	5.8	8.2
Singapore	1963	5.2	0.2	10.2	1.9	3.4	30.5	↓		37.1	↑	6.7	—
	1972	2.8	0.2	23.1	2.2	7.1	24.9	↓		28.6	↑	6.0	—
Thailand	1963	37.3	1.1	14.2	0.5	5.2	18.8	6.9		4.9	6.3	4.5	—
	1972	28.0	1.3	18.1	1.9	5.1	21.4	6.7		6.2	6.5	4.4	—
U.S.A.	1963	3.6	2.2	28.0	2.5	4.4	16.9	6.4		15.4	5.1	12.6	0.2
	1972	3.0	1.6	25.2	2.4	4.9	17.3	6.4		16.8	5.4	14.1	0.3
South Vietnam	1963	28.4	0.3	7.8	0.9	1.3	11.9	3.9		7.3	4.1	17.3	11.8
	1972	39.5	0.2	5.7	0.9	1.1	17.6	4.0		4.9	2.2	18.9	14.6

Source: United Nations Statistical Office.

[a]1963 figures unavailable

[b]1972 figures unavailable

Table 12-5
Foreign Trade and Investment of Pacific Basin Countries, 1968 and 1974
(In Millions of US$ at Current Prices)

	Exports of Goods	Imports of Goods	Exports of Services	Imports of Services	Net Direct Investment
Australia					
1968	3,462	3,692	866	1,903	612
1974	10,663	10,536	2,505	4,660	979
% change	208	185	189	145	59
Canada					
1968	13,143	11,708	2,373	4,079	338
1974	33,220	32,173	5,888	9,469	216
% change	152	174	148	132	(36)
Chile					
1968	908	726	127	490	142
1974	2,046	2,239	156	350	12
% change	125	208	22	(29)	(92)
Colombia					
1968	605	615	182	367	48
1974	1,655	1,342	403	801	28
% change	173	118	121	118	(42)
Costa Rica					
1968	170	193.7	37.9	65.7	4.5
1974	440.8	626.4	91.8	164.5	42.9
% change	159	223	142	150	853
Ecuador					
1968	210.7	212.7	15.2	92.9	29.2
1974	1,187.4	813.8	76.9	441.6	77.0
% change	463	283	406	375	164
El Salvador					
1968	211.7	198.2	25.5	62.5	8.2
1974	471.4	502.6	52.9	165.9	9.6
% change	123	153	107	165	17
Guatemala					
1968	223.5	237.6	35.8	93.1	22.8
1974	588.0	611.8	144.2	244.9	52.3
% change	152	157	303	163	132
Honduras					
1968	181.0	169.4	17.8	60.3	14.4
1974	276.6	377.6	34.9	77.0	(1.2)
% change	52	123	96	27	(108)
Indonesia					
1968	872	831	9	301	(2)
1973[a]	2,954	2,663	91	1,175	278
% change	238	220	911	290	14,000
Japan					
1968	12,751	10,222	2,607	3,913	(144)
1974	54,503	53,025	12,029	17,871	(1811)
% change	327	419	361	357	(1,157)
Korea, South					
1968	486	1,322	394	223	1
1974	4,534	6,239	851	1,218	225
% change	832	372	116	446	22,500

Table 12-5 (cont.)

	Exports of Goods	Imports of Goods	Exports of Services	Imports of Services	Net Direct Investment
Malaysia					
1968	1,331	1,121	186	318	30
1973[a]	2,946	2,300	297	777	171
% change	121	105	60	144	470
Mexico					
1968	1,258	1,892	1,228	1,350	227
1974	3,355	5,779	2,898	3,485	557
%change	167	205	136	158	145
Nicaragua					
1968	161.0	165.2	33.8	75.7	16.4
1973[a]	278.1	327.0	104.3	149.9	13.2
% change	72	98	208	98	(19)
New Zealand					
1968	1,018.0	738.0	115.0	316.0	(5)
1974	2,388.5	2,875.6	479.8	1,186.5	164.3
% change	134	289	317	275	3,386
Panama					
1968	117.5	246.1	210.7	97.3	12.6
1973[a]	159.7	456.3	396.1	225.5	12.0
% change	36	85	87	132	(4)
Peru					
1968	850	673	153	389	(20)
1974	1,572	1,999	303	934	91
% change	85	197	98	89	555
Philippines					
1968	860	1,150	290	401	(3)
1974	2,694	3,144	835	866	35
% change	213	173	188	116	1,267
Singapore					
1968	1,173	1,555	426	164	26
1974	5,496	7,841	2,195	1,019	651
% change	368	404	415	521	2,404
Taiwan					
1968	816	889	216	275	27
1974	5,596	6,422	897	1,203	83
% change	586	622	315	337	207
Thailand					
1968	636	1,035	445	260	60
1974	2,476	2,842	800	717	138
% change	289	175	80	176	130
U.S.A.					
1968	33,626	32,991	18,801	15,769	4,577
1974	98,248	103,774	46,128	36,806	5,043
% change	192	320	145	133	10

Source: United Nations Statistical Office and International Financial Statistics.

[a]1974 data not available

Table 12-6
Export Data for Major Trading Partners of Pacific Basin Countries
(In Percent)

Australia 1973/74	Japan 32.5	U.S.A. 13.1	EEC (except U.K.) 9.4	U.K. 7.2	New Zealand 6.7	
Cambodia 1970	Japan 27.7	France 20.7	Hong Kong 6.5	U.K. 6.5		
Canada 1973	U.S.A. 67.4	Japan 7.1	U.K. 6.3	EEC 6.1		
Colombia 1972	U.S.A. & Canada 36.3	EEC (except U.K.) 24.6	W. Europe (except EEC) 14.9	Latin America 14.9	Soviet Block 2.4	U.K. 2.3
Costa Rica 1974	U.S.A. 28	CACM^a 24	Europe (except W. Germany & Netherlands) 18	W. Germany 13	Netherlands 6	Panama 4
Ecuador 1972	U.S.A. & Canada 37.8	Latin America 19.3	EEC 19.0	Other W. Europe 6	Soviet Bloc 4.0	Other Western Europe 2.0
El Salvador 1973	U.S.A. 33	CACM 31	West Germany 13	Japan 16		
Guatemala 1974	U.S.A. 31	CACM (except El Salvador) 18	El Salvador 13	West Germany 9	Japan 6	
Honduras 1973	U.S.A. 54	W. Germany 12	CACM 4	Japan 3		
Indonesia 1972	Hong Kong 8.2	USSR 3.7	Belgium 1.6	Malaysia 1.0		
Japan 1973	U.S.A. 25.6	S. Korea 4.8	Taiwan 4.4	Liberia 4.3	U.K. 3.7	W. Germany 3.4
	Hong Kong 3.0	China 2.8	Canada 2.7	Singapore 2.5	Indonesia 2.4	Thailand 1.9

Country (year)						
Korea, North 1973	Japan 44.2	France 11.7	Germany 10.4	Rumania 8.0	Belgium 5.9	Other EEC 5.2
Korea, South 1973	Japan 38.5	U.S.A. 31.6	Canada 3.9	W. Germany 3.7	Hong Kong 3.7	U.K. 2.3
Malaysia 1972	Singapore 20.2	U.S.A. 15.6	Japan 10.4	U.K. 7.4		
New Zealand 1972	U.K. 34	U.S.A. 17	Japan 9	Australia 9	France 3	W. Germany 3
Nicaragua 1974	W. Germany 27	CACM 24	U.S.A. 19	Japan 9		
Panama 1974	U.S.A. 42	W. Germany 15	Italy 12	Netherlands 7	CACM 6	
Papua-New Guinea 1972	Australia 41.8	Japan 16.8	W. Germany 13.8	U.K. 10.4	U.S.A. 8.4	
Peru 1973	U.S.A. 34.9	Japan 17.0	W. Germany 7.6	Belgium/Luxembourg 3.9	U.K. 2.9	Italy 2.7
	E. Germany 2.4	France 2.1	Netherlands 1.9	Argentina 1.6		
Philippines 1973	U.S.A. 38.1	Japan 36.3	Netherlands 4.1	W. Germany 3.4		
Singapore 1973	Japan 8	W. Germany 6	U.K. 6	Hong Kong 5	U.S.A. 2.1	Malaysia 1.8
Taiwan 1973	U.S.A. 39.1	Japan 18.4	Hong Kong 7.0	W. Germany 4.7	Canada 4.2	Malaysia & Singapore 3.4
Thailand 1973	Japan 26	Malaysia & Singapore 14	Netherlands 9	Hong Kong 8	U.K. 5	W. Germany 2
U.S.A. 1973	Canada 21	Japan 12	U.K. 5	W. Germany 5	Mexico 4	Italy 3
Vietnam, South 1973	Hong Kong 33	Japan 25	France 14	U.S.A. 1		

Source: United Nations Statistical Office and International Monetary Fund.

[a]Central American Common Market

increases probably reflect the perceived political stability of these countries since apart from Canada, the countries showing decreases are politically unstable.

Table 12-6 presents available data on the major trading partners of Pacific Basin countries. While import figures are more important to aspiring U.S. exporters, nevertheless these export data also indicate the nature of the intercountry relationships.

Financial Stability

Of particular interest to businessmen contemplating investment in the Pacific Basin is the stability of local currency units. Data presented in Table 12-7 indicate wide discrepancies among countries for the period 1968-1974. Thus the sharpest depreciation against the U.S. dollar is for Chile, while other large depreciations are found for the Philippines, Colombia, South Korea, Ecuador, and Indonesia. Interestingly, eight countries have appreciated against the U.S. dollar, and eight have depreciated in the six-year period. Australia, Malaysia, Singapore, New Zealand, and Japan have had the strongest currencies, while a number of others have shown little or no change.

Physical Distribution Variables

In the previous section the data presented focused largely on issues of market size and the product and price dimensions of the marketing mix. In this section the data concern physical distribution.

Transportation

Table 12-8 shows data on transportation modes, specifically automobiles, commercial vehicles, and railways. The absolute figures in the first four columns are translated into per capita figures in the subsequent columns. Automobile use varies markedly from highs of over 300 per thousand population in the United States, New Zealand, Canada, and Australia to less than 10 per thousand population in ten of the countries. The ability to transport goods and services is more directly addressed in the next column, where commercial vehicles on a per capita basis can be seen to vary from over 60 per thousand population in the United States, New Zealand, Japan, Canada, and Australia to less than 5 per thousand in six of the countries. Another seven countries have between 5 and 10 commercial vehicles in use per thousand population. These low figures indicate the paucity of the transportation infrastructure.

Table 12-7
Stability of Local Pacific Basin Currency Against the U.S. Dollar, 1968-1974

	Local Currency Units per $U.S.		Appreciation in Currency Value Relative to $U.S. (Percent)[a]
	1968	1974	
Australia	0.893	0.693	28.7
Canada	1.081	0.978	10.6
Chile	6.9	741.6	(99.1)[b]
Colombia	16.038	26.321	(39.1)
Costa Rica	6.625	7.93	(16.4)
Ecuador	18.0	25.0	(28.0)
El Salvador	2.5	2.5	–
Guatemala	1.0	1.0	–
Honduras	2.0	2.0	–
Indonesia	300.08	415.0	(27.7)
Japan	360.0	291.51	23.5
Korea, South	276.33	405.92	(31.9)
Malaysia	3.061	2.407	27.2
Mexico	12.5	12.5	–
New Zealand	0.893	0.714	25.1
Nicaragua	7.00	7.013	(0.2)
Panama	1.0	1.0	–
Peru	38.7	38.7	–
Philippines	3.9	6.796	(42.6)
Singapore	3.061	2.437	25.6
Taiwan	40.0	38.0	5.3
Thailand	20.8	20.375	2.1

Source: *Wall Street Journal* (various issues)

[a] $\left(\dfrac{1968}{1974}\right) - 1 \quad \times \quad 100$

[b] Figures in parentheses are *depreciations* rather than appreciations.

Data for railways are given in the next two columns, first passenger data and then goods data. The United States, Canada, Australia, and the Soviet Union have high use figures for goods traffic. The figures also show the poor development of the railway network in Thailand, the Philippines, Nicaragua, Indonesia, Hong Kong, Costa Rica, and Cambodia. The final column combines the railway goods per capita with the land area to provide a better indication of the density of railway networks. According to this measure, Hong Kong is the most developed, while Thailand, the Philippines, and Indonesia appear to be the least developed.

Table 12-8
Transportation Modes of Pacific Basin Countries, 1972

	Population (Millions)	I Automobiles in Use (Millions)	II Commercial Vehicles in Use (Millions)	III Railways (Millions of Passenger km)	IV Railways (Millions of Net Ton km)	Col I per Capita (Thousands)	Col II per Capita (Thousands)	Col III per Capita	Col IV per Capita	Col IV per km²
Australia	12.96	4,274	1,024	—	25,603	0.330	0.079	—	1,980	0.26
Cambodia	5.72	27	11	56	10	0.005	0.002	9.8	1.8	—
Canada	21.48	7,401	2,059	3,288	180,535	0.345	0.096	153	8,405	0.84
Chile	8.83	194	152	2,481	2,718	0.022	0.017	281	308	0.41
China	800	—	—	—	301,000	—	—	—	377	0.04
Colombia	22.5	268	87	398	1,198	0.012	0.004	18	53	0.47
Costa Rica	1.84	48	30	57	13	0.026	0.016	31	7.1	0.14
Ecuador	6.5	30	44	62	55	—	—	9.5	8.4	0.30
El Salvador	3.55	38	22	—	—	0.011	0.006	—	—	—
Fiji	0.54	16	6	—	—	0.030	0.011	—	—	—
Guatemala	5.41	43	36	—	106	0.008	0.007	—	20	0.18
Honduras	2.96	14	17	—	—	0.005	0.006	—	—	—
Hong Kong	4.08	125	38	236	41	0.031	0.009	58	10	10
Indonesia	121.63	277	158	3,302	1,042	0.002	0.001	27	8.6	0.0006
Japan	106.96	12,532	9,598	297,888	59,872	0.117	0.090	2,785	560	1.94
Korea, South	22.04	70	72	10,062	7,241	0.003	0.003	457	329	3.36
Malaysia	10.63	29	10	755	179	0.003	0.010	72	17	0.32
Mexico	52.64	1,520	629	4,485	23,878	0.029	0.012	85	454	0.23

New Zealand	2.91	991	201	528	2,733	0.341	0.069	181	939	3.49
Nicaragua	1.99	33	–	35	13	0.017	–	18	6.5	0.05
Panama	1.52	50	16	–	–	0.033	0.011	–	–	–
Papua-New Guinea	2.18	20	17	–	–	0.009	0.008	–	–	–
Peru	14.46	230	118	248	610	0.016	0.008	17	42	0.33
Philippines	39.04	294	191	665	40	0.008	0.005	17	1.0	0.003
Singapore	2.15	177	45	–	–	0.082	0.021	–	–	–
Thailand	36.23	253	141	66	7	0.007	0.005	1.8	0.2	0.004
U.S.A.	208.84	96,420	20,455	13,454	1,135,643	0.462	0.098	64	13,216	1.41
USSR	241.72	–	–	285,792	2,760,823	–	–	1,182	11,421	0.51
Vietnam, South	20.0	58	74	66	7	0.003	0.004	3.3	0.4	0.002

Source: United Nations Statistical Office.

Communications

Tables 12-9 and 12-10 are germane to the question of communication in the Pacific Basin countries. Table 12-9 provides data on the degree of personal communication by telephone, telegram, and mail. The final column, telephones per capita, is a good measure of the communication infrastructure. Once again, the United States, New Zealand, Japan, Canada, and Australia rate exceptionally high, while six of the countries—South Vietnam, Thailand, Nicaragua, Indonesia, Honduras, and Cambodia—have less than one telephone per thousand population.

Of more importance to promotion is the data in Table 12-10, which indicate the numbers of televisions in use and weekday newspaper circulation.

Foreign Supranational Organizations in the Pacific Basin

The extent to which countries in the Pacific Basin are involved in multicountry organizations that affect trade and investment varies greatly with location. None of the eastern countries in the Pacific Basin is a member of such a grouping. Former British possessions maintain some commonwealth preferential ties with the United Kingdom, but as yet the ASEAN organization has no inclination toward developing a trade group.

By contrast, the nations of the Americas belong to a variety of trading organizations, as noted in Table 12-11. The Central America Pacific Basin countries of Costa Rica, El Salvador, Guatemala, Honduras, and Nicaragua belong to the Central American Common Market (CACM). The organization is in fact misnamed; while it has developed a system of internal free trade and a common external tariff, there is little movement toward free transfer of labor and capital, the mark of a common market.

The largest of the organizations, the Latin American Free Trade Association (LAFTA) spans the Americas from north to south. The Pacific Basin countries of Mexico, Peru, Chile, Colombia, and Ecuador are joined by Argentina, Brazil, Paruguay, and Uruguay in an organization whose long-term aims are to achieve complimentarity and integration of their national economies. However, little progress has been made toward that end, although internal free trade is now scheduled to be achieved by 1980. LAFTA has been relatively unsuccessful in moving toward its goals for a variety of reasons, not the least of which is its members' disparate size and economic power.

As a result of the disparity in economic power, the smaller members of LAFTA—Chile, Colombia, Ecuador, and Peru—have joined Bolivia and Venezuela in the formation of the Andean Common Market (ANCOM). ANCOM is moving much faster than LAFTA in the direction of removing internal tariffs and developing a common external tariff. In addition, there is a sectoral program

Table 12-9
Personal Communications by Telephone, Telegram, and Mail in the Pacific Basin Countries, 1972

	Population (Millions)	Telephones Installed (Thousands)	Telegrams Sent (Thousands)	Mail Sent (Thousands of Pieces)	Telephones Installed per Capita
Australia	12.96	4,400	20,081	2,622,000	0.340
Cambodia	5.72	9	—	2,371	0.001
Canada	21.48	10,979	6,536	4,658,000	0.50
Chile	8.83	415	7,604	—	0.041
Colombia	22.50	1,010	17,801	—	0.045
Costa Rica	1.84	78	—	—	0.041
Ecuador	6.51	120	1,554	—	0.018
El Salvador	3.55	43	1,372	28,313	0.012
Fiji	0.54	22	—	14,732	0.040
Guatemala	5.41	54	—	54,167	0.010
Honduras	2.69	16	—	—	0.006
Hong Kong	4.08	795	—	193,800	0.19
Indonesia	121.63	240	3,281	177,542	0.002
Japan	106.96	34,021	58,868	12,381,000	0.315
Korea, South	22.04	755	13,867	610,000	0.023
Malaysia	10.43	211	1,483	267,511	0.019
Mexico	52.64	1,955	53,479	1,243,000	0.038
New Zealand	2.91	1,358	6,028	629,544	0.458
Nicaragua	1.99	19	—	—	0.009
Panama	1.52	100	—	—	0.066
Peru	14.46	269	4,354	—	0.02
Philippines	39.04	391	—	—	0.01
Singapore	2.15	218	1,061	129,779	0.101
Thailand	36.23	235	4,536	131,963	0.006
U.S.A.	208.89	131,108	36,240	86,690,000	0.628
USSR	241.72	13,198	386,532	8,532,000	0.053
Vietnam, South	20.00	43	1,254	76,879	0.002

Source: United Nations Statistical Office

Table 12-10
Mass Communications in the Pacific Basin Countries, 1973/74

		Televisions, March 1973			Weekday Newspapers, Sept. 1974		
	No. of Stations	No. of Black-and-White Sets in Use (Millions)	No. of Color Sets in Use (Millions)	Total	No. of Papers with Daily Circulation over 1000	Total Circulation (Millions)	Total Circulation per Capita (Thousands)
Australia	131	2,950	–	2,950	42	5,101	409
Cambodia	2	30	–	30	n.a.	n.a.	–
Canada	450	6,380	2,680	9,060	115[a]	5052[a]	235
Chile	31	1,000	–	1,000	17	736	73
China	30	300	–	300	32	n.a.	–
Colombia	18	1,200	–	1,200	26	1,194	53
Costa Rica	4	150	0.4	1,504	5	159	87
Ecuador	12	250	–	250	6	241	37
El Salvador	4	108	1.3	109.3	6	273	77
Guatemala	3	105	4.5	109.5	4	84	16
Honduras	5	45	–	45	3	96	36
Hong Kong	4	679	–	679	34	1,967	482
Indonesia	11	150	–	150	35	1,782	15
Japan	204	14,000	133,372	273,272	122	65,213	610
Korea, North	–	–	–	–	1	300	20
Korea, South	11	910	–	910	24	3,387	154
Malaysia	21	296	–	296	24	917	88
Mexico	80	3,700	300	4,000	86	3,668	70
New Zealand	24	717	–	717	21	937	322
Nicaragua	2	60	–	60	2	50	25

Panama	11	183	5	188	6	130	86
Peru	18	450	–	450	13	897	62
Philippines	17	420	30	450	9	677	17
Singapore	2	169	–	169	8	502	233
Taiwan	5	2,000	100	2,100	18	1,661	109
Thailand	5	225	–	225	16	957	28
U.S.A.	927	64,700	46,600	111,300	1,768[a,b]	61,887[a,b]	296
USSR	167	40,000	–	40,000	n.a.	n.a.	–
Vietnam, North	n.a.	n.a.	n.a.	n.a.	4	176	11
Vietnam, South	1	500	–	500	14	201	10

Source: United Nations Statistical Office

[a]Figures are total weekday papers and total circulation. Canadian figures for papers greater than 1000 circulation are 70 and 4375.

[b]English language newspapers only.

Table 12-11
Supranational Organizations in the Pacific Basin

Central American Common Market (CACM)	Latin American Free Trade Area (LAFTA)	Andean Common Market (ANCOM)
Costa Rica	Argentina	Bolivia
El Salvador	Brazil	Chile
Guatemala	Chile	Colombia
Honduras	Colombia	Ecuador
Nicaragua	Ecuador	Peru
	Mexico	Venezuela
	Paraguay	
	Peru	
	Uruguay	

of industrial development whereby product groupings are assigned to individual countries for production, not on a monopoly basis, but instead through head-start privileges. The ANCOM countries have developed stringent rules that tend to discourage foreign investment. In general, the rules aim to make foreign investors minority shareholders in their enterprises. In addition, there are strict rules on profit repatriation.

To the international marketer, the structure and direction of these supranational organizations can be a critical factor in planning. Pacific Basin countries are involved in all three American groupings, all of which have differing goals, are progressing at different rates, and have differing likelihoods of success.

Groupings of Nations

The development of multinational corporations has highlighted the movement toward treating the whole world as the potential market and then selecting some aggregation of individual countries as the target market. Individual countries are thus treated as specific market segments within the target market area. The concept of treating the whole world as a potential market is of great importance, for the firm either develops a series of strategies for countries individually, or it develops a grand strategy into which individual country strategies fit.

Countries can be grouped for the development of the target market groupings on many bases. The most obvious basis is geographical: countries are chosen as potential markets on the basis of their geographical relationships. The basis of this method is efficiencies in the cost of freight and personal travel; economic and cultural similarities are a secondary consideration. Thus the Pacific Basin countries are chosen as a group from all countries in the world. On a finer basis, the countries are grouped as Eastern, Western, Oceania, and the Americas.

The weakness of such a grouping system is that the Pacific Basin countries that are geographically close may have little relationship to one another otherwise. In fact, the choice of the Pacific Ocean as the organizing unit may exclude other countries, such as those in the Indian Ocean, which are more similar to some groups of the Pacific Basin countries than some Pacific Basin countries are to each other.

A second basis for grouping countries is GNP per capita. This dimension enables countries to be grouped on a crude measure of individual income; therefore it is related to the nationals' ability to pay for products or services. When combined with population, this figure gives a measure of market size. When nations of the world are identified on a GNP per capita basis, the Pacific Basin states are spread among the five arbitrarily chosen groupings shown in Table 12-12.

Liander et al. performed a study that grouped countries on variables other than simple GNP per capita data.[1] They grouped eighty-six countries by a variety of multivariate analytic techniques on twelve environmental and societal attributes, the most complex of which was a cluster analysis algorithm. Sethi and Holton have criticized the Liander study on methodological grounds,[2] and they have attempted to correct the problems in a further study, which also used the cluster analysis technique.[3] They studied ninety-one countries and included twenty-nine political, socioeconomic, trade, transportation, communication, biological, and personal consumption variables for 1966. The variables were grouped through cluster analysis into four variable sets: aggregate production and transportation (6), personal consumption (13), trade (3), and health and education (7). Applying cluster analysis to the ninety-one countries on the basis of composite scores of the four variable sets produced seven clusters plus the United States as a unique object. The results are shown in Table 12-13.

Once again it is seen that the Pacific Basin countries are spread across the various national groupings: at least one country is identified with each of the seven clusters, and the United States is classified as a unique object. Indonesia and Hong Kong are single entries in binational clusters 1 and 6, while Guatemala is the sole representative of the much larger cluster 2. Cluster 3 contains countries from South (4), Central (2), and North (1) America, together with four Southeast Asian countries. Cluster 4 is restricted to four Central and South American countries, while cluster 7 contains the four most advanced countries (other than the United States) of the whole Pacific Basin.

One final study, by Sheth and Lutz, attempted to rate foreign countries on their desirability for U.S. investment.[4] They used the six environmental factors—political stability, economic development and performance, cultural unity, legal barriers, physiographic barriers, and geocultural distance—to obtain different sets of 1961-1962 data to form a hot-cold gradient of investment

Table 12-12
Stages of Market Development, 1972

Affluent Societies *(GNP per Capita > $4000)*	*1972 GNP per Capita*
United States	5600
Sweden	5200
Canada	4800
Switzerland	4600
Denmark	4200
Germany, Federal Republic of	4200

Developed Countries *(GNP per Capita $1000-$2500)*	
Norway	3900
France	3800
Belgium	3700
Netherlands	3400
Australia	3200
Finland	2900
Japan	2800
Austria	2800
United Kingdom	2500
New Zealand	2500
Israel	2300
Puerto Rico	2300
Libya	2300
Italy	2200
Ireland	1800
Greece	1400
Spain	1300
Singapore	1300
Venezuela	1300
Argentina	1300
Hong Kong	1000

Semideveloped Countries *(GNP per Capita $360-$990)*	
Uruguay	870
Panama	860
South Africa (including Southwest Africa)	840
Jamaica	820
Portugal	800
Trinidad and Tobago	790
Mexico	780

Table 12-12 (cont.)

Semideveloped Countries (cont.) (GNP per Capita $360-$990)	1972 GNP per Capita
Costa Rica	630
Chile	570
Iran	560
Lebanon	530
Brazil	510
Nicaragua	500
Colombia	470
Turkey	440
Malaysia	420
Ivory Coast	410
Guatemala	400
Dominican Republic	390
Zambia	390
Peru	380
Liberia	370

Underdeveloped Countries (GNP per Capita $90-$350)	
Saudi Arabia	350
Syria	340
Iraq	340
Ecuador	320
Southern Rhodesia	310
El Salvador	310
Algeria	300
Tunisia	300
Honduras	300
Paraguay	300
Korea, South	300
Philippines	290
Jordan	270
Ghana	260
Senegal	250
Morocco	250
Congo, Democratic Republic of	250
Bolivia	220
United Arab Republic	220
Thailand	210
Pakistan	200
Angola	190

Table 12-12 (cont.)

Underdeveloped Countries (cont.) *(GNP per Capita $90-350)*	*1972 GNP per Capita*
Cameroon	190
Sierra Leone	180
Vietnam, South	170
Kenya	170
Mauritania	160
Uganda	140
Togo	140
Cambodia	130
Central African Republic	130
Indonesia	120
Sudan	120
Tanzania	110
Haiti	100
Niger	100
Nigeria	100
India	90
Pakistan	90
Afghanistan	90
Nepal	90
Malawi	90
Somalia	90

Preindustrial Countries *(GNP per Capita < $90)*	
Dahomey	80
Burma	80
Ethiopia	80
Guinea	80
Yemen	70
Rwanda	70
Chad	70
Burundi	70
Mali	50
Upper Volta	50

Source: United Nations Statistical Office

Note: All figures are in U.S. dollars. Underlined countries are Pacific Basin Countries.

Table 12-13
Sethi's Country Groupings

Group 1
Indonesia
Brazil

Group 2
Algeria
Camaroon
Cambodia
Central African Republic
Chad
Dahomey
Ethiopia
Guatemala
Guinea
India
Iran
Ivory Coast
Mali
Niger
Nigeria
Pakistan
Senegal
Somalia
Sudan
Tanzania
Uganda
Upper Volta
Vietnam, South

Group 3
Africa, South
Bolivia
Burma
Ceylon
Colombia
Congo (Leopoldville)
Dominican Republic
Ecuador
El Salvador
Ghana
Honduras
Iraq
Jordan
Korea, South
Lebanon

Malaysia and Singapore
Mexico
Morocco
Nicaragua
Paraguay
Peru
Philippines
Portugal
Syria
Thailand
Tunisia
Turkey
United Arab Republic

Group 4
Argentina
Chile
Costa Rica
Greece
Israel
Italy
Jamaica
Panama
Spain
Uruguay
Venezuela

Group 5
Congo (Brazzaville)
Gabon
Liberia
Libya
Sierra Leone

Group 6
Hong Kong
Trinidad and Tobago

Group 7
Australia
Austria
Belgium
Canada
Denmark
Finland

Table 12-13 (cont.)

France	Sweden
Germany, West	Switzerland
Iceland	United Kingdom
Japan	
Netherlands	*Unique object*
New Zealand	United States
Norway	

Source: S. Prakash Sethi, "Comparative Cluster Analysis for World Markets," *Journal of Marketing Research* 8 (August 1971):348-354.
Note: Underlined countries are Pacific Basin Countries.

climate, where hot represents a positive environment for investment and cold represents a negative climate. The results of this analysis are shown in Table 12-14. As with the other analyses, the Pacific Basin countries are spread throughout the groupings for all countries analyzed.

Conclusions

What, then, are the conclusions to be drawn from the various methods of grouping countries? The most significant conclusion is that from the point of view of a firm wishing to expand internationally, the use of the geographic notion of the Pacific Basin may not be the most appropriate basis on which to make market entry decisions. As the analyses have shown, Pacific Basin countries are distributed across a wide range of groupings. While selecting a group of Pacific Basin countries within a grouping may be a sensible way to proceed to examine market entry possibilities, countries other than Pacific Basin countries within that same grouping may be a far better choice for further examination.

Using Sethi's analysis, if the firm determines that it has the skills and resources to be successful in Thailand, the Philippines, Ecuador, Peru, Honduras, and Colombia (Pacific Basin countries of cluster 3), it may be better off still to enter Syria, the United Arab Republic, Tunisia, and the countries in cluster 3 before entering the Pacific Basin countries in cluster 7, which are New Zealand, Australia, Japan, and Canada.

A second conclusion is that the groupings of countries are a function of the variables upon which the clustering procedure is based. Since the variables chosen by Liander et al. and Sethi differ, so did their clusters. Also, each was different from the single GNP per capita variable clustering. A firm that wants to use one of these methods for developing market entry possibilities should try to identify the variables that are most likely to have a relationship with potential sales of their products and services, and then should perform the analysis on those variables.

Table 12-14
Sheth and Lutz's "Hot-Cold" Gradient, from a U.S. Viewpoint

Country	Value	Country	Value
United States	13.22	Venezuela	−0.40
United Kingdom	4.60	Panama	−0.41
Germany, West	3.44	Costa Rica	−0.47
France	2.64	Turkey	−0.47
Netherlands	2.12	Bulgaria	−0.47
Canada	2.01	Ecuador	−0.52
Belgium	2.00	Libya	−0.60
Denmark	1.33	Bolivia	−0.61
Italy	1.32	Philippines	−0.64
Taiwan	1.16	Egypt	−0.72
Japan	1.13	Peru	−0.73
Sweden	1.13	Lebanon	−0.80
Poland	0.93	Haiti	−0.88
Switzerland	0.86	Guatemala	−0.93
Ireland	0.83	Liberia	−0.94
Argentina	0.81	Ceylon	−0.97
Australia	0.76	Albania	−0.99
Norway	0.73	Thailand	−1.00
Austria	0.73	Mongolia	−1.07
Germany, East	0.72	Paraguay	−1.13
Mexico	0.58	Korea, North	−1.16
Finland	0.47	Iran	−1.23
Brazil	0.46	Indonesia	−1.23
New Zealand	0.40	Korea, South	−1.24
Czechoslovakia	0.33	Ethiopia	−1.25
Spain	0.23	Cambodia	−1.28
Colombia	0.22	Saudi Arabia	−1.31
Greece	0.16	Syria	−1.32
Hungary	0.50	Africa, South	−1.33
Portugal	0.00	Vietnam, South	−1.37
Uruguay	−0.13	Jordan	−1.42
Yugoslavia	−0.16	Iraq	−1.44
Honduras	−0.16	Pakistan	−1.52
El Salvador	−0.17	Burma	−1.55
Chile	−0.18	Israel	−1.57
India	−0.19	Vietnam, North	−1.62
Nicaragua	−0.23	Nepal	−1.68
Cuba	−0.26	Afghanistan	−1.86
Dominican Republic	−0.29	Laos	−1.89
Rumania	−0.29	Yemen	−1.99

Note: Underlined countries are Pacific Basin Countries.

Finally, the analyses presented used data sets developed from different time periods. While the GNP per capita data were for 1972, Sethi used 1966 data, and Sheth and Lutz used 1961-1962 data. Since nations develop along a multitude of dimensions at differing rates, the clusters formed from a given set of variables at time 1 would be expected to differ from those developed from the identical set of variables at time 2. The results presented by the analyses are static and should be interpreted in the light of recent events. For example, an analysis performed today on 1972 data would almost certainly misplace the oil-rich countries of the Middle East, which have had quantum changes on many dimensions as a result of oil price increases in 1973 and 1974.

Notes

1. Bertil Liander, Vern Terpstra, Michael Yoshino, and A.A. Smerbini, *Comparative Analysis for International Marketing* (Boston: Allyn and Bacon, 1967).

2. S. Prakash Sethi and Richard H. Holton, "Review of Bertil Liander et al., 'Comparative Analysis for International Marketing,'" *Journal of Marketing Research* 6 (November 1969):502-503.

3. S. Prakash Sethi, "Comparative Cluster Analysis for World Markets," *Journal of Marketing Research* 8 (August 1971):348-354.

4. Sheth, J.N. and R.J. Lutz, "A Multivariate Model of Multinational Business Expansion," in S.P. Sethi and J.N. Sheth (eds.) *Multinational Business Operations: Marketing Management* Goodyear Publishing Co. 1973, pp. 96-103.

13 The Spread of Foreign Banks into the United States: Far Eastern Bank Operations in California

David K. Eiteman

The "spread" of foreign banks into the United States has received considerable attention in recent banking literature. In fact, it has engendered proposals to Congress that the U.S. banking laws be changed to prevent what some threatened parties deem "unfair" competition. A considerable amount of what has been written stresses the "advantages" or "disadvantages" that a foreign-controlled bank has in competing with U.S. domestic banks.

After a brief view of the structure of foreign banking in the United States and the reasons advanced for changing the country's banking laws, this chapter will address the specific question of whether California-incorporated bank subsidiaries of parent banks in the Far East have financial characteristics that are significantly different from those of domestic banks. Specific attention will be directed toward measures of liquidity and leverage, and toward the very limited data available about profitability.

Foreign Bank Motivations for Entering the United States

Studies about international banking have identified several reasons why foreign banks enter the United States market:[1]

1. Most important, to provide financial services to U.S. subsidiaries of foreign corporations. This reason has its exact parallel in U.S. banks' rapid expansion abroad in the past two decades. Banks from all countries want to stay with their major domestic customers when those customers expand into worldwide operations.
2. To serve as a source of dollars for the foreign parent banks.
3. To establish contacts and links with the U.S. securities markets. In this regard it might be noted that the distinction between commercial banking and securities operations that is so prevalent in the United States is not typical in most of the rest of the world. U.S. statistics on foreign "banking" in the United States include some operations that are directed toward the U.S. securities markets and not toward "banking" as it is traditionally viewed within the United States.
4. To escape banking restrictions in the parent bank's home country.

5. To develop contact with the retail banking market in the United States, especially that of specific ethnic groups.
6. To facilitate settlement of international payments.

Forms of Organization for International Banking

Foreign banks may open offices in the United States under several forms, depending on the laws of the various states in which they might choose to operate.

Branches

Branches are integral parts of the parent bank, with the parent's full resources behind the local office. A branch functions with the parent's name and reputation, and as a consequence, a branch's loan limit is a function of the parent's capital rather than of the much smaller capital of the branch itself. U.S. stockholders or U.S. directors are not necessary. Finally, branches require a much less complicated organizational structure than do other types of offices that are qualified to perform a general banking business.

In the United States, five states have specified statutes allowing foreign banks to establish branches within their borders: California, New York, Illinois, Massachusetts, and Hawaii. Various conditions are required, however; the most important is reciprocity. Banks from foreign countries can establish branches in these states only if the foreign countries in turn allow banks incorporated in these states to operate in their countries.

Seven states specifically forbid foreign-owned branches: Connecticut, Delaware, Minnesota, New Jersey, Rhode Island, Texas, and Vermont. At one time Washington state and Oregon also excluded branches of foreign banks. Washington changed its laws a few years ago and attracted foreign bank branches as well as additional Pacific Rim business associated with the parent countries. Oregon changed its law during the summer of 1975, apparently in part because Oregon feared it was losing Pacific Northwest business to the state of Washington. In the remaining states of the union, specific legislation on foreign banks has not been passed; each state's banking commissioner decides on the appropriateness of each application. However, operations that involve holding companies come under the jurisdiction of the Federal Reserve System.

Branches tend to be the preferred form of organization, especially for foreign banks operating in New York City. In New York, branches must maintain the same fractional reserves against deposits, comply with the same loan restrictions, and make the same reports to the state banking commissioner as domestic banks. In California, branches of foreign banks are severely restricted because to accept general deposits from the public they must be approved for FDIC insurance. The FDIC will not insure branches of foreign banks, however. Since 1969, California "agencies" have been able to operate with foreign but not domestic deposits. Thus to a very limited extent, California agencies can function as limited or quasi branches.

Subsidiaries

A number of states—particularly California, where full-service branch banking is not available to foreign banks—have adopted the subsidiary form of organization. A subsidiary is a separately incorporated bank, owned entirely or in major part by a foreign parent. The subsidiary conducts a general banking business and provides a conduit for relations with the parent bank. Subsidiaries are always organized under state law because all the directors of a national bank must be U.S. citizens. Subsidiaries are eligible for FDIC insurance, and they may also conduct a wide variety of trust operations.

By organizing as subsidiaries and branches foreign banks, with some important limitations, can provide a full range of banking services within the United States. Two other forms allow limited services.

Representative Offices

Representative offices are established primarily to enable the parent bank's clients to maintain contact with their home bank when in the United States. A representative office does not make loans, receive deposits, or conduct general banking business. Rather, it provides information, advice, local contacts for home office business clients, and a location where U.S. businesspeople may initiate inquiries about the bank's services in the parent country. A phone call or letter to a representative office of one Japanese bank in California, for example, led immediately to an exquisite and artistic English language annual report of the parent bank that contained, in addition to financial statements (in both yen and dollar equivalents), detailed discussions of the Japanese economy and of the services provided in Japan by the parent bank.

Agencies

The fourth type of office is an agency. An agency cannot accept deposits from the public, but it may perform many other banking functions, especially those related to international trade. It may arrange loans to finance trade with its parent country, issue letters of credit, and accept, buy, and collect drafts (bills of exchange). Agencies are usually active in the foreign exchange market and, on behalf of their parent bank, in the U.S. securities market. In contrast to the rules for branches and subsidiaries, fractional reserve requirements are not imposed on agencies. Thus there is no limitation on the size of individual loans. The examination of agencies varies by state. The New York state code requires that each foreign banking agency be examined by a state agency, and actual examinations are reported to occur about once a year. California examines agencies about once every two years.

Number of Offices

Foreign banks operating in the United States are free to open as many offices of various types as they can obtain permission for under the laws of the several states. As one illustration, the Bank of Tokyo, Ltd., has operated in the United States as a multistate bank holding company since the enactment of the Bank Holding Company Act of 1956. Bank of Tokyo, Ltd., has branches in Portland and Seattle, and agencies in New York City, Los Angeles, and San Francisco. Representative offices are maintained in Chicago, Houston, Honolulu, and Washington, D.C. Additionally, Bank of Tokyo, Ltd., owns a controlling interest in the Bank of Tokyo Trust Company, a New York Banking corporation; owns 4.9 percent of Chicago-Tokyo Bank, an Illinois state-chartered bank; and owns 5.0 percent of Nomura Securities International of New York. Finally, it owned, prior to October 1, 1975, 52.6 percent of Bank of Tokyo of California. Effective October 1, 1975, Bank of Tokyo of California purchased the assets of Southern California First National Corporation, a one-bank holding company head-quartered in San Diego, and its major subsidiary, Southern California First National Bank. Bank of Tokyo, Ltd., now owns 74.7 percent of the surviving merged bank, whose name has been changed to California First Bank.

In one form or another, Bank of Tokyo, Ltd., has offices in seven states plus the District of Columbia. These offices include banking subsidiaries in three states and branches in two additional states. By comparison, U.S. banks are permitted to operate general banking offices only within one state.

The single exception to the one-state limit for U.S. banks are Edge Act subsidiaries, which can conduct certain kinds of international operations in other states. Briefly, an Edge Act corporation is a subsidiary of a U.S. bank incorporated under Section 25 of the Federal Reserve Act to engage in any of three types of activities: (1) direct international banking; (2) acting as a holding company for the stock of one or more foreign banking subsidiaries; and (3) financing development activities not closely related to typical banking operations. With regard to banking activities, an Edge Act corporation may accept demand and time (but not savings) deposits from outside the United States as well as from inside the United States if these latter deposits are incidental to or for the purpose of carrying out transactions with foreign countries. Edge Act corporations may also make loans and engage in a variety of services such as remitting funds abroad and engaging in foreign exchange activities.

Controversy over Foreign Bank Operations in the United States

Some years ago the statement was made that the only true European banks were the U.S. banks, because they were the only banks in Europe that were taking a continent-wide view of competing for services; also, only U.S. banks at that time were experimenting with modern banking services to businesses such as techniques to expedite fund flows between locations via electronic transfer.

More recently the statement has been made that the only true U.S. banks are the Japanese banks, since it is primarily the Japanese banks that have availed themselves of the opportunity to have banking offices in California, New York City, Chicago, and elsewhere. These offices, whether branches or subsidiaries, provide a competitive service not available from U.S. domestic banks.

Thus has arisen a controversy—a controversy, it might be noted, that did not arise from U.S. observers when U.S. banks went continent-wide in Europe. Should foreign banks, via branches or other forms of organization, be allowed competitive advantages not given to U.S. banks? Posed in this manner, the inevitable answer must surely be no. There are two possible solutions:

1. To pass a federal rule or law preventing foreign banks from opening branches or general banking subsidiaries in more than one state. In other words, confine the foreign banks to the current U.S. rules. This approach is generally favored by small U.S. banks as well as by the multitude of banks in the Middle West and the South.
2. To permit U.S. banks to go nationwide with branch banking, a solution obviously not sought by the midcountry unit banks. However, major internationally oriented banks in money market centers tend to prefer nationwide branch banking, for this solution would permit them to operate and compete with foreign banks in major foreign countries. The pressures on large banks are great, as can be seen from the fact that in 1973 large Chicago banks prevailed on the Illinois legislature to allow foreign banks to operate in the Loop district so that the Chicago banks would not be excluded from operating abroad.

In addition to nationwide branch banking, a second competitive problem arises with foreign banks in the United States. Banks operating under federal charter (i.e., national banks) must be owned by U.S. citizens. This means that all foreign bank subsidiaries must be state banks, which in turn means that all regulation is left to the state governments. State regulation is generally less stringent than federal regulation in terms of reserve requirements. Thus as a competitive matter, state-incorporated subsidiaries of foreign banks are less tightly regulated than are federally chartered national banks or U.S. state banks that have elected to join the Federal Reserve System. (Foreign banks cannot join the Federal Reserve System).

California Subsidiaries of Foreign Banks

American Banker reports that 180 foreign banks are represented in the United States by 62 subsidiaries or affiliates, 77 branches, 72 agencies, and 141 representative offices.[2] The largest concentration is in New York City and California. Within California, some 23 subsidiaries or affiliates, 36 agencies, and 14 representative offices vie for business. Of the 23 California subsidiaries or affiliates, 15 are California-incorporated commercial bank subsidiaries. One is the California branch of a New York banking corporation, which is in turn owned by 6 European banks, and 7 are securities firms.

In addition to the 15 California-incorporated subsidiaries of foreign banks, one California-incorporated bank, Japan California Bank, is owned by a group of 32 Japanese business firms. Technically, this bank is independent rather than the subsidiary of a foreign bank. Operationally, Japan California Bank maintains close ties with Dai-ichi Kangyo Bank, Ltd., of Tokyo, the largest bank in Japan and the ninth largest bank in the world. For purposes of the following analyses, Japan California Bank will be added to the list of California subsidiaries of foreign banks.

These 16 banks are listed in Table 13-1. Of the 16, 7 are owned by Japanese parents, 3 by Canadian banks, 3 by British banks, and 1 each by banks in France, Hong Kong, and Korea.

Financial statements for December 31, 1974, and June 30, 1975, were obtained by mail from the 7 Japanese banks and the Hong Kong and Korean banks. These statements have been used as the data base for the analysis in the remainder of this chapter. The basic purpose of this analysis is to compare liquidity, leverage, and profitability of these Far Eastern-owned banks with similar characteristics for all commercial banks in the Twelfth Federal Reserve District,[a] with the 14,288 commercial banks in the United States insured by the Federal Deposit Insurance Corporation (FDIC),[3] and with a set of aggregate data for all foreign-owned banking subsidiaries in the United States.[4] For convenience of exposition in the remainder of this article, the phrase "of California"

---

[a]The Twelfth Federal Reserve District comprises California, Oregon, Washington, Idaho, Nevada, Utah, and most of Arizona. Data were obtained from weekly releases of the Federal Reserve Bank of San Francisco.

Table 13-1
California Subsidiaries of Foreign Banks, 1974

	Parent (% Ownership)	Total Assets, June 30, 1975	Date Founded
Far Eastern Parentage			
California First Bank[a]	Bank of Tokyo, Ltd. (74.7%)	$1,072,045,408	1953
Sumitomo Bank of California	Sumitomo Bank, Ltd., Osaka (100%)	823,307,719	1953
Sanwa Bank of California	Sanwa Bank, Ltd., Osaka (100%)	161,236,909	1972
Hong Kong Bank of California	Hong Kong and Shanghai Banking Corporation, Hong Kong (100%)	134,524,339	unknown
Mitsubishi Bank of California	Mitsubishi Bank, Ltd., Tokyo (100%)	126,065,028	1972
Tokai Bank of California	Tokai Bank, Ltd., Nagoya (100%)	59,891,473	1974
Mitsui Bank of California	Mitsui Bank, Ltd., Tokyo (100%)	51,080,288	1974
Japan California Bank	32 Japanese corporations (100%)	32,220,039	1974
Korea Exchange Bank of California	Korea Exchange Bank, Seoul (100%)	14,556,319	1974
Canadian Parentage			
Bank of Montreal (Canada)	Bank of Montreal, Montreal		
California Canadian Bank	Canadian Imperial Bank of Commerce, Toronto		
Toronto Dominion Bank of California	Toronto Dominion Bank, Toronto		
British Parentage			
Barclays Bank of California	Barclay's Bank International, Ltd., London		
Chartered Bank of London, San Francisco	Chartered Bank, London		
Lloyds Bank of California	Lloyd's Bank, Ltd., London		
French Parentage			
French Bank of California	Banque National de Paris, Paris		

Source: Annual Reports

[a]Bank of Tokyo of California prior to Oct. 1, 1975

will be omitted from the names of the various California-incorporated subsidiary banks.

Percentage, or common-sized, balance sheet statements for the various banks may be compared with similar data for the three bases of comparison. These data appear in Table 13-2 for December 31, 1974, and in Table 13-3 for June 30, 1975. Data in these two figures show that the two largest banks, California First Bank and Sumitomo Bank, maintained a significantly smaller proportion of total assets in primary reserve form, i.e., in cash and due from banks plus U.S. Treasury securities, than did most banks. Their liquidity was relatively lower. In December 1974, when the Twelfth District banks kept 19.0 percent of assets and all insured banks kept 19.6 percent of assets in primary reserve form, California First Bank had only 12.6 percent and Sumitomo Bank only 10.2 percent of their assets in the same form. The proportion of assets in primary reserve form for all U.S. banking subsidiaries of foreign banks as well as for most of the remaining smaller California banking subsidiaries was typical of both Twelfth District and all FDIC-insured bank averages. The ratios for Japan California Bank and for Korea Exchange Bank are probably atypical because they were founded near the end of 1974. The same general relationships of primary reserves to total assets existed in June 1975.

A measure of bank risk and aggressiveness is the proportion of assets held as loans and discounts, the most profitable asset category. This measure tends to be high when liquidity is low, and vice versa. The proportion of assets held as loans and discounts was somewhat larger (i.e., more risk and potentially more profit) than Twelfth District and insured bank averages for both dates for most of the banks. The proportion was lower (i.e., less risk and potentially less profit) for Hong Kong Bank, Japan California Bank, and Korea Exchange Bank. As was mentioned, the latter two banks were organized late in 1974, so less importance can be attached to their ratios. Although U.S. banking subsidiaries of foreign banks tend to be conservative, having a smaller proportion of total assets committed to loans and discounts, most of the Far Eastern bank subsidiaries exhibit the opposite entity, which is a more risky position.

A composite measure of propensity to trade risk against liquidity on the asset side of the balance sheet is the ratio of loans and discounts to cash items plus U.S. Treasury securities (Table 13-4). A higher ratio indicates a more risky asset policy because loans, the most important earning asset, are larger relative to primary liquidity reserves. California First Bank, Sumitomo Bank, Sanwa Bank, Tokai Bank, and Mitsui Bank measured higher than average, while the remaining banks were lower than the averages used for the comparison. One exception was Korea Exchange Bank, simply because in December 31, 1974, it was a new bank.

A separate measure of leverage, and thus of risk, can be derived from the right side of the balance sheet. This is the ratio of time and savings deposits to demand deposits, shown in Table 13-5. In the Twelfth District, time and savings deposits were 1.84 times demand deposits in December 1974, while nationally the FDIC relationship was 1.37 times. The two largest banks maintained a larger ratio of time and savings deposits to demand deposits, on the order of 3.19 times for California First Bank and 2.69 times for Sumitomo Bank. Hong Kong Bank had a ratio slightly below Twelfth District banks but above FDIC-insured banks, while the remaining Japanese banks had demand deposits roughly equal to or greater than time and savings deposits. For the Korean Exchange Bank, time and savings deposits were 5.23 and 4.16 times demand deposits on the two dates.

The most likely reason why the two largest Japanese banks have a significantly greater than average proportion of time and savings deposits to demand deposits is that these two banks were the only state banks of Japanese parentage until recent years. As Japanese business investment in California grew during the past two decades, loan demand at these banks was very strong. In the early years Japanese businesses, along with other businesses, kept large demand deposits at these banks. Slower business activity and a general liquidity squeeze in both the United States and Japan in recent years has led businesses to reduce their demand deposit balances while, at the same time, loan demand kept increasing. To satisfy burgeoning loan demand from customers, and perhaps to avoid losing clients to the newer Japanese banks, California First Bank and Sumitomo Bank began to pay higher-than-average interest rates on time deposits over $100,000. Seeking "hot money" in this manner permitted continued growth and service to customers, albeit at some sacrifice in profitability, as will be suggested later.

Liability leverage also can be measured by the ratio of total deposits to stockholders equity (Table 13-4). A high ratio indicates a larger amount of deposit liability relative to stockholder investment and thus a riskier mix. By this measure all the banks appear less risky and more conservative than the average for Twelfth District banks. Ranges of between 12.37 and 8.94 for the three largest Japanese banks on December 31, 1974, are slightly above the total FDIC average of 11.76, but it is hard to attribute any significance to such a difference in view of the still higher ratio of 14.52 for Twelfth District banks on the same date. The ratio for all U.S. banking subsidiaries of foreign banks is lower, but the ratios for the remaining banks in the California sample are still lower.

One other measure of risk combines both asset and liability proportions. This is the ratio of "deposits of risk" (total deposits less cash items and U.S. Treasury securities) to "stockholders' capital," shown in Table 13-4. A high ratio indicates more composite risk, since "risky deposits" are greater relative to shareholders' investments. By these criteria, none of the Far Eastern-owned banks are as risky as the average for the Twelfth Federal Reserve District. The larger banks are nevertheless relatively more risky than the smaller banks.

Readers of financial statements of U.S. banks suffer from a paucity of income statement information, especially when viewing quarterly or semiannual statements or when looking for comparative national data. This is presumably because bank regulators are concerned with liquidity rather than profitability,

Table 13-2

Statements of Condition for Far Eastern-owned California Bank Subsidiaries, In Order of Size, and Aggregate Bank Statistics for Comparison, 1974

(In Percent)

	California First Bank[a]	Sumitomo Bank of California	Sanwa Bank of California	Hong Kong Bank of California	Mitsubishi Bank of California
Total Assets	$1047.8M	$797.9M	$153.4M	$123.5M	$117.0M
Assets					
Cash and due from banks	7.9	8.2	20.0	6.4	18.1
U.S. Treasury securities	4.7	2.0	0.4	13.1	2.6
Primary reserves	12.6	10.2	20.4	19.5	20.7
Other securities	15.2	14.9	8.8	4.9	8.2
Loans and discounts	66.3	70.2	67.7	58.5	67.6
Other assets	5.9	4.7	3.1	17.1	3.5
Total	100.0	100.0	100.0	100.0	100.0
Liabilities and Capital					
Demand deposits	20.8	23.9	53.5	29.6	37.9
Time and savings deposits	66.4	64.3	36.6	51.9	38.8
Total deposits	87.2	88.2	90.1	81.5	76.7
Other liabilities and reserves	5.8	4.6	2.3	9.4	14.5
Shareholders' capital	7.0	7.2	7.6	9.1	8.8
Total	100.0	100.0	100.0	100.0	100.0

Source: Annual Reports

[a]Name changed from Bank of Tokyo of California on October 1, 1975.

while many banks see no need to give greater exposure than necessary to their earnings situation.

Japan California Bank's income statement was available, but because the bank had been in operation only half a year by December 1974, comparisons are meaningless. Full income statements were available for California First Bank and for Sumitomo Bank for both dates, and for all U.S.-insured commercial banks for December 31, 1974. Using these income statement data (Table 13-6), and recognizing the very tentative nature of conclusions derived from only two banks, the large Japanese banks appear to have derived a greater proportion of their income from interest and fees on loans than was true for all FDIC banks. This relationship is consistent with the earlier observation that these two banks keep a greater than average proportion of total assets in the form of loans and

Mitsui Bank of California	Tokai Bank of California	Japan California Bank	Korea Exchange Bank of California	Twelfth Federal Reserve District	All FDIC-insured Banks	U.S. Banking Subsidiaries of Foreign Banks
$48.3M	$44.7M	$34.0M	$13.0M	$113,491.0M	$909,285.0M	$11,862.0M
10.2	9.8	20.6	73.5	13.6	13.9	22.4
0	4.4	18.0	0	5.4	5.7	4.5
10.2	14.2	38.6	73.5	19.0	19.6	26.9
0	8.9	0.6	1.5	11.7	15.6	14.8
87.0	75.4	57.8	18.9	62.7	59.7	51.6
2.8	1.5	3.0	6.1	6.8	5.1	6.7
100.0	100.0	100.0	100.0	100.0	100.0	100.0
50.2	43.9	44.4	12.0	28.2	34.5	38.7
37.3	41.7	40.0	62.5	52.1	47.3	38.5
87.5	85.6	84.4	74.5	80.3	81.8	77.2
0.5	0.7	0.9	2.8	14.2	11.2	15.0
12.0	13.7	14.7	22.7	5.5	7.0	7.8
100.0	100.0	100.0	100.0	100.0	100.0	100.0

discounts. Since loans are generally more profitable than investments, one might surmise from this set of data that the Japanese banks should be more profitable than the national average. However, interest paid on deposits as a proportion of total operating income for the two Japanese banks also ran significantly above the ratio for all FDIC banks. Again, this would follow from the earlier observation that these two banks obtained a greater proportion of deposits from time and savings deposits (deposits on which they paid interest) than from demand deposits. Net income for these two Japanese banks, expressed as a percent of total operating income, is smaller for the Japanese banks than for the U.S. average.

Final profitability should be measured by return on stockholders' capital. Data in Table 13-7 show that net income as a percent of stockholders' capital

Table 13-3

Statements of Condition for Far Eastern-owned California Bank Subsidiaries, in Order of Size, and Aggregate Bank Statistics for Comparison, June 30, 1975

(In Percent)

	California First Bank[a]	Sumitomo Bank of California	Sanwa Bank of California	Hong Kong Bank of California	Mitsubishi Bank of California
Total Assets	$1072.0M	$823.3M	$161.2M	$134.5M	$126.1M
Assets					
Cash and due from banks	8.4	10.3	16.1	6.6	19.9
U.S. Treasury securities	4.5	3.0	0.3	10.9	2.0
Primary reserves	12.9	13.3	16.4	17.5	21.9
Other securities	14.9	15.7	11.3	0.8	8.1
Loans and discounts	66.9	67.7	68.4	59.6	65.8
Other assets	5.3	3.3	3.9	22.1	4.2
Total	100.0	100.0	100.0	100.0	100.0
Liabilities and Capital					
Demand deposits	20.8	24.6	45.4	29.6	46.0
Time and savings deposits	67.5	64.8	44.7	52.7	39.4
Total deposits	88.3	89.4	90.1	82.3	85.4
Other liabilities and reserves	4.7	3.4	2.5	9.9	6.4
Shareholders' capital	7.0	7.2	7.4	7.8	8.2
Total	100.0	100.0	100.0	100.0	100.0

Source: Annual Reports

[a]Name changed from Bank of Tokyo of California on October 1, 1975.

accounts in 1974 was 7.88 percent for California First Bank and 8.30 percent for Sumitomo Bank. The data for June 30, 1975, represents a doubling of the six-month net income, rather than a return for the prior twelve months. The figures were 8.22 percent and 8.80 percent for the same two banks. All four measures of return on stockholders' capital indicate that the two large Japanese banks, at least, are less profitable for their owners than were FDIC-insured commercial banks for the year ending December 31, 1974.

Conclusions

Data studied in this survey can be regarded at best as tentative because they are derived from a very small sample of financial statements from Far Eastern-owned banking subsidiaries operating in California. Furthermore, the compari-

Tokai Bank of California	Mitsui Bank of California	Japan California Bank	Korean Exchange Bank of California	Twelfth Federal Reserve District	U.S. Banking Subsidiaries of Foreign Banks
$59.9M	$51.1M	$32.2M	$14.6M	$113,185.0M	$11,714.0M
5.9	10.3	15.1	34.0	12.0	13.1
0	2.9	9.4	0	7.8	3.8
5.9	13.2	24.5	34.0	19.8	16.9
10.1	1.0	17.1	4.1	11.4	15.0
82.3	83.3	52.7	50.3	60.8	55.9
1.7	2.5	5.7	11.6	8.0	12.3
100.0	100.0	100.0	100.0	100.0	100.0
42.6	23.6	42.5	13.3	29.5	30.6
46.3	64.5	36.2	55.6	53.6	43.6
88.9	88.1	78.7	68.9	83.1	74.2
0.7	0.6	5.3	11.4	12.2	16.9
10.4	11.3	16.0	19.7	5.7	9.1
100.0	100.0	100.0	100.0	100.0	100.0

sons are with aggregates for the Twelfth Federal Reserve District, with the 14,288 banks whose deposits are insured by the Federal Deposit Insurance Corporation, and with all foreign-owned U.S. banking subsidiaries. Nevertheless, it does appear that the Far Eastern-owned banks in California are more aggressive in terms of administering their portfolios of assets because a greater proportion is devoted to loans and a smaller proportion to primary reserves than is average for the three standards of comparison. On the liability side, these foreign banks are perhaps more conservative than Twelfth District banks, having lower deposits relative to stockholders' equity. By the composite measure of "deposits at risk" to stockholders' equity, none of the banks appear more risky than average, although the larger ones are more risky than the smaller ones. Very limited data from income statements suggest that the two largest banks are less profitable for their owners than are all U.S.-insured commercial banks.

Table 13-4
Financial Ratios for Far Eastern-owned California Bank Subsidiaries, In Order of Bank Size, June 30, 1975

	Asset Leverage Loans and Deposits (Cash + U.S. Treasuries)		Capital Leverage Deposits (Stockholders' Capital)		Deposits at Risk to Capital Deposits-Cash & U.S. Treasuries (Stockholders' Capital)	
	12/31/74	6/30/75	12/31/74	6/30/75	12/31/74	6/30/75
California First Bank[a]	5.24	5.15	12.37	12.51	10.58	10.67
Sumitomo Bank of California	6.84	5.07	12.22	12.39	10.80	10.54
Sanwa Bank of California	3.32	4.17	11.93	12.25	9.23	10.01
Hong Kong Bank of California	3.00	3.42	8.94	10.49	6.80	8.27
Mitsubishi Bank of California	3.27	3.01	8.74	10.40	6.38	7.73
Tokai Bank of California	5.31	14.06	6.27	8.56	5.23	7.99
Mitsui Bank of California	8.55	6.31	7.30	8.81	6.45	7.65
Japan California Bank	1.50	2.15	5.73	4.93	3.12	3.38
Korea Exchange Bank of California	27.70	1.48	3.28	3.49	0.03	1.77
Twelfth Federal Reserve District	3.30	3.06	14.52	16.60	11.05	11.11
All FDIC-insured banks	3.06	—	11.76	—	8.95	—
U.S. banking subsidiaries of foreign banks	1.91	3.31	9.71	8.10	6.31	6.25

Source: Annual Reports

[a]Name changed from Bank of Tokyo of California on October 1, 1975

Table 13-5
Ratio of Time and Savings Deposits to Demand Deposits for Far Eastern-owned California Bank Subsidiaries

	12/31/74	6/30/75
California First Bank[a]	3.19	3.24
Sumitomo Bank of California	2.69	2.63
Sanwa Bank of California	0.68	0.98
Hong Kong Bank of California	1.75	1.78
Mitsubishi Bank of California	1.02	0.86
Tokai Bank of Clifornia	0.95	1.08
Mitsui Bank of California	0.74	2.74
Japan California Bank	0.90	0.85
Korea Exchange Bank of California	5.23	4.16
Twelfth Federal Reserve District	1.84	1.82
All FDIC-insured banks	1.37	–
U.S. banking subsidiaries of foreign banks	1.00	1.41

Source: Annual Reports

[a]Name changed from Bank of Tokyo of California on October 1, 1975.

Table 13-6
Statements of Income for All Japanese-owned California Bank Subsidiaries and All FDIC-insured Commercial Banks, December 31, 1974, and June 30, 1975
(In Percent)

	Twelve Months Ended December 31, 1974			Six Months Ended June 30, 1975	
	California First Bank[a]	*Sumitomo Bank of California*	*All FDIC-Insured Commercial Banks*	*California First Bank*	*Sumitomo Bank of California*
Operating Income	$78.2M	$64.4M	$68,161M	$39.8M	$31.8M
Interest and fees on loans	81.2	79.7	74.6	81.8	76.8
Interest and fees on investments	14.2	11.5	15.2	13.7	12.2
Other operating income	4.6	8.8	10.2	4.5	11.0
Total operating income	100.0	100.0	100.0	100.0	100.0
Interest paid on deposits	66.7	62.7	40.9	66.5	61.8
Interest paid on borrowings	21.1	3.8	10.1	1.1	1.6
Provision for loan losses	1.5	0.9	3.4	–	
Other operating expenses	21.2	23.0	32.0	22.2	25.6
Total operating expenses	91.5	90.4	86.4	89.8	89.0
Income before taxes and security gains	8.5	9.6	13.6	10.2	11.0
Income taxes	1.1	2.2	3.2	2.4	2.8
Security losses (gains)	0	0	0	0	0
Net income	7.4	7.4	10.4	7.8	8.2

Source: Annual Reports

[a]Name changed from Bank of Tokyo of California on October 1, 1975.

Table 13-7
Rate of Return on Stockholders' Capital
(Net Income Divided by Stockholders' Capital)

	California First Bank[a]	Sumitomo Bank of California	All FDIC-insured Banks
December 31, 1974 (annual return)	7.88%	8.30%	11.21%
June 30, 1975 (semiannual return, multiplied by 2)	8.22%	8.80%	n.a.

Source: Annual Reports

[a]Name changed from Bank of Tokyo of California on October 1, 1975.

Notes

1. See for example, Fred Klopstock, "Foreign Banks in the U.S.: Scope and Growth of Operations," *Monthly Review,* Federal Reserve Bank of New York, (June 1974): Also see Jeffrey Arpan and David Ricks, "Foreign Banking in the United States," paper given at the Academy of International Business meetings, San Francisco, Calif., December 29, 1974; and Francis A. Lees, *International Business and Finance* (New York: John Wiley & Sons, 0000).

2. Laura Gross, "Compilation of Foreign Bank Activities in the United States," *American Banker*, July 31, 1975, pages 186-188.

3. Data was obtained from 1974 *Bank Operation Statistics* (Washington, D.C. Federal Deposit Insurance Corporation, 1974).

4. *Monthly Report of Condition for U.S. Agencies, Branch, and Domestic Banking Subsidiaries of Foreign Banks* (Washington, D.C.: Board of Governors of Federal Reserve System).

About the Editor

R. Hal Mason received the bachelor's degree (1955) and the master's degree (1957) in agricultural economics from Colorado State University. He then joined the industrial economics staff of Stanford Research Institute where he was project leader and program manager with research interests in the economics of food-processing technologies, agricultural mechanization and corporate long-range planning. In 1962 he was awarded a Sloan Foundation Fellowship to attend Stanford's Graduate School of Business where he received the Ph.D. (1966) in business economics. He subsequently joined the faculty of the Graduate School of Management at the University of California at Los Angeles. Dr. Mason's areas of interest and specialty are international business, technology transfer to developing countries and business policy. He is a member of the Academy of Management, the American Economic Association, the Western Economic Association, and the Academy of International Business. Dr. Mason is the author of many journal articles, the coauthor of a book entitled *The Economics of International Business,* and has been a consultant to several private and public agencies.

APR 28 1998	DATE DUE		